True Expat

by

Nicolas Westmore

True Expat

All Rights Reserved

Copyright 2016 Nicolas Westmore

Inquiries should be addressed to nwestmore2000@yahoo.com

Front cover photo by Nick Westmore - Baghdad, Iraq, 2004

Back cover author photo by Rob Clarke Photography
http://www.robclarkephotography.com/

DEDICATION

This book is dedicated. . .

To my children
Kelven
Shenya
Charene
Zarita

To their mother
and my beloved wife Jan
who passed away October 1997

And especially to my wonderful wife and soul-mate Caryl
who has guided and encouraged me to finally get my book published

CONTENTS

PREFACE

This book tells the story of my expatriate life in the oil and gas industry which began with my first overseas contract in 1974. By definition an expatriate is a person who temporarily or permanently resides in a country other than that of their citizenship. In my case my first expatriate assignment was with Aramco in Saudi Arabia but over the years I worked in countries like Malaysia, Azerbaijan, Iraq and others connected with the oil and gas industry.

In Part 1 you will meet True Expats, men who left an indelible mark on my memory.

While away I wrote home, telling my family about them, and now I have the chance to tell you their story too. In doing so I have created a *Hall of Fame* for them - signifying that they are entitled to use a most sacred title… *True Expat*.

In Part 2 I narrate global travel adventures I made whilst on overseas R & R (Rest and Recuperation breaks).

The True Expat and The Hall of Fame

You may ask: "What is a True Expat?" First of all, he's invariably a very likeable guy. Some have a penchant for the opposite sex, often getting into all sorts of fixes, others like the odd drink (or two), others tell outrageous, exaggerated, or risqué stories, and some are really decent guys.

If your True Expat was invited to meet your worldly-wise grandmother, he would soon have her eating out of the palm of his hand. He will convince her that he is the epitome of goodness and light, nigh on celibate, practically tee-total, and given to helping old ladies across the road.

Another characteristic is that he has got the Tee shirt for virtually everything. If you asked him, for example, if he had ever abseiled down the side of the tallest building in the world, then for sure he will have done so and probably abseiled up it as well. Another example is that True Expats have encountered the world's worst drivers. If they had been in Mumbai, then those drivers were the worst. But they would also say the same if it was Rio, Tehran, or Caracas.

And it won't surprise you to learn that True Expats have been to the hottest place on earth, and the coldest, and in getting there have flown in the worst airlines known to man. That, at least, is their story.

The Doubting Thomas

As you can imagine it's inevitable that the True Expat's stories will meet with a doubting Thomas. This poor forlorn soul may mistakenly attempt to prove that our man has finally stretched the truth too far. If he would only take my advice, he would just keep his doubts to himself.

I bend my knee to our True Expat, may he never change. Our lives would be the poorer without him. But should you meet him please don't mention what I have revealed about him. Truth be told he may not recognize himself because I have, how shall I put it, made small changes ... but only to protect his good name.

As for myself, I'm 75 now and it's time to hang up my hard hat and boots. In writing this book I send my regards to those who have trodden the expatriate footpaths of the oil and gas industry. You all have your interesting stories to tell. And to those of you who have not worked overseas I hope that I can bring a taste of our expatriate life.

Nick Westmore, Isle of Wight, August 2016.

PART 1

EXPAT STORIES

CHAPTER 1

THE BEGINNING 1974

Introduction

It was 1974 and our decision was made. I was a project planning engineer working for John Brown Engineering in the UK, 33 years old, married with three young children. I had been offered a job with Aramco (now Saudi Aramco), the oil producing company of Saudi Arabia. So we were off overseas - my first expatriate job in the oil and gas industry. My wife Jan and three young children Kelven, Charene, and Shenya would follow me once I had been assigned married status accommodation. It was an exciting time for us, our first expatriate assignment.

And so we became expatriates (expats). To attract us to Saudi Arabia Aramco offered incentives such as a tax free salary, family accommodation, healthcare, and education expenses. Oh, and we didn't have to pay UK tax – providing we kept within official guidelines regarding the days per year spent in the UK.

My final overseas job ended in 2008 by which time I had lived and worked in Saudi Arabia (on five different occasions), Holland, Qatar, Bahrain, Sardinia, Malaysia, Azerbaijan, and Iraq. It was during those thirty-four years that I met the True Expats that I write about in this book. The seeds of these stories were recorded in letters I wrote to the folks back home, which I have expanded on for clarity. I hope you enjoy my book - and not find fault with my colloquial style of writing!

I arrive in Dhahran

The Saudi Airlines Tri-Star landed in Saudi Arabia at Dhahran airport and from there I was taken to Aramco's headquarters and allocated accommodation. Early the next morning my first port of call was the personnel department. I learnt that I had been assigned housing and would be working at Aramco's offices in Abqaiq. But first I must go to the security department for my mug-shots.

"Won't take long, just a few minutes' walk," was the advice.

True, a few minutes isn't very long but having just arrived in Saudi I found that the 45C temperature was way above that back in the UK!

Personnel advised me that at 6.30 the next morning I would be picked up by a guy named Sam. He duly arrived in his Chevy pickup, shook my hand with a determined grip, and off we went on the road to Abqaiq, some seventy kilometres away. Sam, short and stocky, hailed from Arkansas and as the miles slipped by our small talk moved to an important subject, not about our employer Aramco, or the heat, or even the endless desert stretching to the horizon. Oh no, Sam was recounting a program on African wildlife that he'd seen on TV the previous evening.

"I'll tell you man, that gorilla looks like a real mean son-of-a-bitch."

I nod in agreement, asking myself if this is bizarre or not! Two days ago I was on the Isle of Wight and now here I am, thousands of miles away, driving down a desert road simmering in the heat and talking about gorillas! Sam scratched his stubbled chin.

"Yeah man, that's a real mean mother, but I reckon that if he came up agin one of our grizzlies, he'd be in for a big surprise."

I nod emphatically in agreement.

Disenchantment

We turned off the main highway at the exit to Abqaiq and followed the signs to Aramco's refinery and housing compound. By this time Sam had just finished his doctorate on gorillas and grizzly bears. At the security gate we completed the visitor registration details and headed for the personnel office. Inside the compound life was just like a typical US town - nice bungalows, lawns, sports facilities, a supermarket, a restaurant, swimming pools, tennis courts, and so on.

Imagine my disappointment then when Personnel informed me that married status Brits were excluded from housing on Aramco compounds. No, instead I had been allocated housing outside of the compound in the old town of Abqaiq.

I wondered what that would be like. Najif, the driver assigned from personnel could sense my disenchantment as we drove into Abqaiq. He showed me our future dirty depressing house standing in a baking hot dusty street. There were no other expats living there. I could not imagine telling my wife that this was where she would have to live when she joined me in Saudi. I thought carefully about the consequences if I declined to live there. My mind was made up. I decided that come what may I would tell Personnel that the housing was unacceptable.

The Empty Quarter

Sam was waiting for me after the house hunting visit. We had to check on the progress of a drilling crew working in the Empty Quarter. He had gassed up the Chevy, loaded igloos (water containers) full of iced water, tested his radio and informed the control centre where we were going. A breakdown is no laughing matter and without water and a radio you might not survive. We set off and passed the old city of Huf-Huf where I would be making telephone calls to my family when, three years later, I worked on the Shedgum project.

We turned off the main road and bumped for miles along an endless stony desert track. Sam was really good company and kept me informed with his tales of Saudi life. One story concerned an engineer who was doing a desert pipeline test. As bad luck would have it his truck broke down. He radioed in to report his position. The Abqaiq security guys then took a while to despatch a rescue team. It's not easy to find a truck in the desert so it took them some time to find it. Only to be mystified. He wasn't there. The searing heat was almost 50 degrees centigrade. Hours later they found his body lying beside the pipeline which ran to the Abqaiq refinery.

The conclusion was that he had convinced himself that the rescue team would not find him. So he had decided to chance it and walk back using the pipeline as his directional aid. Only the Bedouin know how to survive in that desert heat. After talking to the drilling guys we returned to the truck and Sam casually asked me to touch the steering wheel. I touched it and withdrew my hand immediately. It was incredibly hot. Believe me, if you like heat then just make for the Saudi desert.

I turn down Abqaiq

Upon return from our drilling site visit Sam pulled to a stop outside the Abqaiq offices. My personnel friend was happy to see me, but I'm not in the mood to make any concessions as far as their offer of accommodation is concerned.
"Didn't you like it?"
"No sir, no way will I ask my wife and kids to live there."
He asked if there was something wrong with the location. I summed up what must have been obvious to anyone who knew Abqaiq. It was isolated, there were no other expat families living there, no expat school, and no decent shops. I had even seen a Saudi squat and relieve himself in the desert sand not far from the house.

I accept an Apartment - in Dammam

Back in Dhahran my meeting with the personnel chief got straight to the point. I explained why I couldn't accept the Abqaiq housing situation. He was most understanding, pulled a few strings and found us a family apartment in Dammam (fairly close to Dhahran). This was much better compared to that dingy dirty back-street in Abqaiq. My wife and children would have company because the whole apartment building housed expats. Schooling was available at the American Embassy in Dhahran. Soon my family arrived and we moved into our nice apartment. Our neighbours welcomed us to expatriate life, showed us the ropes, and in no time we felt at home.

Sam – my first Aramco True Expat

It was a pleasure to make the acquaintance of Sam. In recognition of his tales of gorillas and grizzlies I am pleased to name him as a True Expat, deserving of his place in the Hall of Fame.

CHAPTER 2

WEE JIMMY AND BIG CHARLEY

Introduction

If you've never travelled to the wonderful city of Glasgow in Scotland, then I guess you haven't experienced the need to re-learn the English language. I say this somewhat mischievously because it strikes me that you need help when trying to grasp their speech.

Why? Because I reckon that of all Scotland it's the most difficult to comprehend. Often in their company I find myself apologizing profusely because I haven't understood one word they've said.

Before the peeved folk of Glasgow descend on me in my hideaway on the Isle of Wight I hastily add that I have a great love of Scotland and its people, none more so than for my very first True Expats…

Heathrow Airport Check-in Desk

The Saudi Airlines check-in at London Heathrow airport was besieged with a boisterous crowd of men from all over the UK. The check-in girls, normally accustomed to dealing with well behaved travellers, were now being given the full treatment by men who knew that this was their last opportunity for a bit of fun before jetting off to their oil industry contracts in Saudi Arabia.

One such stalwart was Wee Jimmy who was determined to make an impression on the attractive young girl behind the counter. He told himself that she was surely the most beautiful girl that he had ever seen. True, the girls back in his home city of Glasgow were also very attractive but this was his first time away from Scotland and here was an opportunity not to be missed.

"Guid mornin darlin, what's a pretty lassie like ye doin workin here." Jimmy's countenance showed no embarrassment as to the poverty of this opening remark. "Wha's your name darlin?"
The girl struggled but just about managed to interpret Jimmy's Glaswegian accent.
"Its Becky … may I see your passport please." Becky gave Jimmy a sweet smile.
"Eye, but there's nay hurry Becky … can I ask ye an important question?"
"Depends what it is." Becky had been propositioned by the best of them.
"How about a date? We can have a few wee drinks and then we'll dance the night away."

Becky smiled. She knew that Jimmy was only joking and she liked his outgoing personality.
"Exactly where in Saudi shall we meet?" she asked innocently.
Jimmy looked perplexed but at that point he noticed his buddy Charley at the next check-in desk and shouted out to him in mock pride.
"Hey Big Charley, do ye ken this lassie is my date tonight."

Charley looked down at Jimmy from his six feet four and gave him a contrived look of contempt. They had been best friends since school days and he knew that what Jimmy lacked in stature he more than made up for in his confident personality.
"Behave yourself Wee Jimmy, ye canna take the lassie to Saudi with ye."
Jimmy's face portrayed a look of contrived severe disappointment and, giving Becky an exaggerated wink, was quick to reply.

"You dinna need to be jealous Big Charley, get away and find your own lassie."

Becky completed the check-in, handed Jimmy his boarding card and passport and wished him a nice flight. Jimmy had one last shot intended for his friend Charley.

"I'll see you later darlin, and if ye take my advice ye'll keep well away from that big Scotsman over yon."

The flight to Dhahran, Saudi Arabia

Much to my pleasure I found that having boarded the plane Jimmy and Charley were seated next to me. Charley took no time to introduce himself. Grabbing my hand with a bear-like paw he shook it vigorously.

"How're doing pal, this is Wee Jimmy, and folks call me Big Charley."

I returned the greeting and as soon as he heard my English accent he gave Jimmy a mischievous look.

"Yon boy's a Sassenach (the Scots term for an Englishman) Jimmy, but we'll no hold it agin him."

Both laughed and I could tell that this was going to be quite a ride. The very thought of those two likeable characters still makes me smile. One of life's joys for me is that in my expat travels I rarely met an *average-sized* Scot. They have all either been big or small!

Like me, Jimmy and Charley were going to Saudi for the first time. Whilst I was going on a married status contract where the family accompanies you, theirs was bachelor status which meant that they had to work for four months before having two weeks' home R&R (rest and recuperation). As if that wasn't tough enough, Saudi Arabia does not allow any alcohol whatsoever. We had all been gravely warned by the recruitment agent of the strict anti-alcohol laws and that a prison sentence, lashes and deportation could be imposed if one was found either possessing or being under the influence of alcohol.

But four months without a drink is a daunting prospect for your expat, especially if he is accustomed to a drink in the bars of Glasgow on a Saturday night. Thus Wee Jimmy and Big Charley had determined that if they couldn't drink when they were in Saudi at least they could have a wee dram on the plane. Suffice it to say that they applied themselves copiously to this effect. Consequently, by the time we touched down in Dhahran they were truly under the influence. I found myself behind them as we disembarked and, remembering the warning about alcohol, was convinced that they would be in trouble once off the plane.

Arrival in Dhahran, Big Charley falls headlong

Most airports nowadays have a pedestrian bridge that fits snugly against the aircraft but that was not so on that hot July morning back in 1974. I expect some of you can still remember past days when we had to walk down steep steps from an aircraft and such was the case as Big Charley, followed closely by Wee Jimmy, commenced his erratic descent. Wee Jimmy was clearly concerned for both of them because tackling the steps in their inebriated condition was more than daunting to say the least.

"Be careful where ye are goin' Big Charley, mind that ya dinna fall doon the steps."
This well-intentioned advice was particularly apt because at the bottom of the steps stood four Saudi policemen.
"Nay problem, Jimmy," slurred Charley, "there's nay chance I'll fall doon man."
With a downwards glance at the policemen, he added, "anyone can see that I'm as sober as a judge."

As if to prove this doubtful assertion he decided that entry into this foreign land should be heralded with a rendition of "The Flower of Scotland." With commendable enthusiasm and heavily slurred words he commenced the song.

No true Scot will leave another to sing this stirring anthem alone thus Wee Jimmy joined in with his pal. The four policemen upon hearing their drunken tones looked everywhere for the owners of this cultural exchange and spotted the two inebriated friends just as they reached the bottom of the steps. At this critical point Big Charley thought that he was at ground level.

Unfortunately, he had another step to go. By the time he realized that he wasn't on terra firma he had lost his balance and had fallen headlong onto the tarmac - right at the feet of the startled policemen.

Policemen help big Charley to his Feet

Wee Jimmy staggered to his friends' side, barely able to stand himself. Big Charley lay prone so Wee Jimmy knelt down beside him and proceeded to attempt to take his pulse.
After several failed attempts he started to shake Big Charley's shoulder.
"Charley, are ye still alive man, ye dinna look tae good tae me."
Charley mumbled incoherently and a look of relief crossed Wee Jimmy's face.
"Thank God for that man, I thought ye were dead for a moment there."

Then Wee Jimmy, all five feet two inches of him, tried to get Big Charley, a sixteen stoner, to his feet. Even if Jimmy hadn't been inebriated it was extremely unlikely that he could have lifted Charley, but your Glaswegian is no quitter. With a herculean heave and with eyes bulging he attempted to get Big Charley off the tarmac. But he just didn't have the strength and by now the heat had hit him and he was perspiring profusely. But to his credit Wee Jimmy was not to be beaten so looking at the policemen he gestured towards Charley.
"Would ye mind geeing me a wee hand here, ma friend is nay feelin tae guid."

Much to our surprise two policemen took hold of Charley and with no mean effort got him to his feet. Tottering dangerously, he thanked these Samaritans. Without waiting another moment Wee Jimmy took Big Charley's arm over his shoulder and both lurched unsteadily in the direction of the terminal building. The policemen watched them go whilst the rest of us looked on in amazement, convinced that they were never going to make it.

They Breathe a Sigh of Relief

But they did. On reaching the terminal building Wee Jimmy and Big Charley cast worried glances back at the policemen. They were both very concerned that they might have been followed, fearing arrest for being drunk. But seeing that they weren't Wee Jimmy brightened up and turned to Big Charley with a huge look of relief on his face.

"Would ye believe it Charley, yon policemen are a grand bunch, nay problem at all, eh man."

Big Charley, still leaning heavily on Wee Jimmy's shoulder, declared his approval as to the outcome of their arrival.

"Och ey, they're a great bunch of lads Jimmy, and I ken that Saudi is nay as bad as people make it oot to be!"

I never saw these two characters again but I haven't forgotten them. How they escaped detention for that inebriated entry into Saudi I'll never know. All I can say to Wee Jimmy and Big Charley is that you are my first True Expats, welcome to your place in the Hall of Fame.

CHAPTER 3

MAKING MOONSHINE IN SAUDI ARABIA

Introduction

When I look back on our early expat life in Saudi Arabia it wasn't as bad as we greenhorns imagined it would be. For example, those who liked an occasional drink had been told that they would have to go without. In reality I found that your average expat will tolerate the heat, the long working hours, and even putting on hold the loving attentions of his wife or girlfriend, but it's just not realistic to expect him to remain there and not think about a relaxing drink at the end of an arduous week's work. His problem is where does he get his liquor? He can't go down to the local liquor store because there isn't one.

But all is not lost because amongst the expats is a saviour, a guy who is a master at making moonshine...

Jethro – Master Moonshiner

Any expat who takes on the mantle of a moonshiner in Saudi is in my opinion nigh on crazy. Why? Because he knows that if he gets caught then his Contract is quickly terminated and travel back home may well be preceded by lashes and a prison sentence. So, our moonshine entrepreneur knows the story and assesses the risks. At all costs he must avoid detection.

His first requirement is to be housed on a Western compound, safe from the eyes of the Saudi authorities. Then he must be able to obtain a Liquor Still and equally be well practiced in its use. Finally, he must be able to get his hands on the ingredients which include (I'm not an expert) yeast, sugar, and water. If you were to ask me if I have ever seen a Liquor Still, I can honestly say that I haven't but I understand that in simple terms it's a stainless steel tank and some pipework in which alcohol is fermented and then distilled.

In Saudi and the Middle East this volatile moonshine is named Siddiqi which when translated from Arabic means "my friend," a misnomer if ever there was one! In appearance it looks like water but should you be so brave as to take a mere sip you will feel it burn its way ferociously right down into your stomach.

In my opinion it's a drink of last resort and believe me you really have to be very dedicated to enjoy the stuff. You can dilute it with Coca-cola or Tonic however on the only occasion that I tried it I immediately found that it's definitely not for me. But hey, live and let live.

It didn't take long after my arrival in Saudi before I met Jethro who hailed from Louisiana. A nicer guy you couldn't wish to meet. We both worked for Aramco in their off-shore projects division. Jethro's previous work experience was on the oil platforms in the Gulf of Mexico however he had another expertise not mentioned in his CV… making alcohol from a Still. So, cometh the hour, cometh the man!

Defensive Driving

Although our office was in Dhahran Jethro's preference was to live on the Aramco housing compound in Abqaiq. The down side was that he was faced with a two-hour drive to work. Before long he concluded that the daily drive wasn't such a good idea due to the poor standard of driving, particularly by the truck-drivers.

Let me tell you something right now. If you are driving on a Saudi road and there's a truck coming straight for you on your side of the highway don't expect the driver to put himself out to gain his side of the road. What you must do is get off the road. It's called defensive driving. That way you'll stay alive. So you will understand that Jethro made a wise decision when he arranged to stay with a friend in the Dhahran housing compound during the week, returning to Abqaiq for the weekend.

Soon Jethro had siddiqi customers to satisfy so at the start of the week he drove from Abqaiq up to Dhahran with a consignment of his home-made moonshine in the trunk of his car! Let me tell you something, dread the thought if the police happened to search that car … a fear I'll get to in a moment.

My first Helicopter Flight

It was whilst working in the offshore projects division that I made my first of many helicopter flights offshore. Once there we would review the installation of the new oil platform jackets (that sit in the water) and their topside modules (that sit on the jacket). On that first visit we set off early morning and flew fixed wing from Dhahran to the helo base at Safaniya. Awaiting us was our helo pilot, a veteran of Vietnam.

I still vividly remember that first flight, my stomach in my mouth as we lifted-off and later wheeled over at a steep angle to drop from the sky to a perfect landing on the Platform helo deck. Wow! Fantastic! Our pilot, casually dressed in a Los Angeles Lakers tee shirt and blue jeans gave us the thumbs-up as we disembarked.

I Borrow Jethro's Car

But at the start of the next week a situation occurred which had Jethro worried, very worried. The background is that my apartment was in Dammam which is about ten miles or so from our office in Dhahran. Normally I stayed at work for my lunch but on the odd occasion I would go home. I didn't yet have my own car so I had asked Jethro if I could borrow his car and he had readily agreed.

Due to reasons beyond my control my return back to the office was delayed - the apartment maintenance-man almost electrocuted himself. Thus when I returned to Dhahran I was an hour or so late. As I approached the office parking lot I saw Jethro in the distance walking up and down and upon seeing me he rushed over to the car.

"Nick, are you all right?" There was a strained urgency in his voice. "I've been waiting for you to get back … what's been the problem?" I had never before seen him in such a state.
"I'm sorry I'm late back but I had to get an ambulance for our maintenance guy, he put his hand in the electrical fuse box and nearly electrocuted himself."
Jethro visibly relaxed.
"Man, I've been so worried … and are you sure that the police have not looked in the car?"
"No man, it's been locked, I'm the only one who has used it. Why do you ask?"
"It's just that I forgot to tell you … the trunk of the car is full of Siddiqi!"

Phew! Can you imagine how I felt?

The Explosion

Little did Jethro know that there was another storm cloud on the horizon. Apart from the risk to the moon-shiner being caught making or possessing siddiqi there was the ever-present concern in the hot temperatures of Saudi of a Still over-heating. That spells trouble. But right from the outset Jethro was confident that he had set up his installation correctly and that there would not be any problems.

The site workshop had made a perfect job of welding the stainless steel tank and stainless steel piping. How Jethro managed to get these items off-site and into his housing compound unnoticed one can only wonder. He installed it in his air conditioned garage and started the distillation process.

The next day, after he had driven to work in Dhahran, there was a power outage on the Abqaiq compound. The outside temperature rose to a mid-summer 45C and so too did the temperature in the garage. The powerful electric fan which he had installed to keep the distilling temperature at a steady level was silent. Not a breath of air could be found. The alcohol in the Still increased in temperature and so too did the pressure.

According to his neighbor's wife sometime around four in the afternoon she heard an almighty bang. Jethro rushed home from Dhahran fearing that the Aramco security department would get involved and, worse still, report the matter to the local police. He quickly repaired the Still and to prevent another power outage installed a large battery as back-up to the fan! Jethro was back in business. A cool character indeed!

Warning

Not long after that my contract with Aramco came to an end and I returned to the UK. For all I know Jethro's extra-curricular activities are still going strong. What a special guy he is but just a word of warning, if you should ever meet him don't even think about borrowing his car!

Jethro, for your service to other expats you have earned the right to be called a True Expat. Welcome to the Hall of Fame.

CHAPTER 4

THE EXPAT AND THE SMELLING JUDGES

Introduction

I don't know about you but these days I'm not worried about being breathalysed because I have given up on alcohol. But what of those who do like an occasional drink? I find it interesting that drink-driving legislation has been around for a long time, in fact as far back as 1872. That's when a law was passed in the UK that (amongst other things) banned driving your cattle whilst you were inebriated. For this insufferable offence you could be fined forty shillings and get one month in prison. But, I ask myself, without the aid of a breathalyzer how did they determine if one was under the influence?

Perhaps this account gives us a clue, if not something to smile about …

I meet Jeff

One morning, not long after I joined Aramco (in Saudi Arabia in 1974) I had just settled in my Dhahran office when I heard someone approaching along the hallway. That was when I met Jeff, a fellow Brit from Yorkshire. The trouble with Jeff, in my opinion, is that he's such a happy character. Whilst I was slowly waking up to the day he was whistling a happy tune and the moment he spotted me he grabbed my hand in an iron grip and introduced himself. We became good friends. I learnt that he was married to Sally, his wife of over twenty years, and that they had three teenage girls who, in his words, had all suddenly grown up overnight.

His problem was that he had been made redundant, another casualty of the UK's declining engineering industries. There was little hope of finding work near home and relocation across country was not an option because the girls schooling was at a critical stage. But there was another option - he agreed with his wife that he would seek work overseas and join the Expat brigade.

Jeff makes a good Impression

When he heard of Aramco's job vacancies he wasted no time in submitting his application. The Aramco engineering director conducting his interview was very impressed with his experience and his positive approach to life. A couple of weeks later he received his job offer and after arriving in Saudi he worked hard and made a good impression on the Aramco management.

But that wasn't the only good impression he made because whilst having a social drink with his pals he surprised them in that it had little effect on him. This was quite remarkable because they were drinking siddiqi, a volatile alcohol best left, in my view, to those with greater desire than taste and totally illegal in Saudi Arabia as I explain in more detail elsewhere.

Jeff is arrested

Some weeks later I caught sight of Jeff as he was passing by my office. Missing was the usual happy whistling and positive demeanor. Something was wrong. He joined me, made himself a cup of strong black coffee and slumped into a chair. He then told me about his near-disaster the previous evening. It all started when he and his pals had enjoyed a couple of rounds of siddiqi (or probably more!) in the privacy of his room following which they had gone for a curry at a restaurant in Al Khobar, a local town.

After leaving the restaurant Jeff had set off for the journey back to Dhahran. Within minutes of getting onto the highway he felt nauseous. He pulled over to the side of the road where he was horribly sick. In his distress he hadn't noticed that a police patrol car had pulled up alongside him. The policemen suspected him of drunk driving and in no time at all he was arrested. So off they went to the downtown Al Khobar police station. Jeff was kept waiting for a couple of hours. At last he was taken through to an interview room.

The Smelling Judges

There, awaiting him, seated at a longish table, were three very serious looking Saudi guys. What Jeff didn't know was that he was about to be breathalysed - these were the Smelling Judges. The oldest and senior of the three told him that he had been arrested on suspicion of driving whilst under the influence of alcohol and that he would have to take a breath test. Jeff was understandably very worried. What if he were convicted? A recent headline story in the British press involved a truck driver in Saudi who was apprehended and sentenced for drunk-driving. His sentence was lashes, then imprisonment and then deportation.

His thoughts were halted when he was told to breathe into the face of the first judge.

Jeff was completely taken aback by this unusual request.
"Excuse me … do you mean that you want me to actually breathe into your face?"
The judge nodded and affirmed his request.
"Yes, breathe the breath into my face, and come closer, must smell breath."
Jeff looked around the room but there was no-one he could turn to for confirmation that he had heard correctly. He braced himself, took a deep breath and without restraint gave the judge a full blast - straight into his face. The judge flinched and his expression changed to that of utter repugnance. Jeff gave no visible sign but was very pleased because his breath must have smelt truly awful.

Encouraged, he moved in front of the second judge who undoubtedly had just lost all enthusiasm for his designated task.

"Are you ready for your turn sir?" Jeff asked, innocently. The second judge glanced right and left at his companions but found no sign of compassion. Upon this Jeff gave him an equally abhorrent blast. The judge blanched, the color drained from his face and he appeared about to pass out.

By now Jeff was getting the hang of things so saving his most obnoxious blast for the last judge he lined himself up for the coup-de-grace. Drawing on his innermost strength he filled his lungs and expelled a massive wave of stinking breath straight into the third judges' face. That did it. The poor guy reeled backwards in disgust. All three judges had probably never smelt anything so awful. The senior judge regained an element of composure and directed him to return to the police waiting room.

He sat and waited, and waited. He was deeply concerned as to the outcome of the breath test. Then, without explanation, the policeman who had arrested him curtly told him that he could leave. No-one was more relieved to get out of that police station.

Jeff recalls the Breath Test

"I'll tell you what man" Jeff recounted, "I was nay drunk, it must have been that damn curry we had."
"Of course not Jeff," I replied condescendingly. "No way would Dhahran's champion siddiqi drinker be under the influence."
His face lit up with a thought. He closed the office door and lowered his voice.
"Do you know what Nick, if it hadn't been for the smell of that curry I would now be in prison awaiting lashes and deportation." A further thought then crossed his mind accompanied by a growing smile.
"You should have seen the look of disgust on the faces of the Smelling Judges when they smelt my breath. I'll tell you man, it was a sight I'll never forget."

With that we couldn't control our laughter. Jeff knew that he was very lucky. Not saved by the bell, but saved by the curry! One would have liked to have seen his commendable performance in front of the Smelling Judges. No doubt nowadays they have been retired, superseded by breathalyzers. After sampling Jeff's breath I'm sure that day didn't come a minute too soon for them!

Jeff's unique Smelling Judge story certainly qualifies him for the Hall of Fame – a much liked guy and a True Expat.

CHAPTER 5

THE PRESIDENT'S JET

Introduction

My first visit to Dubai was in 1974. I had flown there on a two-hour flight from Dhahran, Saudi Arabia. I was employed by Aramco for one year as a project planning engineer and we, my wife Jan, and young children Kelven, Charene and Shenya, lived in the port city of Dammam. My colleagues and I were there to review the fabrication progress of the offshore oil platform Jackets (the part that sits in the water) and the Topsides Modules (the parts that sit on the Jacket). Having concluded our visit, we were to fly back that evening to Dhahran. That, at least was the plan, but once again Fate took a hand in things - much to the delight of Don, a true Expat, and his buddies, all Southerners from Louisiana, USA.

Business visit to Dubai

It's been a very hot day. We have been climbing up and down the Jackets and Topsides Modules in the fabrication yard on the water's edge of the Dubai creek. One could easily ring the perspiration out of one's shirt. It's been thirsty work. So when late afternoon we depart for the airport I sense an air of determination.

We disembark from the taxi and I follow my companions who head straight for the airport bar. This is my first trip to Dubai and I'm the only Brit in the group, the rest of the guys are from Louisiana, like Don, a True Expat for my Hall of Fame. In this story I reveal how he raided the liquor cabinet of the President of Aramco's jet on behalf of his buddies.

Our Aircraft develops a fault

Time is of the essence, the return flight to Dhahran is due to take off shortly. The first round of drinks disappears effortlessly and so does the second. But there's a message from Hans the pilot. He can't get one of the aircraft engines to start. What a piece of luck. The guys know that we won't get another cold beer until we come back on our next visit so a third round is duly despatched.

I know Hans quite well; he's an Expat from Holland and lives with his wife and young son in our apartment building in Dammam. He explains that the starboard engine is malfunctioning. It simply won't start. He will have to radio Dhahran and arrange for a replacement aircraft to be sent down for us. The Louisianans suggest that there is no need for him to go to that extreme. They are willing to suffer for Aramco and stay at the Sheraton for the night, adding that there's plenty of time to travel back tomorrow.

The Sheraton, as you may have guessed, is five-star luxury and sits right on the water's edge of the Gulf. Not exactly a hardship to stay there! The Louisianans impress me. Any expat worth his salt would have tried this ploy.

I get a Message to Jan, my Wife

But Hans is on the radio, linked to Dhahran via one of the offshore oil platforms. Yes, they will find a replacement aircraft and send it as soon as possible. The guys groan, disappointed. They won't get their overnight stay at the Sheraton.

Meanwhile I'm concerned that my wife will worry because she's expecting me home by eight, and there's no way it's going to be anywhere near that time. So, whilst my companions continue to apply themselves to the task in hand I ask if I can get a message to her. I'm told that there isn't a direct telephone line to Saudi from the airport (there is now, of course) so it's a case of sending my message via one of the offshore platforms to Aramco's head office in Dhahran and thence by messenger to my wife in our apartment in Dammam. This took quite a while and just as I joined my pals in the bar Hans announced that the replacement aircraft was now on its way down to Dubai.

The President of Aramco's Jet

By now my Louisianans were in a jovial mood. The replacement aircraft arrived and we filed out onto the runway. I wish you could have seen their faces because standing in front of us was the Aramco Presidents' sleek, private jet. Believe me it didn't take us long to climb aboard! For those of you accustomed to flying in such luxury I guess that you wouldn't have found this unusual but we were very impressed. Let me tell me you that this is not your average aircraft. The interior furnishing is five star.

Once on board we had just relaxed in the luxurious armchairs when my friend Don discovered that the President had his own personal drinks cabinet and what's more it was unlocked! Bourbons, Rye whiskeys, Wines, Jack Daniels, a stroke of luck if ever there was one! Now I ask you, if you were the President of Aramco, would you lend your jet, with a full drinks cabinet, unlocked, to a bunch of hard drinking good old boys from Louisiana!

Jack Daniels Anyone?

As we take off from Dubai and head northwards back to Dhahran the whiskey glasses are filled and the bottle of Jack Daniels is looking a shadow of its former self. Don and his pals are now in great form and show no remorse for drinking the president's whisky. I must add that if I were him I would think twice before I tackled them about it. These Louisianans are big, strong, raw-boned men, more than capable of taking care of themselves.

By now the conversation, somewhat inebriated, had gotten on to re-enacting the Civil War. One guy is strongly of the opinion that the

South will prevail should there be a next time. How, someone enquires. The reply, delivered with difficulty, reminded his listeners that most of the North's oil came from the South, so come winter "all we have to do is just turn off the oil then those Yankees will freeze ". This hypothesis was received with great amusement, if not disbelief. Meanwhile the drinks cabinet was not spared, necessitating significant replenishment before the President made his next flight.

Lock your drinks cabinet

That flight was the highlight of my trips down to Dubai. I so enjoyed the company of my Louisianan colleagues. And as for Don, well, he deserves to be in the Hall of Fame, a True Expat. Should he ever visit with you take my advice, lock your drinks cabinet, or say goodbye to your bottle of Jack Daniels.

CHAPTER 6

A FILIPINO EXPAT BUYS PIGS EARS

Introduction

One of the disadvantages of working overseas as an Expatriate is that you often can't get those favorite foods that you so enjoy back home. For example, if you live or have worked in the Philippines then you will know that the nation's favorite food is pork, especially Lechon, a dish that features a whole pig roasted over charcoal. Every year more than a million Filipinos leave to work abroad and I wouldn't mind betting that wherever they are they would jump at a chance to buy some pork, any pork let alone a whole pig. But it may not be that easy, especially if working in a Muslim country where all pork products are banned. This story is how one Filipino expat got around that rule...

In Search of Pork

Many Filipinos work in Saudi Arabia which is the strictest of all Muslim countries. Nonetheless there are those prepared to go to any lengths to get their hands on some pork, as was the case with Ramón, a Filipino colleague and expat friend of mine. He made a plan. He would go for a week-end break across the Causeway which connects Saudi Arabia with Bahrain, stay with a friend from the Philippines who worked in Manama, the capital of Bahrain, and find some pork.

So a couple of weeks later he found himself wandering around the narrow streets of the Souk and at last he came across a butcher's shop where low and behold the guy behind the counter was a fellow Filipino.

They got to talking and it transpired that the shop had no pork joints left, only pig's ears. Ramon was immediately interested and said that he would like to buy them, mentioning that he was going to take them back to Saudi. The shop assistant was obviously wasted in his profession because he immediately foresaw the difficulty that would arise if Ramon was found taking pig's ears back into a country where pork was banned.

So he came up with what I think was a brilliant if not amusing suggestion. Why not put a label on the pig's ears saying that they were lamb's ears? Well, you can imagine how funny I found this idea. Can you visualise a Saudi customs guy examining the label on what must have been very large lamb's ears? Have you seen lamb's ears lately? They don't even look like pig's ears and for sure they are not that large. Don't you just love these guys? Because Ramon got away with it.

Mind you, not having ever eaten pig's ears I can't say what they are like but for Ramón they must have been a feast. Perhaps not quite as good as Lechon but nevertheless a pleasant reminder of things back home.

For his exemplary effort in securing his nations' favourite dish I reckon that Ramon fully deserves to become a True Expat, and his place in the Hall of fame.

Footnote:

From 1994 to 1996 I worked for Mannai Engineering in Bahrain during which time I crossed the Causeway quite a number of times to visit work sites in Saudi. However, going back to 1974 (my first time in Saudi), if my family and I wanted to visit Bahrain for a weekend break then we had to take a Dhow.

CHAPTER 7

JIMMY TWO-RIVERS

Introduction

In 1977 I returned to Saudi Arabia on a single status basis to join the construction project team of Foster Wheeler (an engineering, project management and construction company). We were based at Shedgum and the task was to build the ground-breaking Shedgum Gas Plant. Our client, Aramco, had decided to utilize natural gases previously considered a waste product. Shedgum is located close to the Rub al Khali, meaning the Empty Quarter named because, well, it's empty. But it does have oil. Lots of it. And it was at Shedgum that I met and made new friends one of whom, from the USA, had all the makings of a True Expat...

Cub - my First Friend

It was the evening of my first day at Shedgum. After I completed my meal in the mess-hall I headed for a comfortable chair in an area set aside for relaxation. No sooner had I sat down than I met Cub, an American construction engineer who originally hailed from Montana but had moved to Texas to work in the oil industry.

When I think about it I realise an interesting fact about oil and gas expatriates from the States. Hardly one of them currently lived in the place where they were born. I found this unusual because I thought it natural that one didn't move far from one's roots. I live on the Isle of Wight where, believe this if you will, there are folks in past times that lived in Freshwater that had *never* been to Ryde on the other side of the island. To be fair to them it's a long way to go, over twenty miles!

Jimmy Two-Rivers arrives on site

Cub and I hit it off right from the start and we settled down to talk about how difficult construction works were in such a hot climate. Whilst we were talking a new guy, coffee cup in hand, asked if he could join us. We gestured to an empty chair and quickly took stock of him. He was definitely not your average dude. Tallish, maybe around five feet nine, he was dressed in tight black jeans, an embroidered black shirt, high-heeled black cowboy boots and a black Stetson complete with two white feathers held firmly in place in the headband. His long jet-black hair was tied in a single ponytail. Everything about his appearance was impressive. "Hope you guys don't mind me joining y'all, just arrived today, name's Jimmy, but folks call me Jimmy Two-Rivers." We shook hands and introduced ourselves.

The Little Big Horn

I'm in new territory and just couldn't resist the urge to ask him about his Stetson.
"That's a cool Stetson man, where did you get it?"
"Bought it back home in Montana." Jimmy removed his hat and smoothed the two white feathers which were secured by the headband.
"These feathers are real special man, shows you that I'm a genuine descendent of an Indian tribal chief."

This remark saw Cub's ears prick up, and I could sense what was going through his mind. I was to learn that he was given to observing people, weighing them up, and then asking probing questions of them if he felt they might be stretching the truth.
"Well ain't that something man ... what tribe might that be?"
Jimmy eased his Stetson back on his head and fingered the multi-colored beaded necklace that was visible under his unbuttoned shirt.

"Cheyenne man, ah' can trace my roots way back."

I'm hooked, ready to believe anything. When I was a kid I loved playing Cowboys and Indians, remembering those long summer days when we played around my grandfather's barns and stables and now, wow, here I am face to face with a *real* Indian chief!
"Weren't South Montana mostly Sioux territory?" probed Cub.
"No way man, Cheyenne were the biggest tribe."
Cub could see mileage here, this promised to be good.

"A'h ain't never met a real Cheyenne Indian Chief, I'm sure pleased to meet ya."
Cub's strategy was paying dividends because Jimmy was now warming to his subject.
"Yea man, my great-great-great grand-daddy was chief Crazy Horse, fought against Custer at the Little Big Horn, whipped his ass real good man." Jimmy had a look of pride on his face. This was getting better and better.

Drug Store Cowboys

Following our introduction in the mess-hall Cub and I had become Jimmy's firmest devotees and friends. Mind you, we were not the only ones to be mesmerised by his stories. He was such an interesting guy that in time everyone had been told about his remarkable life experiences. Impressive stories about things he'd done, places he'd been, women he'd wooed. One evening I had another question for him.
"Hey Jimmy, are you telling us that your clothes, boots, and hat are all genuine?"
"Listen man" he replied, "you know those dudes y'all see on TV, dressed up in wild-west clothes, why, they ain't nothing more than drug-store cowboys." His expression showed nothing but contempt for these charlatans.
"Ain't none of them wear the real stuff genuine cowboys wear."

Cub is fast on the draw, his countenance now displaying innocent admiration.
"So you're a cowboy, as well as an Indian chief?"

You have to give it to Jimmy because not even Cub can shake him down.

"Man, there ain't nothin' you can tell me about herdin' cattle."

Ahh.

I breathe a deep sigh of contentment as we settle back for an enjoyable evening, safe in the knowledge that we will be entertained with another unbelievable story. At times, just to be mischievous, we would interrupt with a loaded question, attempting to trap him. But it was futile. Jimmy was too good for us.

Jimmy won't Work at Night

A couple of months later Jimmy, Cub and I were having our usual after-dinner coffee when he indignantly complained that he had been asked to work at night rather than during the day.

"Hell, man, aint no way 'ah came here to work at night."

I had to keep my own council on this one because I had supported the nightshift. We were falling behind schedule on the building foundations because of the blistering heat in the day. Better to do it at night.

Cub was ever ready to exploit the situation.

"Hell man, seems to me there ain't nothing you can do about it."

Jimmy was not to be deterred.

"Well, I'm tellin' you man, ah'm goin to git mah sleep as usual."

Cub's look of concern belied his mischievous intent.

"How can you sleep man, ain't no place to sleep out on the construction site."

"Hell man, I'm goin to tell the site manager I ain't going to work at night!"

The next day I was called to a meeting and the site manager was in a blazing mood.

"Jimmy is a right pain in the butt, tells me he ain't gonna work at night."

Jimmy is Fired

That evening, in the mess-hall, was the last time we would see Jimmy. The site manager had run out of patience and fired him, telling him to get his butt off the site forthwith.

"Sorry to hear you're going man."

Cub's comment genuinely portrayed how we both felt. We'd had some good fun with Jimmy and he had made our days at Shedgum all the more bearable for it. Jimmy smiled and with his cowboy boots lazily placed on the coffee table told us that he had a secret to tell us.

"Hell man, ain't nothin to be sorry about and I ain't got no hard feelin's. Truth be known - ah only come here to see what Saudi is like - never intended to stay but a short while." Cub and I laughed. This was vintage Jimmy. Who else would take being fired so casually? Nothing, but nothing could dampen his spirits.

Jimmy's still telling his Stories

I have often thought about Jimmy Two-Rivers over the years, whether he really was descended from a Cheyenne Chief. If I have any doubts about his ancestry there is one thing I'm certain of - he's out there somewhere, captivating his expat buddies with his entertaining stories. I can just picture him, with his high heeled boots on the coffee table, recounting Shedgum.

"Ah'll tell you man, I told the site manager ah wasn't goin to work no nightshift. Then ah told him that he could shove his job!"

It was a pleasure to make the acquaintance of Cub and Jimmy Two-Rivers. I salute them both as True Expats, deserving of their place in the Hall of Fame!

CHAPTER 8

PAUL'S STORY

Introduction

My travels as an Expatriate in the oil and gas industry have given me rich material for this book. The guys I met and worked with came from all corners of the globe. Each has his own story to tell, with differing life experiences. Once you get to know them, given time, they share those experiences, their ups and downs, joys and sorrows. Who amongst hasn't been there as well? In this chapter I recall my encounter with a genuinely nice guy, proof positive that there still is good in this world - I'm sure you will emphasize with him as much as I did ...

I meet Paul

Paul was one of the quieter, less extrovert expats you sometimes encounter. We first met on a business trip from London to Cuxhaven in north Germany. Swapping stories of Expat life, he mentioned Ras Tanura in Saudi Arabia. We immediately had something in common because it's a place I know very well. His story has stuck in my mind because it's sad yet heart-warming too. Paul grew up in Manchester, graduated from university with an honors degree in Chemical Engineering and chose a career in the oil and gas industry. The years flew by and before he knew it he was pushing forty and still a bachelor.

Paul falls for Fatima

That's when fate took a decisive hand in his life. He had gone to London to work for an international oil Company and that's where he met Fatima. They got on well together and before long she told him her life story. Her Libyan ex-husband, who was a consultant doctor, had divorced her and returned to practice in Tripoli, abandoning her and their two sons. Now, on her own, she was raising the boys without his financial support.

For the first time in his life Paul was smitten, he fell in love with Fatima. They say that love is blind and thus he believed her account of the divorce. They married and she moved into his house with the boys. The first couple of years passed peacefully. Paul built a good relationship with the boys whom he genuinely liked. He and Fatima then discussed whether or not to have children but she wouldn't hear of it. He acquiesced even though he would have liked a child of their own.

Next Fatima pressed Paul to send the boys to boarding school, arguing that it would be good for them. Paul had reservations. What if the boys didn't want to go? Plus, they could hardly afford it. But Fatima prevailed.

Divorce Papers

Several months later he arrived to an empty home. Fatima was absent. On the hallway floor was a large sealed envelope. He was shocked when he opened it to find divorce papers. He had not the slightest inkling that anything was wrong in their marriage. The reason for the divorce was incompatibility. Paul telephoned everyone who knew Fatima and after days of worry he found out that she had left England and returned to Libya. She was living in Tripoli . . . Moreover, she had left without her sons. Emotionally he was shattered and realized that he had been very naive when it came to women.

The divorce went through and Paul was shocked when his solicitor told him that he would have to sell the house, the car, the furniture, and so on. It appeared that Fatima demanded half of everything, mercilessly taking every last penny that she could get. But what really hurt him was the situation with the boys. Following the sale of the house he had no choice but to live as a lodger in a Bed and Breakfast hotel.

The problem was that at the end of the boarding school term he no longer had a place for them to stay. He asked Fatima's solicitor to contact her in order to send them out to Tripoli. A response came back from her – why couldn't he have them? So again he went to her Solicitor and explained that he was living in a B&B therefore he didn't have a place for them to stay.

The next reply was even more indicative of Fatima's cruel state of mind. She suggested that the eldest boy went to live in London with her "ex" husband's sister and that the youngest should join her in Tripoli. To add to the absurdity and heartlessness of this suggestion it was left to Paul to ask the sister if she would accept the proposal. Paul had never met the sister before. Worse still he had to tell the eldest boy that his mother didn't want him. Paul said that it hurt him deeply to see the boys in this situation.

Depressed, homeless, and divorced, this was the lowest point in his life. He just had to do something. He decided to resign his position and seek work overseas because he needed to get back on his feet financially. Fortunately, he found a job with Aramco in Saudi Arabia.

Paul at Ras Tanura in Saudi Arabia

Aramco have a trailer-park for male bachelor employees up at Ras Tanura refinery on the Persian Gulf coast. Paul arrived in the simmering heat of the summer and after surveying the lifeless desert surrounding him he concluded that he had arrived in hell. He felt just about as miserable and unhappy as one could get. Once shown to his trailer he threw his bags on the floor and lay on the bed, deeply depressed. He felt completely alone. He was the new guy in town and had no-one to confide in to exorcise the pain of the previous months.

Sobbing Sounds from Next Door

Suddenly he was aroused from his depression by an unfamiliar sound coming from his neighbor's trailer. What was it? It sounded like someone sobbing. Paul decided to investigate. He made his way to his neighbor's entrance and tentatively knocked on the door. No reply, but the sobbing continued. Paul told me that at this point he was undecided as to what to do. Should he interrupt and enter, or should he quietly go un-noticed back to his room?

After moments of hesitation he slowly opened the door and announced his presence. What he saw was a guy sitting on his bed, clasping a photograph frame in his hands, sobbing his heart out. With tears streaming down his face he looked up at Paul and motioned him to sit down on the bed. Paul said that he had never felt so uncomfortable in his life, not having seen a man so distraught. He understood that the photograph was the cause of such emotion and was curious to know why. So he gradually leant over to take a peek at it. Meanwhile the guy just wept and wept.

Then he showed Paul the photo and between sobs explained that his wife had just sent him a letter saying she was leaving him for another man and wanted a divorce. With this his sobbing re-doubled. He paused for a moment, looked at Paul with pain in his eyes and sobbed "Why has she done this to me?" The guys' anguish tore at Paul's heart. He couldn't help himself and the next moment he too was sobbing - louder than his new friend - for his own awful betrayal by the heartless Fatima.

Heartache is Universal

Life's a funny old thing isn't it? Having met many Expats one hears all sorts of stories including mistresses, marital failure, maintenance debts, multiple girlfriends, angry ex-wives. But this story is the reverse of the usual situation. Here we had two guys whose wives had dumped *them*. And it illustrates that men too can be hurt when their lives take a downward spiral of betrayal and heartache.

Paul - an Expat with a Heart of Gold

But time heals. Paul came through his marriage break-down and banked his expatriate earnings. Eventually he left Saudi Arabia to take up a new position with good prospects in the UK. In telling his story one couldn't detect any bitterness for his ex-wife. Rather he was merciless in taking the mickey out of himself when describing the episode when he had joined his hooch-buddy and sobbed his heart out.

Paul is a genuinely nice guy. He hasn't re-married. The last time I heard from him he had bought a small terraced house in west London. And I was not at all surprised to learn that he had established contact with his eldest step-son who was coming to stay with him the next weekend.

Paul, you've got a heart of gold, you deserve your place in the Hall of Fame. You're a gentleman, and a True Expat.

CHAPTER 9

SOCCER IN THE DESERT

Introduction

The 2022 FIFA soccer World Cup is scheduled to take place in *Qatar*. It has been reported that this will be the first Arab country to host the soccer World Cup. But hey, hang on a minute, what about the soccer played back in 1977 at Shedgum in Saudi Arabia? Surely history should record the formation of the Shedgum soccer league, the desert sand compacted into a pitch, the fierce rivalry between teams from different countries, and the absence of a referee - that is until Rob arrived on site...

Huge Interest in Soccer

It was 6pm on a July evening at the soccer pitch, located near the huge Shedgum construction site. The 40C desert heat was subsiding and the spectators were gathering to watch the evening's games. To be honest originally there wasn't actually a recognisable soccer pitch – in fact beyond the living accommodation lay the construction site, and surrounding both was the desert. You can appreciate, therefore, that after the day's work was completed there wasn't much for the guys to do. So imagine the huge interest shown when a soccer league was proposed, something that many amongst the multinational workforce could throw themselves into either as players or spectators.

The Founding Fathers

Soon an organising committee was formed. The first task was to make a soccer pitch - to be located close by the accommodation cabins. Accordingly, heavy rollers were borrowed from the construction site and an area of sand the size of a soccer pitch flattened and hardened. The perimeter was then marked by rope borrowed from the site stores. The goal posts were made from timbers which had formerly resided in the carpentry shop. As for goal netting, well, there wasn't any. But such minor deviations didn't worry the founding fathers of the inaugural Shedgum soccer league.

And so from each nationality a number of teams were formed and a league table published. All games starting at 6pm. Unfortunately, what the founding fathers hadn't foreseen was that the games became very competitive. Foul play went without being penalised and there was a real danger that WW3 could erupt on the pitch.

A Referee Needed

What was needed was a qualified referee. There being none available a guy who was a Manchester United fan was dragooned into service! Pity him. His first game between the Korean and Turkish teams was a referee's worst nightmare - they gave him a lot of four letter abuse when they didn't like his decisions. Subsequently it came as no surprise when he indignantly told the founding fathers that he had never been so abused in his whole life. He then resigned forthwith. This sent ripples of mirth around the site because if there's one thing he didn't lack was a very thick skin, plus he could swear and curse with the best of them!

Cometh the Hour, Cometh the Man

The founding fathers were now at a loss. Order had to be restored or else the soccer games would have to be permanently cancelled. But fate has a way of intervening in life and cometh the hour, cometh the man. One evening I was relaxing with my pals Cub and Jimmy Two-Rivers when a new guy, Rob, introduced himself. From his accent I could tell that he was a fellow Brit.

If you put two or more Brits together sooner or later the subject of soccer is bound to arise and glory be: our man had an encyclopaedic knowledge of the game. Sensing where this was going I asked Rob if he had ever played the game. He confided that he had retired as a player but was now a referee. And not just your local park referee, oh no, he had regularly officiated in games in the top English soccer league.

Just what we were looking for. Had he by any chance brought his referees strip, whistle, law book, etc?
"Why?" he asked. Whereupon we told him of our dire need for someone who was qualified and could bring control to the soccer games.

You can imagine our delight when he told us that he had come prepared should his services be needed. Alleluia, we had our soccer referee. Shamefully we didn't enlighten him as to the volatility involved less he should get cold feet and withdraw his welcome offer. So now the players would have to toe the line or be penalised for transgressing. Take my word for it - the players never realised what a rude awakening awaited them!

Over-Forties vs. Under-Forties

There were two soccer games that July evening. The curtain-raiser, fifteen minutes each way, pitted the over-forties against the under-forties. To be followed by a longer game between the two best sides in the league. In my infinite wisdom I had proposed that the over-forties play against the younger guys. I can now admit that this was a mistake! To begin with I found it difficult to find eleven older guys who were willing to play on sand in a temperature unlikely to be much below 30C. If you haven't yet played a sport on sand, then let me tell you that it's very exhausting!

I Dragoon Chris into Service

After constantly badgering those who looked reasonably fit I at last had ten players, but at a loss to find the eleventh. Desperate times need desperate measures so I suppressed my misgivings and approached Chris, a smashing guy, but believe me in normal circumstances he would be the last one to ask. To start with he was overweight and he definitely wasn't fit. In fact, he confided in me that he hadn't played any sport at all since his early twenties and at 46 he wasn't sure that he could play in the heat, and on a sand pitch to boot! This reservation was accompanied with a cloud of his cigarette smoke followed by a hoarse cough.

I hesitated, wondering if I was doing the right thing in asking him to play. But we needed him. To put his mind at rest I told him that he could play in defence with me. To his great credit he agreed to play. What a relief. We had our team of old men at last.

Under-Forties 5, Over-Forties 2

Out onto the pitch ran the younger guys, full of vigour and looking much too fit by far. The first half was played at a merciless rate and the young guys scored two goals. At half time we were tiring, feeling the strain. We clustered around each other, strategising our second half. The whistle blew and we trouped back onto the field, all of us, that is, except Chris. I looked around for him but he was nowhere to be seen.

Amazingly we drew even, and suddenly the game became a battle of nerves. Could we hold on, keep the score level until the final whistle? The younger guys had different ideas, they wanted to win. The crowd watching the game cheered our side, willing us to keep going. But we were totally exhausted. This was our undoing. The young guys scored three more goals, and the score at full time was 5-2 in their favour. Man, were we tired! But where was Chris?

It transpired that at half time he had collapsed with heat exhaustion and was rushed off to the sick-bay. It took three days for him to recover after which he vowed, between puffs on his cigarette, to never play soccer again!

The Referee establishes Order

We didn't hang around to see the next game but we had vivid reports of the proceedings. The two top teams faced up to each other even before the kick-off. Battle lines were drawn. Then Rob, attired in his official referees strip, took to the field. The players' mouths were agape. Who was this guy? They were soon to find out. The game started and from that point onwards Rob strictly applied the laws of the game. Foul play was penalised and instead of the usual free for all the players had to toe the line and do as they were told.

Rob, our Referee, is accepted

The next day a downtrodden deputation of chastised players complained to the founding fathers - Rob being the villain. The founding fathers told them that the future of the game depended on the laws being correctly applied. The players got the message. From that point onwards Rob was accepted. The soccer became very popular both for the players and for the many that stood at the sidelines supporting the games.

Two worthy True Expats

So I have no hesitation is naming Rob as a True Expat – worthy of the Hall of Fame.
And what of Chris? He too has justly earned himself a place in the Hall of Fame as the un-fittest True Expat of all.

CHAPTER 10

WHEN ST PETER SEES ME COMING

This poem was written over forty years ago by a group of men working for the George A. Fuller Company in Hufuf, Saudi Arabia. If you have been an expat in the Middle East, you will understand how those guys felt when writing the poem. And to those of you who have not had that pleasure I hope that their words bring an understanding of what expat life can be like. One more thing. I dedicate the poem to those George A. Fuller guys.

Somewhere in the Arabian Desert,
Where the sun is like a curse,
And every day is followed,
By one that's slightly worse.

Where the dust and flies are thicker,
Than the endless desert sand,
Just one of the many tortures,
Of this God Forsaken land.

Somewhere near the Gulf of Persia,
Where a woman is never seen,
Where the skies are never cloudy,
And the grass is never green.

Where the drinking water is colored,
Like the drainage from the sink,
And a man can't drown his sorrows,
Cause there's not a beer to drink.

Somewhere near the tropic waters,
Where the nights are made for love,
The moon is like a spotlight,
And the stars all gleam above.

Now all the gleam and glitter,
Of a lovely tropic night,
Is merely a waste of beauty,
For there's not a girl in sight.

You can have this Arab country,
Where the mail is always late,
Where the Christmas Card in Summer,
Is considered up to date.

Where the camels are all crummy,
And the donkeys slightly worse,
And we really must be crazy,
Where we start to writing verse.

Take me back to the good old USA,
The land I love so well,
Away from this desert oven,
A substitute for "HELL".

And when St. Peter sees me coming,
I'm sure that he will yell,
"Come in you men from Hufhuf,
You've done your hitch in "HELL".

CHAPTER 11

EXPAT IN YANBU, SAUDI ARABIA

Introduction

To get to the Red Sea town of Yanbu in Saudi Arabia one takes a flight to Jeddah and then drives northwards for three hours on an endlessly boring road. Soon after my arrival to work on the construction of a billion-dollar new oil refinery, I was intrigued to discover that Yanbu has a Tourist office located way out of town on the road which we took to work each day. Well, I just couldn't contain my curiosity because I never saw Saudi as a tourist destination. So one lunchtime I found myself at the enquiry desk. A young Saudi guy greeted me … in Arabic. Ummm.

Problem in communication. After several fruitless questions he had a brainwave – why not communicate through his computer? Right … So first I typed in my question which he, using Google Translate on his computer, changed to Arabic. Back and forth we went. (Did you know in 2016 Google Translate supports 103 languages and 200 million people daily)?
Question: "What tourist things to see?"
Answer: "Well, there's the big oil pipeline that runs alongside the main road."
Question: "And what else?"
Answer: "Beaches north of the city."
Right, I thought, I won't be rushing to put much on Trip Advisor then!

Pigeon Problems

Sometime in the dim and distant past there was one species that found that it could survive virtually anywhere and, for no particular reason, someone named it Pigeon. Now Pigeon determined that wherever he lived he would have the right to choose where he laid his head to rest at night. Now Pigeon had a son, named Pigeon and Pigeon's son had a son, and he was named Pigeon too. Thus it was that Pigeon survived and multiplied.

Eventually Pigeon found his way to the desert lands of Saudi Arabia and there in the ancient Red Coast city of Yanbu he lived in peace for many generations.

Time passed then one morning, shortly after Pigeon had taken his bath in the local oasis, he spotted man approaching. Changes were afoot and soon man commenced the construction of an oil refinery. So Pigeon called a meeting of his fellow pigeons and it was decided that a reconnaissance flight should be sent to find out what this unwanted intruder was doing.

They spot a Warehouse

Upon arrival at the refinery construction site they spotted a large building called a warehouse. Being of an inquisitive nature Pigeon swooped down and found a sign saying "Entrance". So leading the way he swept inside whereupon he found the most wonderful pigeon home, protected from the hot rays of the remorseless sun and sheltered from the frequent sandstorms. So Pigeon took up residence in the warehouse and threw a massive Pigeon house-warming party. They were so happy. Life was good.

But the owners of the refinery were very concerned. Pigeon was not welcome so instructions were issued that Pigeon must leave. Meantime it was rumored that there were pigeons flying right across the Red Sea to join their brethren in this most luxurious of roosting homes. And so at our next refinery construction meeting a new agenda item was added "Pigeons in Warehouse." But the meeting had to first deal with a more urgent problem, that of radio communication. The refinery was soon to be tested prior to start-up.

The test engineers had their two-way radios, which were absolutely essential, but they couldn't talk to each other because the radio aerials had not been erected.

Meet Randy

Randy Scott settled his lanky frame into his conference room chair, awaiting the arrival of the Chinese contractor's management team. Outside the thermometer hovered around 45C. The sweat clung to his brow even though he had only walked a short distance from the parking lot. The summer heat in Saudi Arabia was exhausting and as he brushed back a lock of grey hair that fell over his forehead he ruefully reflected on what he might have done wrong to be given this job as construction manager on a site that was manned by a Chinese contractor.

Project is behind Schedule

He had been an expatriate for many years but he had never experienced anything like this. Prior to this assignment he had a record of getting construction completed on schedule. His boss back in Houston had every confidence that Randy would enhance his reputation on this $billion project. True, the Chinese management team were extremely hard working and dedicated, but they lacked experience in international contracting. The result was that they had fallen well behind schedule. In turn this was costing money, big money.

Randy had to put them under pressure in order to recover the lost time but there seemed to be no end to the problems that they brought to him to resolve. Today he knew that he would have to concentrate on the missing radio communication aerials. And as if that wasn't enough he had to face the problem of unwanted pigeons in the warehouse! When would it ever end? He needed patience.

Meet the inscrutable Chinese Contractors

The door opened and the Chinese site management team filed in. Dress code was standard, each man looking like a pea out of the same pod. Blue trousers, blue jacket and short haircut. Each man bowed in respect as they greeted Randy. Jiang-pong, the contractor's project manager, took his seat opposite Randy.

Close inspection was not needed to see that he was verging on overweight. Next to him sat Chong-ping, their construction manager, known to rarely giving a straight answer to a question. To his right sat Chang-Wi, the purchasing manager, wiry and bespectacled, and a keen advocate of making a mountain out of a molehill. Foo-dong, the contract's manager, made up the foursome, completely inscrutable. One could be confident that if he won the lottery he wouldn't display an ounce of emotion.

Communication Chinese-style

The greetings were completed and Randy addressed the first agenda item.
"Mr. Jiang-pong, when are you going to install the radio aerials?"
"Earholes, Mr. Randy, solly, I dun un-stan, what earholes?"
"No, no, not earholes, aerials."
"Ah, you wan know abou earholes - Mr. Chong-ping in charge of constructon, he know about instor earholes."
"Mr. Chong-ping, can you throw some light on the aerials please?"

As usual, Chong-ping was evasive.

"Light ... you mean you wan we have install electeric light poles?"
"No, no, Chong-ping that was just a figure of speech."
"Figga of spich, what that mean, we dun un-stan?"
"Well, what we mean is can you tell us about progress on the aerials that have to be installed on the control room roof?"
"Ah, you wan know about earholes on control room roof?"
"Yes, Chong-ping, earholes on the control room roof, when are you going to install them?"

Chong-ping, true to character, continued to make things difficult.

"Oh so solly, we got mistook. We thinking you say wan install aerials on roof."

"That's all right, Chong-ping just a slip of the tongue, its earholes of course, sorry, our mistake."

"Slip of tong, what you meen, slip of tong, you got probrem with tong, so solly to hear it."

"No, no, Chong-ping, my tongue is very good thank you, that was just another figure of speech."

"Ah, you make two figgas of spich, you velly cleva." Haaaa.

"Yes, yes, Chong-ping, very amusing, but getting back to the earholes."

"Ah-so, earholes, what you wan know?"

"When are you going to install them, you are holding people up."

"What you meen, hole peeple up, we not hole peeple up, we not strong enough to hole peeple up." Haaaa.

"Yes, yes, Chong-ping, velly, I mean very funny, thank you for that. But look here, we simply can't go on all day like this, so tell us, exactly where are you with progress on the earholes?"

"Ah, that velly difficool question to answer."

"Why, you should know by now if you are able to finish the job."

"Ah-so, can finish job, but need earholes first."

"Are you telling us that you haven't even ordered the aerials?"

"Order yes, but deliveery to site, not see them yet here."

"But at last week's meeting you said that they were due in a few days, what's happened in the meantime?"

"Wha you meen, meentime, solly but we don un-stan what you sayig us."

"We mean what are you doing about the missing earholes, you must have some idea where they are?"

"Ah, yu wan know where they are … you shuud have say so, you need ask Mr. Chang-Wi, he purchasing manager, he know all about earholes."

"Mr. Chang-Wi, tell us, do you know where the missing earholes are?"

Chang-Wi was well prepared. Here was his chance to make matters worse than they really were.

"Ah, that velly good question Mr. Randy, earholes is probrem, they gone wong prace."

"Wrong place, why have they gone to the wrong place Chang-Wi?"

"Earholes they was sen to flence contactor by mistook … velly silly people these earhole suppiers, they not know difference between flence and earhole."

"Are you telling me, Chang-Wi, that the fence contractor has the aerials?"

"Ah so, flence contactor velly worry, in terribull state, he not know what do with earholes."

"Well, it's easy Chang-Wi, just tell him to send them to the control room building … tout suit."

"Solly, I dun un-stan toot-sweet, you wan sen to control beeldin or to toot-sweet beeldin, which one you meen plis?"

Randy is fading fast, but drawing on his inner-most strength, continues.

"Mr. Jiang-pong, what we mean is can you send them as soon as possible … we simply cannot go on like this can we?"

"Ah so, is probrem, so solly, but flence contactor velly difficult to understand, no speekin good Engleesh like us…"

Beeg Probrem - Pigins

Jiang-pong's countenance was a picture of grave concern.

"Mr. Randy, regardin beeg probrem in warehoose, pigins still comes inside, and make nests everywhere."

Randy was impressed. So far the Chinese contractor had problems but now they had a big problem.

"I'm very concerned too, Jiang-pong, but surely all you have to do is to keep the warehouse doors closed?"

"It not work, we tlied but pigin he get in when we not lookin, he velly cleva that pigin."

Chong-ping interjected, here was an opportunity to deviate from the question.

"Is beeg probrem cos all pigins in Saudi Arabia come to warehoose."
Haaaa.
Randy tried a different approach.
"Have you tried to hand over the warehouse to the client?"
Foo-dong adopted his inscrutable look, it was his responsibility to obtain acceptance of the works. If he was worried he didn't show it.
"Ah so, I tlied Mr. Randy, Clynt he says not accept pigin in his warehoose."
"Foo-dong, tell us, what did the client say to you."
"Client he say velly upset, velly, velly upset."
Foo-dong's face portrayed how upset the client was.
"Yes, yes, Foo-dong, but what did he tell you to do about it?"
"Clynt he no wan pigin in warehoose, he say must making pigin go nother prace."
"OK, Foo-dong, what do you suggest that we do about the problem?"
"Well, I ask my flend in Shanghai, he got pigin, make fry in races."
"And what did he suggest?"
"He like pigin, say he feel solly for pidgin."
"Quite so, but how can we stop them from getting into the warehouse?"
"My flend he says try put pigin net up at warehoose enrance and hexit."
"Ummm, so he thinks that will do the trick eh?"
"Solly, don un-stan, wha you meen, do trick?"

At this juncture Randy felt an overwhelming desire to slip away quietly and end it all but instead he advised Foo-dong to get the netting and have it installed as soon as possible.

Pigin Probrems on the Agenda

The next meeting found Pigeons now elevated to the first item on the Agenda.
"Chang-Wi, about the pigeon netting, have you placed an order yet?"
"Ah so, velly difficult to prace order, probrem coming."
Randy tried hard not to show his frustration.
"Excuse me, pigeon netting is a problem, why is that?"

"We wan velly leeetle squere mitters but supprier he charge velly much plice."
"Why?"
"Suprier say cannot give leeetle squere mitters, must take full woll."
"How much is on a full roll?"
"Two hundred mitters, so we say onery wan cover warehoose enrance and hexit."

Randy is losing the will to live.

"Did you try our suppliers in Jeddah and Riyadh?"
"Ah so, still tiling, but no have small squere mitters netting anywhere in Saudi Arabia."
"Well, how about getting it from China?"
"No need pigin netting in China, they eatin pigins so not probrem."
Haaaa.
"Now look here guys, you must get this problem sorted out."

Just Joking

Chong-ping was ready.

"Maybe we getting Rambo come with machine gun and shootin pigins, then no probrem."
At this suggestion the whole Chinese contingent creased up with laughter. Randy realized that once again he was up against odds that he couldn't beat. The subject was left with the Chinese to resolve. The next thing he heard was that a delivery of Chinese firecrackers had been delivered to the stores.

Randy was worried and called a meeting.

"Jiang-pong, what exactly do you intend to do with the firecrackers?"
"No probrem, just make pigins fry away then we put netting at enrance dol."
"Do you mean entrance door?"
"Ah so, at enrance dol."

Chinese Firecrackers

Randy had his doubts but confirmed that he would be present when the exodus was in operation. He arrived at the warehouse to find dozens of Chinese workers brandishing firecrackers. With a signal from Jiang-pong there was an almighty series of deafening explosions. The resident pigeons, happily snoozing on their mid-day siesta, were scared out of their wits and with a flurry of feathers they exited the warehouse en-masse. A loud cheer went up from the men and Randy, somewhat mollified, returned to his office.

Just Joking - Again

The next week's meeting should have been pigeon-free but no sooner had Randy asked for a report on the progress of construction then Jiang-pong was on his feet looking very glum.
"Mr. Randy, Sir, we velly solly but have another beeg probrem."
Randy tried to remember when there was a small problem.
"What sort of problem?"
"Pidgin netting beeg probrem, no keep pidgins out of warehoose, come back in las night."
"How can they get back in? You have put the netting up haven't you?"
"Must ask Mr. Chong-ping, he in charge of construction."

Chong-ping adopted a straight face.
"Probrem is warehoose men velly silly, put net in wong prace."
"Wrong place, what do you mean?"
"Put net over hexit dole instead of enrance dole, velly silly, should know pigin come in through enrance dole."
Randy sighed, and was about to respond when the four Chinese burst into laughter.
"So solly Mr. Randy, we make joke for you, no more beeg probrem, no more pigins in warehoose. Now we velly happiness."

Randy heaved a sigh of relief. Should his boss in Houston ask what his biggest challenges were he would immediately respond ... firstly we had missing Earholes and, secondly, we had "beeg probrem - Pigins in Warehoose."

Randy, you are a True Expat. Well done, if you haven't expired from the heat, ulcers or heart failure - then welcome to the Hall of Fame.

CHAPTER 12

THE DONKEY RACE

Introduction

Some 6,500 years ago successive waves of people migrated into a land which is now known as Iran. These ancient Iranians established the first recognizable civilization with a workable system of government. Their other achievements included the invention of wheeled vehicles, the use of a written language, and the development of the scientific practice of agriculture.

Oil was first discovered in Iran in 1908 bringing a new wave of people – oil workers. This story takes place in the boom days of the 1970's when three True Expats from Newcastle in the north-east of England found life on an oil refinery construction site extremely boring on their day off, and set about putting that right...

Another boring Friday

Mike returned to his cabin after breakfast and slumped into a chair, morosely contemplating yet another boring Friday. Most single status expats who have worked on construction sites in the Middle East know that empty feeling. Mike had been told by HR that his job building the new oil refinery in southern Iran would entail a six day working week, with one day off. However, what they hadn't told him was that the day off would be on Friday... which is the Muslim day of prayer. In consequence even if Mike had wanted to he couldn't go and leisurely wander around the nearby Souk because it was closed. In fact, everything was closed.

What Mike needed was company, someone to cheer him up, so he called his pals Bobby and Jack. They had known each other back in Newcastle and had gone to Iran because there wasn't employment for them at home. Gone were the skilled jobs in the shipbuilding yards, the steel-making plants and the engineering industries, all were now closed. When Mike was joined by Bobby and Jack he solemnly placed a bottle of siddiqi on the table and, pouring liberal glasses of the fiery liquid, wished them good health.

Siddiqi is not for the faint hearted. Distilled into a pure alcohol it was bravely imbibed by expats where no other alcohol was available. For a while they drank quietly, absorbed in their own thoughts.

Then Bobby broke the silence

"I'll tell you what man, there's nowt to do in this place on a Friday, and that's the truth."
This observation elicited nods of agreement followed by a re-filling of the glasses. As the contents of the bottle decreased so their depressed mood lifted. Of the three Bobby was the one who could be relied upon to cheer his pals up. And by now the siddiqi had taken hold.
"Look here guys … the sun is shining, it's a beautiful morning, and as your social chairman I'm inviting suggestions as to what we can do today."

His announcement was greeted with a time-honoured response (unprintable) leaving him in no doubt as to where he should go. But it took more than that to faze him.
"Come on Jack, what shall we do today man?"
Jack, broad-shouldered and as strong as an ox, declared that they should arm-wrestle and that the loser should provide the next bottle of siddiqi. There were no takers. Bobby weighed in at nigh on seventeen stone and none of them could beat him. The next suggestion by Mike grabbed their attention.

"I've got a great idea - let's have a donkey race" he slurred. His difficulty in speech was a tribute to the siddiqi.

His pals eyed him with disbelief. Bobby was confused.
"Don't be daft man, where are we going to get donkeys from in this god-forsaken hole?"
Mike paused for a moment, he was fairly tipsy and putting thoughts into words took a little time.
"Nay problem man, I think I know where we can borrow some donkeys." As an after-thought he added "And we're in luck because they'll be doing nowt today – it's Friday."

Bobby and Jack had no idea where Mike got this hair brained idea from, or even if it would work. But they weren't worried ... the siddiqi had mellowed them. So Mike's suggestion was endorsed, followed by the disposal of the final contents of the bottle. This was going to be no ordinary Friday!

Donkeys for Transportation

Throughout the Middle East in those days it was quite common to see donkeys carrying bulky loads on their backs or pulling wooden carts loaded with goods. Back when the new refinery commenced construction there was a need to transport locally supplied items to the construction site.

And thus it was that early one morning Amir, turbaned and bearded, appeared at the site main gate. Next to him stood his prized transportation vehicles - three donkeys harnessed to dilapidated wooden carts. Whatever the site needed he could supply, be it drinking water, soap, toilet rolls, cans of paint, and so on. Amir and his donkeys soon became a regular sight, well known by everyone. It was obvious that he had a great affection for his donkeys and in return they responded to him with an almost telepathic understanding of what he needed them to do.

One could visualise that as a young boy he was taught by his father, walking alongside the donkeys, stick in hand, as they carried their loads tied firmly to their backs. And after his father retired Amir modernised the business, acquiring donkey carts and stabling his donkeys under cover, albeit an old ramshackle shed on the outskirts of his village. He never mistreated his four- legged friends and lovingly watered and fed them. And most of all he ensured that on Fridays when he attended prayers they were given a day of rest.

Little did he know of a crazy plan about to take place on that fateful Friday morning.

Mikes idea of a donkey race was probably allied to the fact that he liked horse racing which in turn led to the odd bet here and there. If one were to meet Mike it would be advisable not to mention horse racing because he would bore you to death with facts and figures. He knew which jockey, wearing whose colours, riding what horse won the UK Cheltenham Gold Cup, The Derby, and the Grand National for the past umpteen years. For him his suggestion of a donkey race was divine inspiration. His hair brained idea could make him a killing … by placing a large bet on his donkey to win. Winner would take all. Brilliant. By what means he would assess the racing qualities of each donkey was not clear but such a small matter wasn't going to spoil his day. So without pause he proceeded to outline his plan.

Racing Colors

"Have you guys seen Amir with his donkeys delivering materials to site? Well that's who we are going to get our donkeys from."
His pals looked at him in amazement.
"Don't be daft man, there's no way he will let you have his donkeys, they're his pride and joy."
"I wasna thinking of asking him man…" He waited for the statement to sink in.
"Not asking him? Well how do you propose to get them without asking?" said Bobby.
"No problem man, we'll just go down to his stables and borrow them for a while. He'll be at the mosque all morning and be none the wiser."
"You canna just walk in there and take the donkeys," added Jack.
"Sure you can, they're not locked up, it's no problem man."

And then Mike had another brilliant thought.

"We'll need some cans of paint so we had better get away doon to the stores to get some."

"Paint, what do we want paint for man?" Bobby and Jack were losing their ability to keep up with Mike.

"For our racing colors man, you canna have a donkey race without racing colors."

"You mean to say we are going to paint the donkeys?"

Bobby could hardly believe his ears. But Mike, an expert on racing colours, was now on home turf.

"Aye, we'll paint them in different colours ... and then we'll have a bet on our own donkey to win". Looking sternly at his pals he added, "and winner takes all."

With that the three lurched unsteadily out of Mike's room.

"Come on then ye Geordie layabouts, let's get away doon to the construction site stores and get the paint."

With that they piled erratically into his pickup and with a great effort of concentration he managed to start the vehicle and engage gear. With a sudden lurch and a screech of tyres he shot off at an alarming speed, making for the stores. Fortunately, they were deserted. In no time at all they seized cans of red, green and blue paint. Just as they departed Jack dashed back into the stores and emerged with a can of black paint.

"What do you need that for?" exclaimed Bobby "You're not going to paint your donkey black are you?"

"Just wait and see" said Jack. "Come on, let's go, time's getting on, and Amir will be in the Mosque by now."

The Donkeys Are Painted

Our three expatriates got back into the pickup and as they drove erratically to Amir's stables they were engaged in a very important discussion – what color to paint their own donkey. Jack wanted red, Bobby chose green and Mike, casting a superior look at his pals, chose blue because it always turned out to be a winner for him. This didn't impress his pals at all because his success in choosing winners, and losers, was well known to them.

Soon they reached the stables and, finding that they were alone, carefully approached the unsuspecting donkeys with paint cans and brushes in hand. Without delay our inebriated heroes began splashing huge dollops of paint on the poor innocent animals. It was fortunate that they were quite docile and in no time at all they were covered from head to foot in bright paint. Jack had one last touch to apply. Opening the can of black paint he proceeded to paint the donkey's tails with the black paint. What a sight it was!

The Race

And so the stage was set and our three friends, doubled over with inebriated laughter, opened the stable gate and commanded their magnificent steeds to take up their starting positions. The plan was to make them run down the main street which ran through the centre of the village. First donkey past the Mosque would be the winner. But the donkeys displayed little appetite for this unwanted Friday excursion and it was with great reluctance that they took to the street.

The bets were placed and on the word "go" each punter gave his donkey a resounding whack on the back. This was not well received and had little effect. So our pals resorted to raucous unprintable yells of encouragement and, coupled with wildly flailing arms, they so alarmed the donkeys that they broke into a panic-stricken gallop. Mike's blue donkey was in the lead and the closer they got to the finishing line at the Mosque the more he urged his donkey on. His pal's donkeys followed close behind but, just as they got within yards of the Mosque, disaster struck.

Amir emerged from the building with his fellow worshippers.
The sight that met the poor man froze him to the spot. He couldn't believe his eyes. Without pause his beloved donkeys went careering wildly past him whilst our heroes, caught red-handed, made an erratic about-turn and fled in the opposite direction. But they didn't get away from the scene un-recognised.

Amir enlisted the help of his fellow worshippers and after a wild chase managed to return the terrified donkeys to their stable. Early the next morning the construction manager was surprised to find Amir waiting at his office door. Before he could even open his mouth Amir launched into a wail of woe: his poor donkeys had been painted all the colors of the rainbow and had been made to race at a tremendous speed through the village.

Amir is Recompensed

By now our Geordie heroes had sobered up and hearing of Amir's complaint admitted to being the perpetrators of the dastardly deed. Compassionate action was urgently needed in order to avoid the situation growing worse so the three guilty culprits put their hands in their pockets and amply rewarded Amir for the use of his four-legged friends. This cheered him up enormously and he left the site in a happy mood.

Amir becomes a Proud Man

But the fact was that no matter how much he tried he couldn't get the paint off the donkeys' coats. They say that it's an ill wind that brings no good because before long he and his donkeys became celebrities. People flocked from the surrounding villages and towns to admire his painted donkeys and Amir, ever ready to capitalise on a good thing, would pose proudly with them for endless photographs. The news spread and he became famous throughout the region. Amir was a proud man.

True Expats

I am pleased to nominate our three Geordie heroes as True Expats. Long may they grace the Hall of Fame. They initiated the first-ever painted donkey race in Iran. To this day Mike remains slightly aggrieved. If it hadn't been for Amir issuing forth from the Mosque at that critical moment, then he was certain that his donkey would have won the race. What a shame because blue almost turned out to be Mike's winning color. Ah well, some you win, and some you lose. That's life, isn't it!

CHAPTER 13

LIFE ON AN OFFSHORE PLATFORM

Introduction

Holland has long been a producer of offshore gas. Their North Sea platforms are connected to pipelines that come ashore at Den Helder where they have their natural gas processing stations. It's from there that the offshore platform workforce fly out to their lonesome homes in the North Sea.

Offshore platforms are subject to regulated maintenance Shutdowns to ensure their safe and efficient operation. Falling behind the Shutdown schedule results in a huge loss of income for the platform owners. In the North Sea there is a crucial window of time before adverse winter sea conditions affect the supply boats, cranes and barges servicing the platforms.

I and a colleague Donald were on secondment to a Dutch offshore company called NAM, owned by Shell and ExxonMobil, to help get the Shutdown schedule back on track and to streamline the supporting logistics so essential to the offshore shutdown season. In this chapter I recall a trip offshore to platform T14.

It had been many years since I had flown offshore and I had almost forgotten how isolated and constricted it is living and working on a platform. Platforms are in a production mode 24/7, around the clock, all year long. The operations staff work a twelve-hour shift, seven days a week on a rotation basis, typically two weeks on and two weeks off.

On T14 I was in for a big surprise to discover that a fellow Islander — and True Expat — was the chef…

Den Helder, North Holland

It's 6am and a cold north-east wind is blowing as my colleague Donald and I set off from the Motel Akersloot near Amsterdam on quiet early-morning roads to drive the two-hour journey up to Den Helder in the north of Holland. Our destination was the NAM heli-port which is located right on the coast of the North Sea. From there we will fly offshore to T14 gas platform.

On arrival at Den Helder dawn had broken. We headed for the helicopter departure building where we put on our survival suits, bright orange, definitely not suitable for a night out on the town! Upon being called we made for the helo pad and minutes later we were airborne, on our way to T14. This was my first helicopter flight over the North Sea although I had flown offshore many times when working for Aramco in Saudi Arabia.

Life on an Offshore Platform

For those of you who have never been on an offshore platform you're not missing much. It's an isolated life and not for everyone. Your nearest neighbor may be a platform many miles away and it's not as if one can mosey over there for a chat. Visitors are few and far between, mainly being the workboats that bring materials and supplies, plus the crane-barges needed for heavy lifts during the shutdown and maintenance period. And don't even think about having your favorite tipple because the platform is "dry". In what little leisure time you have there is nowhere to go so basically all one does is work, eat and sleep.

Hot Bedding

Space on an offshore platform is very limited so one doesn't have one's own room, instead there is what is known as "hot-bedding."

Whilst the day-shift guy works, the nightshift guy sleeps. When the nightshift guy goes on shift, the cabin staff clean the room, change the bedding, and then the dayshift guy sleeps. Two people – one bed. And if your sleep has ever been disturbed by noise then just spend a night on an offshore platform when the maintenance is taking place. Your slumbers will be accompanied by the noise of compressors, cranes, welding machines, all thundering away just outside your door. Remarkably, after a period of adjustment, you get used to this and sleep despite the noise.

Dangers of offshore Helicopter Travel

Travelling offshore by helicopter is a regular part of life for platform workers and is largely accident-free. *But not always so.* In 1986 the worst accident to date occurred when 45 people died in a Chinook helicopter crash. The twin-rotor helo ferrying oil workers from Shell platforms in the UK's North Sea Brent fields plummeted into the sea only two miles and one minute's flying time from Sumburgh airport in Shetland. I'm familiar with this airport because when we were building the Sullom Voe oil terminal back in the early eighties I flew there from Aberdeen.

After the Chinook crash everyone travelling to a UK offshore platform had to take a mandatory offshore survival course. It applied to employees and visitors alike, irrespective of the length of the visit, whether it be for a two-week rotation or one afternoon's survey. There are four elements involved – Safety Induction, Sea Survival, Firefighting and Self Rescue, and Helicopter Safety and Escape. Let me tell you right now that you won't get me to do the Helicopter Escape. No sir! Why not? Well I'll let you judge for yourself.

Helicopter Ditching Course

My expat colleague Gerry once described it in detail to me which put me off for life. He and three other guys were togged out in head-to-toe survival suits and strapped into a mock helo cabin which was suspended over a large tank filled with sea water. They were to undergo a simulated helo ditching into the sea and learn how to survive it.

Gerry recounted that the instructor explained that upon ditching they should not attempt to exit the cabin until it was about half full of water. He admitted that he was scared.

Down went the cabin hitting the surface of the water with a crash. Almost immediately it started to sink and water poured into the cabin. Only then did the instructor signal for them to escape. At this point in his story Gerry paused, his mind going over the experience. He then told me that he still has nightmares about it and never, ever, wanted to do that course again!

The Platform "Muster Station"

The flight from the Den Helder helo base to the platform took about one hour. Below us the cold grey waves of the North Sea threw up white sea horses whilst the noise of the engine drummed loudly in our ears. Upon landing on the platform helo deck the routine is to be immediately shown to your muster station. This is the assembly point that you must go to in the event of an emergency.

It's a sobering thought that most of the men who survived the North Sea Alpha Piper platform disaster of July 1988 did not or could not go to their muster stations. Some risked death by jumping one hundred feet into the sea, whilst others were able to jump from the cellar-deck. This lies at the bottom of the platform, about twenty feet above sea level. Those who went to the muster stations were amongst the one hundred and sixty-seven men who perished in what remains the world's worst oil platform tragedy.

Following the muster station visit Donald and I were shown to our cabins. We couldn't actually go inside because the nightshift guys were sleeping in the bunks that we would later sleep in. So we got on with the purpose of our visit, holding meetings to discuss and agree the way forward in order to improve logistics and get back on schedule.

The Best Expat Chef – and Food – in the World

And now we come to the best part of platform life - namely the food! In my view it's five star, better than the Ritz hotel! And T14 was no exception. Can you imagine my surprise to find that the chef, Russ, was a British expat and moreover he too came from the Isle of Wight! Never mind those TV chefs who woo us with their recipes. Let me tell you that Russ is the best chef in the world, bar none.

T-bone steaks, mouth-watering fish dishes, vegetarian choices, salads, fresh fruit, ice cream, yoghurts, the choice extensive and the food excellent. And what I also like about Russ is that he has charisma. As soon as you meet him he puts you at ease. Mind you, one has to be broad minded because he's more than likely to entertain you with a delightfully risqué story or two.

And so having completed our meetings we flew back onshore. It would be great if one day I could meet up with Russ again because I'm sure that he has more of his outrageous stories to tell. And may he continue forever as the world's best chef!

Good luck Russ, you're a True Expat! Welcome to the Hall of Fame!

CHAPTER 14

FINGER PRINTING AND QUEUE JUMPING IN QATAR

Introduction

This story is set in 1991 in Qatar, a small Gulf state situated on the Persian Gulf. It wasn't until 1949 that the first Qatari oilfield commenced production. Up until that time this small desert country was relatively unknown, a peninsular protruding into the Gulf from the land-mass of Saudi Arabia. Its people were pearl divers, fishermen, boat-builders or employed in simple industries. In 1973, Qatar General Petroleum Company (QGPC) was formed and took control of the fledging oil sector.

Today Qatar is known to have the largest off-shore gas field in the world. And that's not all. Because back in the day I arrived there it was also known for the joys of finger-printing and queue jumping, as I soon found out …

My arrival in Qatar

Our Qatar Airways 747 was descending into Doha. The visibility was perfect and I could see Bahrain below and the Causeway stretching across to Saudi Arabia. As we approached the airport the blue surface of the Gulf shimmered in the sunlight and the fishing dhows, wakes streaming, were returning to port having spent the night at sea. My mind went back to when I first lived in the Middle East and I recalled how warm the Gulf waters were. After a year spent in Saudi Arabia I could never swim in the cold waters of the UK again!

The wheels screech and we are on Qatari soil. I breathe a sigh of relief and utter a silent prayer for another safe flight. The terminal is thronging with men wearing white galabiyyas whilst the women are black-veiled and wearing the head to foot black abaya. Everywhere there are blue-uniformed porters, dark-skinned, from India, Bangladesh, and Sri Lanka. One of them flashes me a friendly smile, his white teeth lighting up his face. He takes my suitcase and places it on a trolley.

Once in the arrivals concourse we find a guy with my name on a placard. I introduce myself and within minutes I'm in the air-conditioned comfort of a sleek Chevrolet sedan. We take the inner ring road and are soon at the Guesthouse, the transit point for new employees and a stop-over for those on their way out on R&R. The sign above the door welcomes me to QGPC.

Choosing our new home

The next morning, I was taken to QGPC's offices to report to the Personnel department. My main aim was to push hard to get a house allocated. I wanted my wife Jan and youngest daughter Zarita to join me as soon as possible from the UK. That afternoon I was taken to view a number of houses reserved for married-status employees. The house I liked best was brand new and located close to the Centre, Doha's popular shopping mall. Just what we needed so I asked for it to be furnished without delay.

The Trials of Finger Printing

Back at Personnel I was told that I must go to the police station to have my fingerprints taken, a government requirement for foreigners. So the next day at 6am in the morning I arrive at the police station only to find that about three hundred Third Country Nationals (TCN's) have beaten me to it. The place is jam-packed, massed around the entrance door.

Believe me those guys had no idea what waiting in line means! So there I was stuck at the rear of these guys in what felt like a massive rugby scrum with no referee, waiting for the police station to open. In a way this was part of my learning process as an expat. Next time I'd know what to do. *What not to do* is to wait one's turn. Oh no, forget about good manners, forget about normal behavior. As they say, when in Rome ...

Learning Queue Jumping

The police station door opened and there was a huge surge forward. I found myself enveloped in a heaving, shoving, every-man-for-himself mass of humanity, each intent on being the first through the door. If one had said to those guys that the first one through the door would be given a million dollars then I swear that you wouldn't have noticed one iota of difference. So I found myself at the very back having been queue-jumped by the dozen or so others who arrived after me. The sun was getting hotter by the minute; I was perspiring and mighty fed up with the queue-jumping.

The Police Finger Print Me

At last I got inside the door only to witness a scene that reminded me of the dark ages. Standing behind a long table were half a dozen short-tempered Qatari policemen. On the table were six steel plates about eighteen inches square on which was spread black finger-print ink. As we approached the table a policeman barked an order in Arabic which no-one understood. He then impatiently grabbed one's hand and bending the thumb pressed it onto the ink-blackened plate. This was followed by each finger; the prints being placed onto a postcard-sized fingerprint record sheet. If the print wasn't clear the policeman would get extremely grumpy and make one repeat the process.

To be honest I was offended by the manner in which the TCN's were being treated only to find that I was treated in exactly the same way. I had done what the policeman told me but still one of my prints was not clear. So he raised his voice and forcibly made me repeat the process. No, I wasn't a happy bunny but I bit my lip and followed his terse instructions.

Soap Anyone?

When the fingerprinting was finished I was directed to the exit door. Out one goes, holding blackened hands away from one's clothes and wondering how to remove the ink. A friendly TCN ahead of me pointed to a tap mounted on the outside wall of a nearby building where a bunch of his friends were crowding around it trying to wash their hands. I joined them and it soon became patently obvious that water didn't make one bit of difference. The ink stubbornly refused to come off. What we needed was soap but the fingerprint policemen were only interested in getting our prints and clearly couldn't care less about us after their job was done.

I looked around me vainly hoping that some soap would materialize, but it wasn't to be. I rinsed and rinsed my hands but all I managed to do was to make matters worse. In the end I gave up and returned to where the driver was waiting for me. I showed him my hands and he nodded sympathetically, probably having seen many expats before me in the same predicament. I sat in the car like a robot, my hands held in the air, trying not to touch my clothes or the upholstery.

Back in the Office

Back at the office I headed for the men's-room and gratefully grabbed a bar of soap. I washed, and I washed, and again I washed my hands. I then took some paper towels and wiped them. A little bit of ink came off. I kept this up for about five minutes, intermittently wiping them on the paper towels. At last a small sign of white showed through the black ink. With renewed enthusiasm I continued to soap my hands, lathering them again and again.

By now the bar of soap had all but disappeared and my arms were aching with the effort. I towelled my hands for the umpteenth time and told myself that it would have to do. Back in the office I showed my colleagues my hands, ruefully acknowledging that they were not truly clean. They all had a good laugh and told me that everyone had to go through the same nightmare.

A Rude Awakening

Having moved into the new house I retired for the night and slept well …until I was awakened by a deafening noise. I sat bolt upright in bed and tried to figure out what on earth was going on. Then suddenly it dawned on me – it was five o'clock in the morning and this was the call to prayer. My spirits dropped. Standing literally just across the street was a mosque. The loudspeakers were surely the loudest in the whole of Doha! At last the noise stopped and I rued the fact that I had not noticed the mosque when I chose the house. I dreaded having to tell my family that I had chosen a house next to a mosque but thankfully when they learned the bad news they took it in their stride.

Subsequently every morning at five a.m. we were awakened by the call to prayer but funnily enough we were soon able to fall back asleep again once it had finished. Nonetheless when shortly afterwards a colleague informed me that he was moving to a new house I lost no time in rushing around to the housing department and reserving his house before anyone else could do so. When I explained that we wanted to move because of the early-morning noise from the mosque the housing guy saw the funny side of it and laughed uncontrollably. When he had managed to recover his breath he remarked that such a situation happened all the time.

So we moved to the Al-Saad area of Doha where we were very happy. Time flew by and not long before the end of my first year with QGPC I was asked to visit their refinery at Umm Said, a town about thirty kilometres south of our Doha offices. I had been told that before I went to the refinery I must submit my passport in order to get a security pass – issued by the Qatari national police force. I wasn't happy about handing over my passport because being without one in any foreign country is not to be recommended.

My "Lost" Passport Saga

One week later I checked to see if the pass had been issued. The duty policeman was as usual sitting with some buddies engaged in their favorite pastime of talking and drinking tea. No, he hadn't heard back from Umm Said police station but not to worry, give it a few more days and then come back. I duly returned but still no news. I was then told that once the paperwork was in the hands of the police no-one could do a thing to speed them up.

 At last I received the bad news. Umm Said police had no record of ever seeing my passport. In other words, they had lost it. I was totally dismayed. The police procedure required that the loss be reported to the CID headquarters in Doha. It came as no surprise when the CID accepted that my passport was lost. Which meant that I must place an advertisement in the daily newspapers requesting that should anyone have found my passport to kindly hand it in to the CID.

I felt that this was pointless but I placed the advertisement and was told that I would have to wait three weeks to allow time for its return, should it be found. When I heard of this delay alarm bells really started to ring because our R&R was coming up in just four weeks' time. Having been overseas for one year we were eagerly looking forward to going home on leave.

I waited impatiently for the three weeks to pass knowing that the passport would never be found. My sole thought in life was to get my new passport in time for our R&R. You can imagine that with only one week remaining before our departure I was just a little bit anxious! At the end of the three weeks no one had returned the passport. I could now go to the CID office and get the clearance needed to apply for a new passport. And guess what? I had to go and be fingerprinted! To say that I wasn't looking forward to that procedure again is an understatement but if it had to be done in order to get the new passport then so be it. One thing was for sure. This time I knew how to survive the chaos.

Queue Jumping Mastered

The next morning, I arrived at the finger-printing police station at six am. I was armed with a bar of soap and a hand towel. This time I shed all of my Western queuing habits. I shoved and pushed my way to the front but no one seemed at all perturbed by my bad manners.

The moment the doors opened I was the first to burst through. I rushed to the first available ink-plate and before the policeman could open his mouth I had ink on my fingers and thumbs. He watched amazed as I distorted my finger and thumb joints to impossible angles in order to get good prints. In no time at all I was finished. I shot out of the door and seconds later was washing the ink off my hands. I then watched with grim understanding as other luckless guys tried, without soap, to wash the ink off *their* hands.

As I was about to leave I gave my soap to a young Bangladeshi guy who was obviously new to the system. He gave me a grateful smile and as I walked from the compound I glanced back and gave him a wave. He waved in return and held his hand aloft . . . triumphantly grasping the bar of soap.

In the Nick of Time

The following morning, I had another chance to practice my queue jumping skills! I was the first through the doors at the British Embassy. Crowded behind me were the luckless people who had been ahead of me when I arrived. I had made up my mind that I would not be queue-jumped again. The lady behind the desk looked at my documents and asked for my old passport. I explained that it was lost and that the CID papers provided proof.

This was a new situation for her so she disappeared to seek guidance from a senior colleague. I was shown into a small interview room and had to explain the situation all over again to her superior. I stressed that I was very anxious because I was due to go on R&R in a few days. He commented that a new passport might not be available by my departure date. Let me tell you that I was not happy with his response!

But all's well that ends well and the day before we were due to depart I received my new passport - but only in the nick of time as they say.

So, my dear reader, if you *must* lose your passport overseas make sure that you carry a bar of soap for finger-printing and be prepared to master the art of queue-jumping like I did.

CHAPTER 15

HERMAN THE GERMAN

Introduction

I met Herman the German when I was working for the Qatar Petroleum Company in Doha. We were late in preparing the schedule for a refinery shutdown and we needed a planning engineer on board at very short notice. In spite of our earnest endeavors days went by and we found no one available. Then Herman's CV landed on my desk...

Bad News

We had to act quickly. Herman was available immediately so whilst having reservations about his experience we had little choice but to go ahead and hire him. He arrived in Qatar and we sent him to the refinery to prepare the shutdown schedule. The problem was that, having expressed the urgency, he responded with the most ponderous rate of progress that one could imagine. In fact, he was still preparing the schedule when the shutdown started. This was very bad news! The schedule was critical to the timely execution of the shutdown works.

Herman's Wonderful Wife

One day he paused from his work to chat. Had he told me that he had the most wonderful wife? I replied that he hadn't. In that case I should know that she was extremely talented, and furthermore she was a very shapely woman. Sensing that I could keep this going I encouraged him to continue. He hardly needed to be asked. I was to learn that she was an acclaimed artist and that she was so beautiful that she had been one of the worlds' leading models. There was no holding Herman back. He enthused that his wife had given art exhibitions here, there and everywhere and had modeled in the major centres around the world. And, (I should have guessed!) she was *very* wealthy in her own right.

Man and Dog

These glowing attributes amused me. Nonetheless I congratulated Herman, assuring him that it wasn't often that a man was so fortunate. But there was more to come. What he hadn't mentioned was that, whilst having the most beautiful wife, the real love of his life and his best friend was his dog! Herman described in reverent tones how gifted and intelligent was his beloved four legged friend. But to top it all he said he had *telephone conversations* with his canine friend.

When Herman saw the look of doubt on my face he said that he dares not forget to phone the dog *every* day (he didn't bother with his wife) because if he didn't then apparently the mournful mutt went into a sulk. My curiosity was aroused. What language, I asked, did the two faithful friends use for communication, and what did they talk about? Herman seemed surprised by my questions.

Canine Calls

He gave me a patient look. Didn't I know that there is an exceptional empathy between man and his dog? Thus their telephone conversations ranged across various subjects, the weather forecast, the result of the dog's recent visit to the vet, and other matters of mutual interest. When hearing this it was all I could do to keep a straight face. What could I do but to tell him that he was a very lucky man to have such an intelligent dog in his life. I don't know about you but up until that time I had never met anyone who had conversations with their dog via the telephone!

Herman Moves On

Herman never did finish that shutdown schedule. We managed to complete the works without it. After the shutdown was finished he moved on to another unsuspecting employer who no doubt was driven to despair by his slow rate of work. But there was a plus side because no doubt they too were soon acquainted with his beautiful wife and his intelligent dog. Even now, all these years later, I can picture Herman's dog lounging beside their swimming pool, wearing dark sunshades, telephone cupped to one ear, patiently awaiting Herman's daily call.

Wherever you are Herman, step forward, it gives me great pleasure to recognize you as a True Expat, and your dog too! Welcome to the Hall of Fame.

CHAPTER 16

THE WATER BUFFALO

Introduction

In April 2000 I set off for Malaysia to join Kvaerner Engineering's management team over-seeing the engineering and construction of two new Chemical plants for Petronas – the national energy company. It's a wonderful country consisting of seven States each of which is ruled by a Sultan. Every five years these rulers convene to elect among themselves the Malaysian head of State. This story recalls experiences I'll treasure forever, meeting new friends like Berserah the water buffalo, and Aziz the chicken chopper.

Saturday, my Day off

It was Saturday, my day off, and I had motorcycled from my apartment at the Awani Kijal beach resort in Terengganu State down to Teluk Chempedak beach in Pahang State. Having parked under the trees by the food stalls I liberally applied my sun block and then set off along the shore bound for Berserah village.

On leaving the shore I headed inland to make my way up the incline of the jungle path. The humidity hit me and I was perspiring heavily by the time I left the path. Ahead I could see the azure waters of the South China Sea. I walked across the soft sand to the water's edge. A warm breeze silently embraced me as the waves washed gently ashore. The beach was deserted. Another day in paradise.

My Volvo T-Shirt

Today I'm wearing my favorite hat which proclaims that I have been to my company's Family Day gathering. I've now taken to wearing it at all times because recently, whilst jungle trekking in Sarawak, Borneo, I had gone without it and as a result got painfully sun burnt. I'm also wearing my favorite Volvo T-shirt because it gives me a pretension of affluence …
"I drive a Volvo, what do you drive …   a Toyota … so sorry for you".

I must tell you how I acquired it. It was on a Saturday afternoon in Kuala Lumpur, the capital of Malaysia. I was enjoying a walk through the city centre when I was attracted to a large crowd watching a Volvo promotion event given by a group of four very extrovert Australian performers. As I joined them the guys had just finished bashing away on some drums and the crowd were applauding. It was precisely at that point that my path to fame or, more aptly, acute embarrassment, occurred.

"*Someone* isn't applauding", the leader of the group pretentiously proclaimed, his outstretched arm pointing in my general direction. This caught the attention of the crowd … who could the culprit be? They watched the progress of one of the performers as he wove through them towards where I was standing.

I glanced around apprehensively, wondering if I could make a discrete departure before he chose me. It was true that I hadn't clapped but in my defense I had only just joined the crowd. Maybe he would pick on someone else. That was wishful thinking and any thought of escape was cut short when, with a crescendo of drumbeats, the smiling emissary grabbed hold of me. The crowd loved it. The guilty one had been identified! I'm sure that they were very relieved that it wasn't one of them!

Was my face red. I found myself propelled onto the stage. What followed was another of the most embarrassing moments of my life. The four guys involved me in their fun and shenanigans. I have to admit that I felt a complete idiot. But the crowd rapidly increased in size, clearly appreciating my Malaysian stage debut. Greg, their leader, congratulated me in a friendly Aussie twang. "Well done mate, wait there a moment" whereupon he presented me with a Volvo T-shirt which I've worn with pride ever since although, to be honest, I haven't heard that as a result Volvo car sales have suddenly increased. On the other hand, it's not every day that one becomes a star performer in Kuala Lumpur is it!

The Walk along the Shore

As I walked along the shore I saw movement under the trees ahead to my left. As I got closer I saw two dogs - my solitude wasn't guaranteed! But they seemed amiable companions and after a while they disappeared from view. At last I reached a rocky outcrop jutting out to sea. I paused to watch some villagers fishing from the rocks, always ready with a friendly wave and smile. I descended back onto the beach which stretched way into the distance. Ahead I could see fishing boats pulled above the high water mark at a village called Kampung Tanjung Api.

Suddenly my attention was caught by tiny movements on the surface of the sand. I stopped and observed what I can only describe as a fascinating sight - literally dozens of busy small seashell creatures with different colored shell patterns. I thought of David Attenborough, the English broad caster and naturalist, of how he would have described this little community in his unique manner, their names, their shapes, and their diversity.

Lunch in a Hawkers Stall – Malaysian style

I couldn't watch for too long because lunch was calling. So I resumed my progress along the beach and there, sitting right at the water's edge was the restaurant that I was heading for. Well OK, it's not a restaurant as we think of one but a Malaysia hawkers' stall. Open air seating, no air conditioning, no toilets, and no frills and graces. But I had grown to love it there - my favorite hawkers' food stall.

Soon I was seated under an awning where I could feel the breeze coming in off the South China Sea. The staff consisted of the owner Faridah, her daughter Zubadah, and their friend Norhassila. They smiled and greeted me whereupon I swung into impressive action with my two words of Bahasa, Malaysia's language.

"Selamat Pagi" (good morning). They responded with the same greeting. Then with effortless ease I reverted to English and requested my meal. They knew what I wanted because I ordered the same every week!

My food arrived in the usual soup dish, accompanied by tea in a glass, known as Tay-O. As I ate my meal I took care not to bite on the pieces of splintered chicken bones! These no longer surprised me and with accomplished ease I copied my fellow diners and threw the bones onto the sand next to where we were sitting. The thought came to me that there weren't many restaurants back home where one could or indeed would do that!

When I first did battle with the chicken bones I concluded that the supplier had definitely not been taught the finer points of his profession! I visualized a dedicated chicken-chopper, using one of those hand choppers that I had seen at the local meat market, bone splinters flying in all directions.

Berserah the Water Buffalo

When my lunch was finished I bid farewell to my friendly lady hosts and continued along the beach intent on visiting my friend Berserah, the water buffalo. His owners were a Chinese family whose fish sheds stood on the edge of Kampung Berserah. I looked out to sea and sure enough there was the green-painted fishing boat, lying at anchor.

After fishing at night the crew had come inshore as far as possible where they had off-loaded their cargo of fish onto a smaller boat. This in turn had been brought into shallower waters where Berserah the water buffalo stood harnessed to the shafts of an ancient wooden-wheeled cart. The yolk across his powerful shoulders was tied to the shafts with nylon rope and it was on this yolk that he would bear the weight of the fish baskets loaded onto the cart.

And so he waited patiently until the men maneuvered the fishing boat towards him. The cart driver cracked a stick over Berserah's rump and guided him alongside the boat. He stopped in exactly the right place to allow the offloading of four large baskets full to the brim with fish. It was cooler there in the water, much better than standing in the hot sun. He plunged his great head under the water and as he surfaced he snorted several times, the sea water discharged in a jet of spray from his nostrils.

The driver gave an instruction and slapped the rein on Berserah's left side. The end of the rein, tied in a knot, passed through Beserah's nostril. He turned his huge head to the left and his powerful thighs took the strain. The cart started to move away from the boat and as Berserah straightened up for the beach he again plunged his head under the water, his final opportunity before leaving the sea. Now he must make the arduous journey to the nearby fish sheds.

I walked beside the cart and waved hello to the driver. He smiled, his face lined and wrinkled. He was wearing a headband, tied tightly, and his shirt was tucked into what we would call a skirt, and what the Malaysians call a labuh. As Berserah neared the path taking him through the dunes to the fish sheds the sand became much softer. He slowed, laboring as the going became increasingly harder.

The driver used his stick to lightly slap Berserah on the rump, urging him to pull harder. Berserah responded, lowered his head, his magnificent curved horns now almost level with the ground. His shoulder muscles bulged and one could see his power and strength. At last, breathing heavily, he passed over the dunes onto level sand.

Without further instruction he made for the fish sheds. Once inside the driver jumped down from the cart and standing in front of Berserah flicked his nostril with the rein. Berserah knew the command and backed the cart towards a truck whereupon the fish baskets were loaded for transport to the fish markets of Kuala Lumpur. As I took my leave I watched as Berserah turned and made his way back to the fishing boat to collect yet another heavy load.

What an impressive animal! As I studied the ancient cart and the weathered fish sheds I wondered how long this lifestyle had existed. Probably for generations. And what of the future? Would we still see Berserah leaving the water's edge, his magnificent black coat shining, his muscles straining under another heavy load? Or would he be superseded by a more modern conveyance? I hoped not. Because some day in the future I knew that I would return.

Footnote: I meet Aziz, the Chicken Chopper

I was intrigued – who was the bone-splintering chicken-chopper who supplied my beach-side hawkers' stall? Eventually by pure chance I met him. I must tell you how. Most Fridays I rode my bicycle from my apartment at the Awani Kijal beach resort to a local town called Chukai. It was there that I would have lunch in a small hawkers' stall in the busy marketplace.

One day whilst eating my meal a guy joined me and took a vacant chair at my table. His name was Aziz and he told me that he had a business selling chickens. Umm. My interest was aroused. Were they ready for the table I asked? Aziz said that they were. In no time I had selected one. Having weighed it Aziz brandished his menacing meat chopper and with true abandon and scant finesse chopped the carcass into pieces. It was as if that chance meeting with Aziz whilst having my lunch was pre-ordained. I had found my man – there in Chukai was the bone-splintering chicken-chopper.

That was the beginning of a friendship that has endured to this day. And what of the hawker stall owner where I met Aziz? He too is a good friend. His name is Malik. Both now have successful businesses. Selamat Pagi, my friends, please excuse my laziness for not learning Bahasa.

CHAPTER 17

MOTORCYCLING MALAYSIA TO THAILAND

Introduction

Sometimes Fate decides things for us. For example, if I hadn't passed by that motor cycle shop in Kuantan, Malaysia then I probably wouldn't have bought the motorcycle. It's not that I'm given to making rash decisions. Not at all. I'm the type that has to think things over carefully, weigh up the pros and cons before committing myself. So why did I throw discretion to the wind?

In my defence I was simply swept off my feet. Love at first sight.
There was this red and black beauty with gleaming chrome exhausts and laid back easy-rider handlebars. The funny thing is that I hadn't owned a motor cycle since my early twenties, family life dictating the need for a car. But there I was, nigh on 60 and smitten by this sleek beauty.

It wasn't as if I needed transport because we were all allocated a company car. No, the fact is I just couldn't help myself. That's how I became the proud owner of a Honda 600 cc touring motor cycle. I proudly rode it back to my apartment knowing that soon we had a long weekend off from work. That would give me the opportunity to head from Malaysia up to Thailand for a few days – a 350km adventure trip ahead of me.

My Trip Begins

It was dark when I set off from my apartment but a warm sunny morning as I crossed the border post into Thailand. High above the blue sky was flecked with white clouds as I cruised the road to Pattani, a two-hour ride. Grazing contentedly at the roadside was a water buffalo tethered by a rope threaded through a ring in its nose. Thai farmers keep their animals tethered to prevent them being a hazard to motorists whereas in the villages of Malaysia the opposite is true.

Motoring on village roads there can be dangerous should a family of cows or water buffalo gallop across in front of the unsuspecting motorist.

Breaking the speed limit?

Something flashing in my wing mirror caught my eye. I looked again and saw a white police car approaching very fast, headlights on full beam, siren sounding a warning. Damn. I checked my speed. I was doing 100km, was that too fast? I slowed down and in seconds the police car swept by me at high speed, followed by three black Mercedes with darkened windows and unmarked license plates. The rear was guarded by another police car. Breathing a sigh of relief, I took my speed back up to 100km and tried to ease the discomfort of having been driving my motorcycle for nigh on 200 kilometres.

I reach Pattani and Khae-Khae Beach

At last I reached Pattani, checked into my hotel and after asking directions, I headed for Khae-Khae beach. Stopping at a small beach-side cafe I found a seat under the shade of some pine trees. I gazed contentedly out onto the shimmering water of the Gulf of Thailand. My seat was a stone bench and in no time at all a bottle of cold Singa beer was placed on the stone table in front of me.

As I stretched my aching limbs my attention was attracted by a cat with three kittens. The kittens played on the beach whilst mother cleaned herself. A lone cat approached and one of the kittens playfully ran to this newcomer who hissed, warning the kitten off. Instantly the mother ran to the scene, stopped close to the intruder, ears flat, body tensed. The intruder sensed danger and slowly moved away. Then the mother cat, happy with the security of her kittens, relaxed and resumed her cleaning routine.

I dine on Yellow Rice and Chicken

Finally, my meal arrived. I had struggled to understand the menu so I hoped that whatever I had ordered would be edible. The plate of yellow rice and fried chicken leg was just about par for the course but the plate of cucumber and raw cabbage, topped with ice cubes was a new development. Paper napkins were strategically placed in a green condiment container, together with toothpicks and a small bottle of red sauce. Please be careful if you happen to like the contents of those innocent looking bottles because man, are they hot!

A black cat joined me, perhaps sensing some scraps. I finished my chicken leg and threw the bone several feet away, wondering if I could tempt her but she ignored it.

Beach Life Thai Style

My meal finished I strolled along the beach where I came across some teenagers, two girls and three boys, aged about sixteen or so. The girls said hello and with Thai friendliness asked me to have a photograph taken with them, which I did. Further along the beach I heard them chattering and laughing and it occurred to me that they were just the same as teenagers the world over. Carefree - full of fun.

Further on I came across a guy standing in about two feet of sea water, using a fishing net. Around the bottom periphery of the net was a light chain, presumably to weigh it down. He threw it in a perfect arc across the water then pulled it slowly towards him. I stood and watched. The sea dappled in the setting sunlight and the only sound was that of the waves as they washed gently ashore.

Exploring further North

I love being near the sea so the next day I set off on my motorcycle to explore the coast north of Khae-Khae. I found myself following a winding tarred road which soon deteriorated into a dirt track. I was about to turn back when in the distance I spotted a small food-stall. I was hungry so I stopped for lunch. The owner didn't have any customers so within no time at all he served me with fish and the ever-present rice.

By chance I had discovered a place called Ta Chi Cape. The fact that I was the only customer encouraged my Thai host, who I later learned was called Pappi, to talk to me albeit I couldn't understand a word he said. Given the remoteness of his food-stall I wondered where his customers came from. But the lack of business didn't seem to concern him and, taking a seat at an adjacent table he too sat eating a meal.

Nearby was a small lake which doubled as a shrimp farm. A young guy in a rowing boat progressed slowly across the water, one hand regularly sweeping across the surface, spreading shrimp food. Nearby was a complement of chickens looking for scraps of food. One found a scrap and when challenged by the others made off at a fast pace, seeking safety. This went on for what seems like ages. Let's face it chickens are not that intelligent are they?

Pappi covets my Specs

At last I was ready to leave and on reaching my motorcycle I took my specs off in order to put my crash helmet on. Pappi had followed me and, picking up my specs, he removed his own reading glasses and tried on my long distance ones. This done his expression changed to one of surprise and pleasure. The reason was that he could now see distant objects with clarity. This led to embarrassment for me because he wanted to keep them!

I return to Ta Chi Cape Months later

If you have ever been to a place that brought you a sense of peacefulness and serenity then you will understand how I felt about Ta Chi. I couldn't wait to go back. So two months later I set off once more. Having bought myself a new pair of spectacles I wanted to give Pappi the old pair that he liked so much.

The dirt track to Ta Chi had worsened since my last visit causing me to ride slowly, the vibration from the rough surface shaking my motorcycle. At last I saw the food stall ahead of me. I stopped, but there was something different this time. It was deserted, Pappi was no longer there. I dismounted and wandered inside. There was an air of silent loneliness. So I left and rode on to where the track ended at the water's edge. I was disappointed because I had looked forward to giving the specs to Pappi. Now it seemed unlikely that I would have the pleasure of doing so.

In Search of Pappi

As the waves gently rippled onto the shore my mood improved. I set off on foot to walk along the beach. It was just wonderful, golden sand stretching in a curve to the point of the Cape. Then I saw a young guy standing in the water ahead of me. As I reached him I could see that he was floating a large palm-tree leaf in the sea secured by a string tied to rock lying on the seabed. I stopped and asked him what he was doing. I gathered that later in the day when the sun went down the fish would swim under the palm leaf. He then caught the fish.

I was truly impressed. I asked him if he knew Pappi, the food-stall owner and, if so, did he know where he lived? The conversation was typical of many that one has when traveling - very hard work! He couldn't help so I left him and continued along the beach.

On to Budi Village

I hadn't gone far before I met two young guys with hand-fishing nets so, determined to find Pappi I repeated my enquiry. Whilst we were talking an older guy (with about three remaining front teeth) joined us and soon they were engaged in an animated conversation. Then they turned to me and gestured towards the end of the Cape and the name "Budi" was repeated several times. I asked if Pappi lived in Budi and they nodded their heads in affirmation. I was thrilled, thanked them, and immediately headed in the direction that they had indicated. After a twenty minute walk I came across two men and a woman repairing their fishing nets and discovered that one of them spoke good English.

As we were talking the same three guys joined us and finally I got confirmation that Pappi, my food-stall friend, did indeed live in the village of Budi. Which, fortunately, just happened to be where the three guys lived because they offered to show me the way there. The three-toothed guy owned a motorcycle taxi with a flat-bedded sidecar, the type commonly used in Thailand to transport just about everything under the sun. In no time at all the two young guys had jumped onto the sidecar and once I had fetched my motorcycle I followed them as they set off for our destination.

After a couple of miles, we found ourselves entering Budi village. The houses stood on stilts right next to the seashore. From the centre of the village I could hear the call to prayer.

At this point I wasn't sure if I was in the right place. What if there had been a mistake in communication? What if Pappi didn't live in Budi? I bade farewell to my guides thankful that they had shown me the way to this remote village. I was thirsty so I parked next to a village food stall and bought a Pepsi. Within minutes I was surrounded by a bunch of inquisitive village children.

From the interest shown in me I wondered if other tourists ever came there but concluded that it was unlikely because how would anyone ever find the place? I smiled at the children and the girls shyly moved away. The boys, on the other hand, returned my smile. I thought that those kids were so charming, especially the girls. Dark skin, beautiful slanted black eyes, sparkling with a natural happiness.

My Guide Celebrity impresses his friends

Soon we were joined by adults and I asked for help, explaining that I was looking for Pappi. Apparently he wasn't there. However, a good looking young guy came forward and offered to take me to him. One has to remember that in such circumstances one has very little idea of what the other is saying! My new guide hadn't any transport and without asking he jumped onto the pillion seat of my motorcycle. As I retraced my way through the village he was greeted with jovial remarks from his friends. He was now a celebrity which was clearly much to his liking.

I was reminded of a Billy Connelly story in which his taxi drivers wife asked if she could have a lift in Billy's taxi to the theater where he was appearing that evening. "Certainly", said Billy. But instead of riding in the front with her husband, which he had expected, she sat next to him in the back seat. As they approached the theatre she called out of the open window to the throng of theatre goers "look who I'm riding with - Billy Connolly".

Likewise, Celebrity was determined to make the most of his golden opportunity to impress his village friends. I had great difficulty in driving because he was standing up on the foot rests and waving exuberantly to his audience which made me wobble all over the place. At last we left the village and after a while Celebrity directed me across an undulating grass track taking us to a sandy beach.

Pappi at last

Celebrity jumped off the motorcycle and headed towards a man who was just getting into his car. They talked animatedly and after gesturing in my direction they finally approached me. I was hoping that this would not be a mistake. The guy with Celebrity certainly bore a similarity to Pappi, medium build, about fifty or so years old, wearing spectacles. Using sign language, I asked him if he remembered my visit to his food stall three months previously. I showed him the spectacles and these drew a dawning realization. With warm smiles we shook hands but he was quite shy which made me hesitate – I would give him the spectacles later.

He then gestured in the direction of the village and indicated that I should follow him. Celebrity preferred to ride with me and before I could persuade him that the car would be the better option he hopped back onto the pillion seat! The track which Pappi took twisted and turned, sometimes steeply downwards requiring me to accelerate furiously to get back onto level ground. Believe me it was a relief when I found myself back in the village. Celebrity bid me farewell, I parked my motorcycle and Pappi beckoned for me to follow him.

We took a hardened dirt path winding between the close-knit wooden homes. Pappi went ahead and called to the women of the house, advising them to cover their heads with their headscarves. I held back to allow them time to do so and then he gestured to the entrance door of their house. I removed my shoes before entering the main room. It had no furniture whatsoever so I sat on the floor, resting my back against the wall. My presence didn't take long to be communicated throughout the village because Pappi's whole family plus neighbors soon arrived. First came the men and children followed by the women, a semi-circle of curious happy faces sitting facing me.

I meet Pappi's Family

I don't know about you but I cannot sit cross-legged like the Asian people. How do they do it! I would be in agony in five minutes after sitting like that! So I sat with my legs stretched out on the floor in front of me. The children sat and stared - I smiled and encouraged them to smile back. Magic. Don't you just love the innocent ways of small children, their mannerisms, not being able to keep still for longer than a few seconds!

There was a little guy near me no older than a year. He hadn't got a diaper on. A girl barely a year older picked him up and he struggled and yelled because he wanted to stay with me. Pappi then sat cross-legged in front of me surrounded by four young men, his sons. They could speak a little English and we swapped our names. The oldest son told me that Pappi had six daughters and five sons. So now he became Pappi to me too.

Pappi asked me if I would like something to drink. Could I have black tea with sugar? They hadn't any, so one of the older daughters returned with a jar of Nescafe coffee. "English coffee" she proclaimed. I accepted and soon a tray arrived on which were two cups of coffee and two small cakes, for myself and Pappi. All the while the room was filling to the rafters with the arrival of more and more people.

One of the ladies announced the arrival of a male friend who could speak English. That was a lucky breakthrough because I then learnt all about Pappi and his family. My most pressing question concerned Pappi and the food stall, I needed to be sure that he was the man that I had met on my previous visit.

Yes, it was him, and he did remember me. By now the family reverted to functioning as normal. Pappi's eldest son had found a space and laid his prayer mat on the floor a few feet away from me, and proceeded to make his prayers. The one-year-old boy was crying, probably tired. Would I like a photograph taken with Pappi? I indicated that I needed to go back to my motorcycle to fetch my camera. Outside the entrance door I put on my shoes.

By now it was dark and as I walked between the houses a small hand grasped mine. I looked down and it was one of the boys from Pappi's house. Obviously it was no place for a stranger to be walking at night on his own! I was touched by this simple act of friendship and as I returned with the camera I held his hand and let him know that he was the leader. He in turn had taken a liking to me and as Pappi and I sat together on the floor, arms around each other's shoulders, smiling for the photograph, I found the little boy sitting close by my side.

Invited to Stay

At last it was time to go. But one of Pappi's daughters who could speak a little English urged me to stay the night in their house. Pappi smiled at me encouragingly and there was lots of support for the idea from all the family. That was a special moment in all my travels – to be invited to stay in a Muslim home. I explained that I had already paid for my hotel but they remained insistent. I thought it wise to show them the hotel receipt to convince them. They were so genuinely friendly. It was now pitch dark outside and I wondered how I would find my way out of the village back onto the Pattani road.

I return to Pattani

Pappi's eldest son came to my rescue. He owned a taxi and was about to go into Patanni to do an evening's work. As I was about to leave I placed the spectacles into Pappi's hand. He put them on then embraced me, it was his way of saying thanks. I bid the whole family and neighbors' farewell and followed the taxi into Pattani, and arrived safely back at the hotel.

Fond Memories

I may not see Pappi and my Thai friends from Budi village again. That's sad, but I'm glad I met them. They enriched my life. I hope that they won't forget the Englishman who came from Malaysia on his motorcycle, searched for and found Pappi, met his family, and gave him the spectacles. But who knows? Someday I may go back and with any luck get to drink English coffee with them once again.

Footnote

Pattani province is on the east coast of southern Thailand. The people who reside there are an integration of Thai, Chinese and Islamic cultures and many belong to the large fishing community. Their uniquely painted fishing boats, known as Korlae boats, are very attractive particularly the bow section which is decorated with vividly-colored intricate paintings of battling mythical beasts. In my lounge, in pride of place, is a wonderfully painted model of a Korlae boat which I bought in Pattani, reminding me of those motorcycle trips from Malaysia.

CHAPTER 18

ANYONE FOR TENNIS?

Introduction

Azerbaijan has been linked with oil for centuries. Apparently medieval travellers to the region would remark on its abundant supply. By the 19th century Azerbaijan was by far the frontrunner in the world's oil and gas industry, having drilled its first oil well in 1846. This, by the way, was more than a decade before the Americans discovered oil in Pennsylvania. By the beginning of the 20th century Azerbaijan, amazingly, was producing more than half of the world's supply of oil. Today, over 80% of Azerbaijan's oil production comes from offshore – the Caspian Sea.

From Malaysia I headed for Baku in Azerbaijan. Our project team were there to design the expansion of an oil terminal, increasing its capacity to receive oil from new offshore platforms located in the Caspian. And whilst we are on the subject of history - what about my participation in a Baku tennis tournament...

Remembering my Rugby Days

As I walked into our Baku office on that pleasant Azerbaijan summer morning little did I know of the chain of events which would soon take place. Our notice-board displayed a poster inviting anyone interested to sign up for the up-coming SOCAR tennis tournament, slated for September 2002 at the Gangelik tennis courts. Until my assignment in Baku I had never played tennis. I had watched a bit on TV and was quite envious that it was so easy to score 15 points with just one bash of the racquet.

This envy emanates from the fact that in rugby, which is my favorite sport, we had to slog away for ages to get any points at all. For example, when I started playing for Saunders Roe Apprentices Rugby Football club in 1957 (on the Isle of Wight) we had to wait for the whole season to end before we won a single game, leave alone score 15 points. If I remember rightly in that first season we played fourteen games, lost thirteen, and won one.

And it would be remiss of me if I failed to mention the after-match shower facilities. Take for example the showers at the Isle of Wight Rugby Club, at that time located at a decommissioned airport lying on the outskirts of a town called Ryde. Long abandoned, the airport boasted a motley collection of tawdry dilapidated buildings outside of which was the former grass runway, converted by the more zealous of the club's members into a resemblance of a rugby pitch.

Shoppers of today wandering around the new Tesco supermarket will not realize that right next to the Deli counter stood what was then loosely described as the rugby changing room.

This august wooden building, long past its best days, was equipped with one household bath and a water heater. Now, for those of you who are not familiar with the game of rugby there are thirty players, plus a referee. In the bigger clubs they also have linesmen, but we were never that lucky. Indeed, if we were able to get the required fifteen players onto the pitch it was a miracle, and out of those at least three or four would be suffering from an almighty hangover from over-imbibing the evening before.

Not for us the strict puritanical life of today's players where almost all human pleasure is sacrificed for the sake of the game. Not at all. But we did have to share, *all* of us, that one bath. Can you imagine the scene? And spare a thought for the referee because if he had officiated without upsetting either side then he stood as good a chance as anyone else of getting into the bath. But dread the thought that he had blown his whistle having spotted two aggrieved players throwing devious punches at each other in a scum. He would have been the last to have gotten into that bath.

But back to Tennis in Baku, Azerbaijan

The poster informed those interested to telephone Natasha in the engineering department, which I duly did.

"Can I speak to Natasha, its Nick, calling about the invitation to tennis players."

"Oh, 'ello, Natasha ere speekin, you vant play tennis in tournament, yes?"

"Well, er, yes, I suppose you could say that."

"Neekolas, vat good you are play tennis, you very experience player?"

"Not exactly experienced Natasha, just a beginner."

"Vat, you no play tennis before… how old you Neekolas?"

"Uhumm, I'm sixty-one."

"Vat! You sixty-one and you never yet play ze tennis, vy not?"

I detected a hint of fun in the question and later was to find that she had a great sense of humor.

"That's a good question, guess I never had time before, but now I'm very keen to play."

"OK, Neekolas, you come see me and put name on list."

Natasha, dark-haired and attractive became my coach. My goodness, that girl was blessed with a lot of patience! She informed me that there was another beginner in the office who I might like to contact, Lenny Walters. Neither of us had ever played tennis before, we didn't have tennis racquets, we didn't know the rules and we desperately needed lots of practice. But all was not doom and gloom - at least Lenny was a youngster because he was only fifty-four!

In search of Tennis Courts

Before I go much further I fully understand that there may be those of you who have not yet heard of the SOCAR tennis tournament. Please don't let this worry you because just about everyone outside of

Azerbaijan hasn't either. SOCAR is an oil group in Azerbaijan and they were the sponsors of the upcoming weekend's play.

Police Encounter

I immediately set about searching for practice Courts and had a stroke of good luck when I learnt that the Baku police force had a sports centre on the Boulevard, just a ten-minute walk from my apartment. That evening found me boldly knocking on their front door. There was no response. So I tried to open it. No luck, it was locked.

I persevered and after several minutes of rapping on the door a policeman, revolver at his hip, appeared. From his stern countenance I gathered that he was not keen to talk to me and without giving me a chance to speak waved me away. Now I'm not one to give in easily so I gave him a big smile and tried the friendly approach. After a moment or two of his Russian and my English I was fading fast and all looked lost.

Then I had the idea of telling him, in sign language of course, that I was here to play tennis. So I threw an imaginary tennis ball high above me and with right arm flailing empty air I smashed the ball at well over 100 mph into the opponent's court. In a flash my imaginary opponent miraculously managed to return this formidable serve but made the fatal error of forgetting my killer forehand smash.

No Speak Russian

The policeman nodded in recognition and without tempting me to demonstrate any more of my awesome powers unlocked the door and I was inside. Step one accomplished. But the next step was a greater challenge because I now needed to speak Russian and at that time my vocabulary consisted of only a few Russian words. In fact, to this day it still consists of only a few words which I put down to the fact that I'm very lazy when it comes to learning languages.

This has caught me out many times. For example, in September 2007 I was in France for the rugby world cup and upon finding myself stranded in Cannes was helped by a really friendly French lady. After we had conversed in English for a while she asked me if I spoke French. I told her that all I had was from my school days. She gave me a warm look of disapproval and said "Nicolas, you really *must* learn to speak French, it's essential, n'est pas?" I couldn't argue with that!

And here I was again, this time it wasn't French but Russian that was my Achilles heel. The duty policeman ushered me to the reception desk where I found to my great relief that the police officer could speak a little English.

"Sir, I have come to ask if we can use the tennis courts."

"Tennis courts no play, only vor ze policeman's."

"But sir, we are willing to pay."

"Not allowed, only vor ze policeman's."

"We won't interfere with your guys, just an hour in the evening, that's all that we are asking for."

"Is policeman's court, only vor ze policeman's."

I was beginning to lose the battle and then a sudden thought occurred to me.

"Sir, we are playing in the SOCAR tennis tournament at Gangelik stadium."

His demeanor changed and a look of recognition crossed his face.

"Gangelik, you plays ze tennis at Gangelik?"

"Yes sir, we are playing in the tournament – it's only two weeks away and we need to practice – it really is urgent you know."

"OK, you cum tonight, pay ze twenty Manat, 'ave court one hour."

I thanked him and as I departed I shook hands with the now friendly duty policeman who quickly locked the door behind me. Phew, that was a close thing. So too were the near misses by cars as I negotiated my way back across the road towards the Old City. This wide road doubles as a favorite racetrack for Azeri drivers. It doesn't matter which direction the traffic is travelling the objective is to reach maximum speed before slamming on the brakes at the next set of traffic lights. But I safely negotiated this hazard and walked back through the Old City, up the hill next to Fountain Square and home to my apartment.

Our First Practice Session

That evening Lenny and I had our first-ever practice game. The balls were flying here, there and everywhere, that's how bad we were. On one occasion I hit a ball right over the perimeter fence which is at least twenty feet high. We hurried outside to recover the ball but after an extensive search we gave up. It wasn't until a later occasion that Natasha told us that there was very little chance of ever seeing the ball again.

With our first evening practice game over and flushed with new-found enthusiasm Lenny and I went in search throughout our office for other novice players with whom we could practice. This however was a lost cause because we were the only ones who were beginners so I hit upon the idea of persuading a couple of young expatriate Indian colleagues, Sri and Rao, to join us. They too had never played before but quickly got the hang of things.

The Tennis Tournament

The tournament was to be played over a Saturday and Sunday and come the Saturday morning we arrived at Gangelik in our best tennis clothes. My tee-shirt, a memento from my days in Malaysia, proudly announced that Volvo is the best car in the world. I had been presented with it one Saturday afternoon in Kuala Lumpur as a reward for impulsively volunteering to join a group of Aussies in their entertainment act outside of a shopping mall. Lenny went one better than me. His previous job had been in Ireland thus he sported a shirt proclaiming that Guinness is best. No true Irishman will disagree with that!

Before we took to the court I thought that it would be wise to have a team talk.

"Lenny, when I serve I want you to go up to the net and if you see the ball heading in your direction bash it back as hard as you can, and don't forget to then run back for the long ball."

He looked at me dubiously, clearly something was worrying him.

"Right, but what are you going to be doing while I'm running around like a blue-assed fly?"

I must admit that I hadn't anticipated this question so I had to think fast.

"I'll tell you which way to play it, you know, give you a few tips."

We both laughed not least because we knew that I had little idea about the game. Our confidence was soon put to the test when we saw the other super-fit contestants, dressed in pristine white tennis clothes, warming up on the courts. Hell, what have we done, it's going to be sheer murder out there.

Natasha encourages Us

Natasha arrived and told us that our first game was against a couple of young Azeri guys who were also beginners.

"Yu vill vin this match, they not so good at play tennis."

"Do you really think that we can actually win?" we asked incredulously.

"Sure, just get ball bak over net and yu vill be OK."

Oz – the Umpire

This cheered us up. We made our way to the court and said hello to Oz, our umpire. He was one of the guys from our office who had volunteered to help out. If nothing else he had a good sense of humor.

"G'day mates, what are you two old boys doing here, got lost or something?"

Lenny gave him a withering look which only encouraged him more.

"Over there, Lenny, is the tennis court, and that string thing in the middle, well mate, that's called a net."

"Now look here Oz" replied Lenny, "just make sure that you get the score right, after all you can barely count at the best of times."

Lenny knew Oz well and it soon became clear that they took no prisoners when it came to taking the Mickey out of each other. Next he announced our opponents.

Our Opponents

"On court One we have Walters and Westmore versus Ramovich and Gavosky."

Our opponents, who were standing nearby, came to join us when they heard their names mispronounced.

"Zir, ze name is Ramonaveech, and ze other name is Gavarisky."

"That's correct mate, Ramovich and Gavosky, right first time." Oz beamed with good humor.

I gave Lenny a glance of amusement and he was clearly holding back from killing himself with laughter.

"Right mates, shall we get on with it then?"

"OK Lenny" I muttered, "you watch out for Ramonaveech, he looks good to me."

The Match Begins

Oz was now getting into his stride.

"Ramovich to serve to Walters."

Lenny stood on the baseline where he presented an engaging picture in his Guinness shirt, his legs protruded from his shorts like two white sticks. Concentration creased his forehead and he held his racquet at the ready. Ramonaveech served. Lenny missed and it was fifteen-love. I prepared to receive the next serve. Ramonaveech was looking too cocky for my money so in my determination to get the ball back I sent it far over to the right of the Court into some waste ground.

Oz can't contain himself.

"Thirty-love. Crikey mate, what sort of return do you call that?"

Lenny returned the next serve and we saw our first glimmer of hope because Gavariski, brimming with confidence, made a wild swipe at the ball and missed completely.

"Thirty-fifteen, bad luck mate, you only just missed it."

Up in the commentary box Oz is having fun. The next serve was to me. The ball bounced nicely and I made a lucky return. Thirty-all. Next Lenny beats Gavariski with a nice return shot. Thirty-Forty.

Oz Loses Concentration

Oz is uncharacteristically silent and as we look up at him we realize that he isn't even watching us but eying the four ladies playing on the next court. Lenny is quick to take advantage of the situation.
"Uhuumm, umpire, what's the score?"
Oz is torn away from his revelry and the worried look on his face tells it all, realizing that he's been caught on the hop.
"Thirty-all?" asked Oz, hopefully.
"Come on Oz, you can do better than that, you're the umpire, have a guess what it is."
Oz could see that Lenny had him on the ropes but he clearly had fast powers of recovery because without further hesitation he declared the score as thirty - forty.
The look on Lenny's face portrayed mock admiration.
"Hell Oz, excellent umpiring."

Meanwhile supporters in the form of Sri and Rao have arrived. They were competing later in the morning having made amazing progress. I had encouraged them to enter the tournament consequently they had approached Natasha.
"So, you vant play tennis, vat you are, beginner or experience?"
"Well, until a few days ago we had never played tennis but we have practiced and now we are getting better."
"Who you with practice?"
"Well, actually with Nick and Lenny."
With this Natasha fell about in convulsions of laughter, unable to contain herself with the thought.
"OK, put names on list."

Back on court I quietly remark to Lenny that if we can play the ball to Gavarisky then we stand a good chance of winning the set. What happened next was bizarre. Ramonaveech served and with a desperate backhand stroke I expertly hit the ball with the handle of my racquet. It spun up into the air and dropped just over the net. Gavariski just managed to get it back only for it to bounce just in front of me. Without taking my eyes off the ball I hit it with my thunderous forehand smash.

Unfortunately, Ramonaveech happened to be standing right in the way of the ball which was heading for Armenia at about two hundred miles an hour. It hit him slap bang in the middle of his face and with a pitiful groan he collapsed onto the ground. After rising groggily to his feet he declared that he was going to withdraw. Oz, who was as usual ever ready with a quip, declared us the lucky winners.

"Game, set and match to the old boys. Good on ya mates. Now you can buy me a beer."

Game one was over. We were winners! This called for a celebration. In no time we were on our third round of drinks. We staggered onto Court for our next game. Our Azeri opponents, two of the fittest looking guys I have ever seen, were waiting for us. Oz attempted to climb the four steps of the ladder to the umpire's chair. It was painful to watch.

"Jush a moment guys, wait till I get to my poshishon."

We were never going to win because we simply weren't good enough.

Next Monday in the office Oz was in his element. Anyone and everyone had to know.

"Had a good time at the tennis mates, but you should have seen the funniest thing."

"Oh, what was that Oz?"

Oz's face wrinkled in a wicked grin.

"Well, you should have seen Nick make his forehand smash, man, it was **awesome** ..."

Lenny, an inveterate globe-trotter, went on to better things because he headed off to a job in South America. The last time I heard from him he was impressing his fellow expatriates with his tireless running to all four corners of the tennis court. I'm proud to say that he has me to thank for that.

As for me, regrettably my tennis is still as awful as ever. But I don't let such minor matters stand in my way. I still play whenever I can find a doubles partner brave enough to partner me. I have grown accustomed to that growing look of dismay as they have to run from one end of the court to the other, fatigue etched on their face. By the way, if you have been one of them you'll know what I mean.

True Expats

Thanks Lenny. You're a star. So too are you Oz. You both deserve the title of True Expat. Welcome to the Hall of Fame.

Natasha

Finally, how can I forget the pained exhortations of my wonderful Azeri tennis coach, Natasha: "Neekolas, pleeze, ow many times I says to you … must hit ze ball *over* ze net."

CHAPTER 19

ALI'S SEARCH FOR TRUE LOVE

Introduction

They say the search for true love doesn't run smooth and never was this saying more true than for a certain expat from Turkey who I'll call Ali. We met in 2001 while I was working for Kellogg Brown & Root (an engineering, procurement and construction company) in Baku, Azerbaijan. Here is his story of unrequited love…

Baku in Winter

There was a bitterly cold wind coming in off the Caspian Sea as I made my way to the gym, located in the Palace of Sports at the end of the Boulevard in Baku. Not that the temperature inside the gym because it had no heating whatsoever.

Teymur, my friend the Azeri gym instructor, smiled happily as I vigorously rubbed my hands to get some circulation going. My breath hung in a white cloud in the cold air. To look at how I was dressed you would think that I was heading for the North Pole. On top of my gym clothes I had a thick track suit, a long wind-cheater, my scarf, gloves and my woollen hat which I had pulled right down over my ears. But I was still cold. Having been in Azerbaijan for going on three years I had grown to enjoy the springtime, summer, and autumn, but I didn't care too much for the winter.

Theoretically Baku shouldn't be so cold because I had been told by Pete, with whom I worked in Malaysia, that the winter temperatures rarely reached freezing point. Oh no, then why is the city covered in snow? And what about the fact that one has to walk very carefully to avoid slipping up on the icy pavements! Pete, you've got it wrong.

A devious thought crossed my mind. His next expatriate assignment was to be in Moscow and old-timers have told me that it's very cold there in the winter, with months of snow. Serves you right Pete, that'll teach you to tell me that Baku is mild in the winter!

My fellow Azeri gym enthusiasts were definitely tougher than me, seemingly oblivious to the cold, exercising with resolute determination. I told myself that man and boy they grew up here thus unlike me they don't feel the cold. In my defense my previous expatriate job in Malaysia with its year-round warm climate probably made my blood thin. My mind went back to those sunny times, the warmth, the beach walks in shorts and tee shirt at the weekends. Ahh … those were the days!

Fate brings Ali into my Life

Immediately after my arrival in Baku in January 2002 my first objective was to find an apartment. The next was to find a gym and by the end of the week both objectives were achieved. My apartment was in an ideal location being right by Fountain Square and the gym was in the Palace of Sports at the end of the Boulevard. I could get there in ten minutes by walking down the side of Fountain Square, through the Old City, past the Maidens Tower and along the Boulevard.

It wasn't long after joining the gym before I was satisfied that I had made the right decision. I had considered the more modern gyms frequented by other Baku expats but in choosing the Palace of Sports I was able to meet many of the local Azeris – and one Hall of Fame Turkish expat called Ali.

Fate decreed that I should meet Ali a couple of months after I had joined the gym.

I was doing my exercises when he introduced himself - a handsome guy of about twenty eight years of age, five feet ten tall, with jet black hair. And he was still single. As I got to know Ali I looked forward to our conversations because I knew what was coming … he would tell me that he was in love.

Girlfriend # 1: Connie

The first girl was Connie who working for USAID, a US government organization. Ali had been hired by USAID as an interpreter and soon after he and Connie had fallen in love. So much so that by the time Connie's contract ended he wanted to marry her. Connie returned home to the USA promising to get him over to the States so Ali waited patiently for the call to join her. But one evening he gravely told me that he had received a message from Connie to regretfully say that she no longer loved him. I commiserated with him and said that perhaps it was inevitable that it ended that way, being so far apart.

Girlfriend # 2: Lisette

After that Lisette appeared on the scene and new love was in the air. She had assured him that she would help him travel to France when she returned home from her job at the French embassy. But, uncannily, things went the same way and another love disappeared down the drain.

Girlfriend # 3: Ingrid

By now I'm beginning to get the hang of Ali's stories. Thus some months later when Ingrid from Stockholm appeared on the scene I was fully prepared for the steps which would follow. Sure enough Ingrid eventually disappeared off the radar screen just as her predecessors had done.

As time passed it dawned on me that the story for each girlfriend was the same. Initially the romance went well but then the girlfriend completed her stay in Azerbaijan and returned to her home country resulting in the end of the love affair. Only to be replaced by a new love which then also sadly suffered the same fate. I never actually met these girls but after being told chapter and verse about them by Ali I felt that I knew them quite well. The interesting thing about them was that none of them were Azeri. This realization came to me when Ali related the story of Ingrid.

By this time, I had become his mentor, girl-friend counselor, and potential world-travel adviser. The latter position was needed because if Ali should at last be told by his loved one to get on a plane and make haste to be with her then my help would be essential because he would be so stunned that he wouldn't know which way to go.

Ali Dreams on

But Ali was no quitter. A couple of months after Ingrid's departure he informed me that he wouldn't be in Baku much longer because he would be joining an uncle who was in Bulgaria running a successful fruit and vegetable business. Time went by and the deadlines for Ali's departure came and went.

As before this too came to nothing. By now I had learnt to accept his stories and instead of doubting their authenticity I sympathized with his position. Here's a young well educated university graduate speaking fluent English yet only able to get a job as an interpreter. Who can blame him for wanting to better himself? What I admired about Ali was his never-say-die approach to life. No matter how often his dreams were dashed, he picked himself up and tried again.

Ali plans to go Sturgeon Fishing

My last conversation with Ali was not in the gym but down on the 25th May Street. I had gone to change some money at the street-side money-changers when I bumped into him. I happened to remark that it was unusual to see him in this area of the city. He gave me a serious look that told of something new in the air and informed me that he was now in a business partnership with a friend. Doing what, I asked. Fishing, he replied. What a surprise! Ali patiently explained that he and his buddy, who had a boat of sorts, were going to fish in the Caspian Sea for sturgeon. "Good money to be made," he said. I wished him luck, shook hands, and we parted.

That's the last time I saw Ali because not long after I was demobilized from Baku and on my way to Baghdad in Iraq.

I would like to bet that Ali's sturgeon-fishing days didn't last long. Whatever his plans are I wish him well. After all, it's the Ali's of this world who give us encouragement to accept our setbacks but never give up. And who knows, he may still find love and the girl of his dreams.

Ali, my good friend, you are a True Expat. Welcome to the Hall of Fame.

CHAPTER 20

MR GLUM AND MR BOOK

Introduction

The walk from my apartment in Baku, Azerbaijan to the gym in the Palace of Sports took me right past the Maiden's Tower. But how did it acquire that name? Legend has it that in past days the King was going to force his daughter to marry a man she didn't love. She escaped by asking her father to first build a tower for her, and when it was finished she committed suicide by jumping from the top of it. But in modern times, other legendary figures are needed...like these two entrepreneurial characters I've called Mr Glum and Mr Book.

The oldest Bathroom Scales in the World

I have a great regard for those who are self-made. You know, the type who have an eye for a business opportunity! It has to start somewhere doesn't it? Take for example
 the guy that I often walked by on my way to the gym in the Palace of Sports at the end of the Boulevard in Baku. He had located his corporate business headquarters half way along the Boulevard, next to the fountains and close to the boating lake. It's a sensible position selected because it is on one of the busiest pedestrian routes. It's there that he placed his prized business asset – his bathroom scales.

I don't want to be mean but one could be forgiven for thinking that they were the oldest, not just in Baku, but in the whole world! And I ask you, when did you last stand on a pavement of all places and be weighed ... and of all things on bathroom scales?

How much?

And what does this entrepreneur charge for this service? A whopping 250 manat - about four pence. But, despite the low price, business is not exactly brisk. Maybe the folk passing by think the age of the scales would not tell them their correct weight. After all, it would be a bit of a blow if, upon being weighed, you were informed that you were 10 lbs/5kg heavier than what you hoped, wouldn't it? And what if a really large Bakuvian stood on this ancient measuring device, surely it would realise that its days were numbered and that it should make way for the younger, stronger generation.

Mr Glum

But what really amused me was the demeanour of our man. Not for him the welcoming smile or a confident composure designed to entice the innocent passer-bye into spending their 250 manat. No, not at all, because he had the most sombre face of any man I've ever met. That's why I have named him Mr Glum. Mind you, I had tried to get him to smile, or even acknowledge that life is not as bad as his countenance portrays. But no, every time I greeted him his dead-pan features never changed.

But who am I to judge? He probably loves his job. And what does he tell Mrs Glum when he gets home after a day at work.? One can only imagine. My guess would be that he would, at length, recount the three people or so whom he had weighed, noting that each had a look of total disbelief when told of their increase in weight!

Business improving

I'm pleased to report that Mr Glum seemed to be faring better the following summer because he had gone to the trouble of purchasing spanking new bathroom scales. The strollers along the Boulevard were obviously impressed, figuring that there was now a good chance of being weighed correctly. What's more he pegged his price to the previous year's level, still only a few pence - it doesn't come much cheaper than that!

Mr Glum's Wife

On the many occasions that I passed Mr Glum he was always on his own so imagine my pleasant surprise when one evening I saw him relaxing at his business headquarters with a lady, who I presumed to be his wife. This sight immediately appealed to my sense of humour. I'll tell you why.

Mr Glum is as thin as a rake and about five feet one inches tall. His lack of height is exacerbated by the fact that his trousers are two inches too long resulting in folds at the bottom. On the other hand, his wife is quite plump and is several inches taller. The other difference is that she seems to be a jolly person with a happy personality, quite unlike her husband and thus more suitable for attracting customers to step up and be weighed.

I meet Mr Book

Low and behold a little while later I came across another entrepreneur, Mr Book, who had just opened a second hand book shop. Located just a short distance from the Russian Embassy he had spread his books on pieces of weathered cardboard which were placed on a patch of earth bordering the pavement.

Day in and day out he displayed his ancient collection yet I never saw anyone buy a single book from him. But he didn't seem to mind and like many who love books was often seen reading from one of his collection. It was sad that there was a dearth of customers so in my mind I imagined that one day a Baku book connoisseur would pass by and be immediately enthralled. After deep thought, and a wary eye on his budget, he would make a purchase for a few pence and leave with his treasure clutched to his bosom.

He moves his Book HQ

And so on my daily lunchtime walks I continued to pass by Mr Book, ever eager to see if anyone showed the slightest sign of making a purchase. Goodness only knows what I would have done if our man had actually sold a book because I'm sure that the excitement would have been too much to bear! Imagine my surprise when a few weeks later Mr Book moved his business Headquarters. I say surprised because he had only moved about one hundred metres. It was clearly a strategic decision because he was now located by the bus-stop right outside the front of the Russian Embassy's visa department. This, I presumed, provided the potential to attract more customers.

He sold a Book!

He still had the same stock of old books and as before they were displayed on cardboard but now placed at the side of the pavement. Perhaps he figured that the patient line of folk who were waiting for visas were bound to get bored. What better way to pass the time in the queue than by surveying his relics from the past? But wait for it ... can you imagine how pleased I was when, shortly after his move, I witnessed someone actually *buying* a book from him. This was an event of historical importance! Furthermore, I noticed an increase in those browsing around his shop. I found that quite heart-warming.

Go visit Mr Glum and Mr Book

If you should ever visit Azerbaijan and find yourself at a loose end in Baku I suggest you take a stroll along the boulevard. When you get near the boating lake look to your left where you will find Mr Glum and his new bathroom scales. Do me a favour please and get yourself weighed. It will help his cash flow won't it?

And should you have finished your current novel why not make for Mr Book's pavement shop outside the Russian Embassy and buy a book from him? Mind you, you will have to learn Russian in order to be able to read it. Don't let that stop you, after all the purchase is in a good cause isn't it?

CHAPTER 21

LIFE IN BAKU, AZERBAIJAN

Introduction

Azerbaijan is bounded by the Caspian Sea, Dagestan, Georgia, Armenia, Turkey, and Iran. The capital is Baku where I and many expats worked and lived. Having gained independence from the USSR in 1991 the Azeri's finally had freedom from Soviet rule. Yet many of the older generation told me that conditions were better in the Soviet days. There were jobs for everyone, good schooling, hospitals, and much more. However the younger generation liked the freedom, they could travel, enjoy western music and culture. I found them, young and old, the most likeable people.

Socialising

What if you lived in an apartment building in Baku and wanted to gossip with your neighbour? Unfortunately, you don't have a garden fence to lean over so the solution is that each apartment has a balcony. This is your garden fence so to speak. I often saw my neighbours having a chat to each other in this way. And guess what? It's the women who did most of this form of socialising!

Now, you men will probably feign mock surprise, maintaining that it's women who talk the most. Well of course this is not so, proven beyond doubt because everywhere one goes in Baku one can see the

Azeri men socialising in the countless small cafés. There, for hours on end, they sit and talk and play their favourite games of dominoes and backgammon. Yes, the men do their fair share of talking too.

Finding an Apartment

After arrival in Baku one's task was to find an apartment. Joined by my friend Raj we set off armed with a list provided by the housing agent. Office colleagues recommended the central Fountain Square area, having popular bars, a range of good restaurants, and nightlife for those so inclined. By the time we had viewed the sixth apartment we were both sure that we had found the ideal place.

The agent was as pleased as punch that he had not one but two prospective tenants until we revealed that we both wanted the same apartment! This really stumped him. I agreed with Raj that whoever won the toss of a coin would have first choice. Sure enough Raj won the toss! But it all worked out for the best because my second choice was equally as good, plus it was right on the edge of the Square.

Power Outages

Not that my tenancy got off to a good start. I had been told of power outages so I specifically asked the housing agent if my apartment building would be affected. He confidently assured me that I had nothing to worry about. Famous last words because having set off from the office on that cold dark January evening I arrived at the ground floor entrance door to find the whole building in total darkness. A power outage!

Unprepared, I fumbled with the keypad and finally managed to enter the numbers only to find that when I got inside the building it was darker still. I mean pitch black darkness, necessitating painstakingly feeling my way forward inch by inch. Just my luck because I had to ascend the stairs to the fourth floor.

When I eventually reached my apartment I still couldn't see a thing. I tried several times, unsuccessfully, to get the key into the door lock. I was about to give up when my neighbour's door opened and upon seeing my plight quickly lent me a candle. That simple act of kindness later developed into a lasting and valued friendship with Ruislan and Ileyna, my Azeri neighbours.

The Lada Taxi

After I had lived in Baku for a couple of weeks I got the hang of travelling around the city by minibus. But to start off with when I had just arrived I sought the advice of Alex, our front desk security guard. Did he know of a reliable taxi driver? He promptly disappeared out to the roadside and hauled a taxi-driver into the office. Enter Ilham. Parked outside was his beloved old Lada taxi.

This Russian economy-built car was spread across the Soviet satellite countries and despite the jokes it inspired it just kept going for ever and ever. Upon seeing his aging vehicle, I remembered that I should ask if it had seat belts. Alex interpreted for me. Ilham confirmed that yes, seat belts were available. Apparently Azeri law requires the use of seat belts but from my experience few Azeri drivers take any notice of the requirement.

That evening after work I joined Ilham in his taxi and to be fair there was a passenger seat belt. I took it off its hook and fastened it only to observe its voluminous slackness as it lay forlornly on my lap. In what was a futile gesture I gave it a sharp tug to see if it locked. I should have known that it wouldn't. Instead it extended to the limit of the slack available, stubbornly refusing to lock and adamant that it would not assume a protective position across my chest. I gave Ilham a sideways glance knowing that I was not going to achieve anything if I mentioned it. After all, he had told the truth - there was a passenger seat belt. Unfortunately, I had forgotten to ask whether it actually worked!

Stopped by a Cop

We set off in his Lada and we hadn't gone far when I heard a siren whooping behind us. Sure enough it was a police patrol car. Ilham stopped the car, fished out his driver's documents and spent several minutes with the policeman. Discretely placed inside his driver's licence was a fifty Manat note. He returned, gave me a wry smile, and off we went. Since then I was told that it was not unknown for the traffic police to pull aside a driver for a traffic "violation." Rather than go to Court the easiest resolution was to pay the "fine" on the spot. Ah well, when in Rome...

Women Road Sweepers

Early each morning the company minibus driver would pick us up to take us to our Baku office. And summer and winter alike as I stood at the top of Fountain Square at my pick-up point I would see the road sweepers already at work. Not men, but women. Stout, hardy, wearing a yellow smock, they dressed for the weather, particularly on the cold winter mornings when they wore volumes of warm clothes. They scrupulously cleaned the streets and pavements with old-fashioned brooms.

When did you last see a gang of female road-sweepers cleaning your streets? Only in Baku. Yet, if I'm philosophical about Baku then I'd say that life goes on much the same as anywhere else. You see the children, noisy, laughing, playing in the narrow side streets. The house-wives doing their shopping. The traffic buzzing around the busy city centre; and you can see the guy driving his beat-up Lada on the one hand, and on the other, a posh guy swanking around in his shiny Mercedes Benz.

Just call me Richard

There is only one Catholic Church in Baku and not long after attending Mass I offered to be a reader. This led to acquiring a new name, Richard! The reason was quite simple. You see, the priests were both from Slovakia and whilst they spoke some English they had difficulty in remembering our first names. You would think, in a Russian-speaking country, that my name, Nicolas, would be easy to remember. But not so with our priest. I had to learn that when he asked for Richard, then it was me he wanted.

The first occasion that I realised that I had this new name was one Sunday when he needed someone to read the bidding prayers. In a quiet voice he looked at the congregation and asked for Richard to come forward. I normally sat near the front and I could see that he was looking in my direction. I caught his look but, thinking that it was someone else that he wanted, I didn't move.

His voice became more urgent so I glanced around behind me to see if Richard was coming forward. It was evident that everyone else didn't know who Richard was either because not a soul moved. I looked at the priest again and could see an agonised look on his face. Instinctively I went forward. His look of relief was palpable.

After Mass I gently reminded him that my name was Nicolas. He laughed, and apologised. I'm smiling to myself as I recall that conversation because some time later, just before Easter, he stopped me.
"Richard" he asked "would you be a narrator on Palm Sunday?"
Ah well, you can't win them all, can you?

Tea with a Sugar Lump

The people of Baku are naturally friendly. On one of my weekend walks I stopped in a little street-side café and in no time there was a nice pot of tea on the table, some chick peas served in a saucer, and sugar lumps in a small dish. It's rare to see ground sugar because you don't put the sugar into your teacup. Rather you put a sugar lump in your mouth and then sip the tea, thus sweetening it. The staff in the cafe were all women, with the exception of a young guy of about eighteen, who brought me the tea.

A Marriage Proposal

One of the women came over to talk to me and I gathered that she was the owner and that the young guy, Valiyev, was her son. She gestured towards the kitchen and called out to an elderly lady to join us. She then told me with a glint in her eye that the woman would like to marry me and come to England with me.

Well, I don't reckon that she was a day younger than 70 but the sparkle in her eyes told me that she was full of fun. So I went along with the joke and taking my new lady friend by the arm made as if to leave the café with her. Everyone had a good laugh. Once again I found, as I have everywhere that I have travelled, that the friendliest folk are often the ordinary working class people. These women were not dressed in the latest designer-clothes - in fact the opposite. I was invited back to have an Azeri meal so the next Friday I joined them again.

I have much to be thankful for the kindness of such warm-hearted people.

The Butcher's Shop

I don't know about you, but I wouldn't want to be a young steer tied up outside a butcher's shop in that side street in Baku. No, I would much prefer to be in the open fields, without a butcher in sight. Because if you were that steer the chances are that the next day you would be hanging on the hooks suspended from the rails inside the shop. When Mrs Baku wants to buy some beef for her husband's lunch, she wants to know that it's fresh, and make no mistake it definitely *is* fresh.

And none of your waste either, if you don't mind. The hooves, the gut, the head are all on display for purchase by the discerning shopper. The thrilling thing is that neither are the steers deposits ignored either! These are saved in a low-walled repository immediately outside the door of the butcher's shop. I guess if Mrs Baku wanted to fertilise her balcony flowerbox then these too can be ordered. No doubt that whilst one haggled for the lowest price for the beasts' head, hooves or whatever, one would be suffused with a pungent fragrance as it drifted in through the open shop door.

But let's not think ourselves too sophisticated and look down our noses at these working class Baku folk. Surely it wasn't so long ago that many an English village garden had a pig-sty and old Grampy would slaughter the pig, smoke or salt it, then feed the family for a good period of time.

Second-hand Carpets

Often of an evening in Baku I would go to the gym. I would walk through the Old City where I would pass by the souvenir shops many of which sold carpets. Now I can tell you that close inspection is not needed to reveal that they were not new, rather they showed signs of wear, in my book definitely second-hand. Personally I don't see much point in buying a carpet that is part-worn, but there's no accounting for taste is there? I hasten to add that I know very little about the value of part-worn carpets!

Courting Couples: Baku

My route would take me along the Boulevard which, bordering the Caspian Sea is a pleasant part of the city. It includes wide pedestrian ways, trees, fountains, cafes, children's rides, a boating lake, altogether a very popular place for a family day out. And for courting couples. Yes, in plain view seated on benches under the shade of the trees one would often see courting couples. Call me old fashioned if you like but I found it nice to witness their reserved behaviour, content to just sit and talk and enjoy each other's company.

I found this very interesting. Having worked in a number of Muslim countries I was quite surprised at the freedom given to them. After all, over 95 percent of the Azeri population practices the religion of Islam. However, their Constitution gives everyone the right to freedom of conscience. Religion is separated from the state and all religions are equal before the law.

Courting Couples: Bangladesh (The Love Garden)

Those Boulevard courting couples reminded me of another "Love Garden" I once visited thousands of miles away and if I were to tell you that it can be found in a very conservative Islamic country then you might be surprised. I had travelled to Chittagong whilst on a visit to Bangladesh. The service from the hotel reception desk was non-existent because the receptionist, lounging on a settee, was watching an exciting movie on TV. I wanted directions to a beautiful lake which lay in the hills to the north of the city. But, hotel guest or not,

I had to wait. Eventually he gave me directions and following negotiations with a taxi driver I was soon at my destination.

I hired a boat to take me on the lake. What a lovely setting. Surrounded by wooded slopes it was very picturesque and peaceful. As my boatman rowed along I saw courting couples sitting quietly side by side on the lakeside slopes, so I asked my guide for the name of the place. "Ah," he replied with a sanguine smile, "we call it the Love Garden."

And those courting couples in Baku. Who knows, they may by now be married with a family of their own, at weekends to be found strolling past the very place where they sat and fell in love.

CHAPTER 22

SOMEWHERE IN GEORGIA

Introduction

Being new to the office in Baku, Azerbaijan I hadn't previously met Tom but right from the start we got along well. We had a lot in common. We were both in our early sixties and experienced expats. And we were both avid rugby union fans. But he was in a class of his own when it came to energy levels, just one example being his plan to re-furbish on old dilapidated Russian passenger bus.

Baku, Azerbaijan - My Dress Sense

There isn't anyone better to arrange the farewell party for one of our expat colleagues than Tom. That's because he's very familiar with the best bars in Baku. He's told us to be in the Caravan Bar in Fountain Square at 8pm this Saturday evening. I'm confident that I can find the bar because I live right on the edge of the Square.

Just before I set off from my apartment I check my dress sense. I'm wearing one of my garish multi-colored shirts adorned with mythical dragons and some sort of Chinese picture-story. Proof positive that I have no dress sense whatsoever. My route to the pub in Fountain Square couldn't be easier. Turn right from my apartment building, walk thirty yards or so along the pavement, cross the road when I get to the newspaper kiosk and there's the steps leading down to the square.

The Pub is on the Corner

As I descend the steps a cold wind is blowing. Ahead I can see the water fountains, illuminated by spotlights, the white spray caught in the wind. Across to my left is McDonalds outside of which is the Clock that has become the meeting place with Gus and Raj, my Friday evening fellow-diners. I check Tom's directions. There's the ABC shop, a firm favorite with every expat in town, selling pirated CD's, DVD's, and Software of all descriptions. Here's the first road branching off the Square and not far past it is the second road, which goes to the boulevard. This should be it because Tom said that the pub is on the corner, right here.

The problem is I can't see a pub anywhere. Am I in the right place? Doubt sets in. I retrace my steps and try to work out what has gone wrong with my navigation. By now it's nearly 8.30pm and I'm about to give up and return home. There is a building on the corner but it doesn't look like a pub.

The curtained windows give no sign as to what lies inside and the gold lettering painted on the window is in Russian, so I can't read it. Just as I'm about to turn away a young Azeri couple, muffled with scarves and wearing ankle-length coats open the door to go in, permitting me a chance to look inside. To my relief I see the guys from the office, seated at a table. As I hang my coat a cheer goes up from my friends the Pipers (piping designers). They had seen my shirt. It had to be the Pipers didn't it? I swear that there's no corner on this earth that you can escape having the Mickey taken by them!

Tom's amazing Energy

My insight into Tom's amazing energy came when he had returned from his recent rest and recuperation (R&R) break. In confidence he confided in me that he had jetted off to Venezuela for a job interview. Upon arrival in Caracas he had presented himself at the client's office, full of his usual vigor. The fact that he had flown from

Azerbaijan to London and then straightaway to Caracas didn't seem to have affected him at all.

I was intrigued. Had he been offered the job? Yes, he had but had turned it down, it wasn't quite what he wanted! The very next day he had flown back to London because he had another urgent task waiting. "Why the haste?" I asked meekly. "Well," he replied, "it's all about the problems I'm having with the patents for my engineering company."

Tom visits Japan

Patents? Engineering company? What engineering company? Tom then explained that one of his hobbies was model engineering. After he had graduated with a degree in mechanical engineering he had started to play around with designs for model railway engines. Years later and purely by chance he met a fellow enthusiast. Cutting a long story short this guy advised Tom to form a Company and Patent the designs.

That's where the Japanese came in. "The Japanese?" I'm struggling to keep pace with him. Apparently they had infringed copyright law and were producing model railway engines in Japan to his patented designs. That's why he had to get back to London – so that he could fly to Tokyo to see a Japanese lawyer and stop the copyright infringement.

Visibly weakening I asked how things went in Japan. He told me that unfortunately there was nothing that could be done about the situation because Japanese law doesn't help in such copyright infringement situations. I felt exhausted just listening to him. From Baku to London, then Venezuela, then Japan, then back to London. I remarked that after all that travelling he must have been glad to get back home to the UK to take a well deserved rest for the remaining few days of his R&R. Well no, he replied, actually he had no time for a rest. No rest? "Why not?" I asked. Because he had arranged to drive his Bus on an outing! What Bus? What outing? We had no more time so I had to wait for an answer.

Tom's love of old Buses

Soon there was another excuse for Tom to arrange a get-together so once again we descended on the Caravan pub. I had been waiting for a chance to ask Tom about his Bus so I grabbed him and pressed him for more information. He told me that some years previously he had bought an old double-decker bus, parked it in a barn at a nearby farm and spent many hours restoring it to its former glory.

Tom's Charity Work

He had then joined a group of like-minded bus owners and out of that had grown the idea that they should put their restored buses to good use. They decided that they would do some voluntary charitable work by taking disabled adults, children, and senior citizens to interesting places for a day's outing. He duly applied for his PSV (public service vehicle) driving license. Upon attending the driving test, the Examiner's mouth fell open when he saw Tom's gleaming ancient bus. Tom passed the PSV test, recruited a volunteer support group and commenced taking groups on outings. He modestly played down his part. In his words he "just did the driving."

Tom buys an old Russian Bus

Time went by then one-day Tom had some news for us - he was now the proud owner of an old Russian-built passenger bus which had been languishing in a Baku garage. His plan involved the garage owner overhauling the engine then one of his pals from the Caravan pub would drive the bus all the way back to the UK. This pal apparently knew the ideal route - from Azerbaijan through Georgia, onwards to Turkey, and so on up to Calais.

Somewhere in Georgia

My employment contract in Baku came to an end in 2004. I couldn't leave without saying farewell to Tom and to ask if his old Russian bus had actually been delivered to the UK. "No... not exactly," he replied. "What do you mean?" I asked. He paused for a moment and then said that he wasn't quite sure where the bus was but believed that it was en-route "somewhere in Georgia."

For all I know it may still be there because I never did find out if his pal delivered the bus. So Tom, if you are reading this account, please let me know if your bus made it to the UK or if it's still listed as missing "Somewhere in Georgia!"

It gives me the utmost pleasure to nominate Tom as a True Expat. Welcome to the Hall of Fame.

CHAPTER 23

THE AZERI WEDDING RECEPTION

Introduction

I guess all of us enjoy going to a wedding so imagine our pleasure when we were invited to attend an Azeri wedding reception in Baku, Azerbaijan. Getting married were Dunya, a girl from our office, to Ahmad her fiancé, an accountant. Times have changed in our society but the wedding tradition is one of the most significant of the Azerbaijani people. Thus we were privileged to be present.

The Wedding Palace

There's an air of expectation in the Wedding Palace where the guests are already seated awaiting the arrival of the bride and groom. The staff have clearly been very busy because the eighty or so tables are laden with enough food to feed an army. And there's no shortage of drinks - soft drinks, beer, champagne, and yes the inevitable vodka. No event in Azerbaijan could possibly pass muster without vodka. Meantime I'm standing outside on the forecourt watching the road because I want to get a photograph of the happy couple on their arrival.

At last, in the distance, I spot the wedding entourage approaching, car headlights blazing, horns blowing continuously. They certainly don't do things by halves here in Baku. I have often seen a wedding car followed by the cars of family and friends whose clear intent is to make as much noise as possible - this is no time to get in the way, there's a wedding going on here! And it impresses me to see the traffic police and city-hardened drivers giving way to the wedding procession.

The wedding car carrying the bride and groom glides smoothly to a halt at the entrance to the Wedding Palace. I take some photos and then position myself strategically in the entrance of the foyer where three musicians are assembled to welcome the couple. They strike up the welcome tune. One has a long flute, another an accordion, and the third a hand-held small drum which he plays with his fingers. It's traditional Azeri music and to my Western ear it sounds somewhat discordant.

I make ready with my camera. Here comes the chief bridesmaid, carrying a heart shaped mirror which she holds chest-high, pointing forwards. Next comes the bride looking beautiful in a white off-the-shoulder wedding dress and the bridegroom, looking very smart in his wedding suit.

The bride, groom and wedding family now assemble at the entrance to the reception room. By now all of the guests are seated at the tables. I join my colleagues from the office. They have been waiting for ages and are just about to start on the food. But there's an announcement in Russian and the house-band, about ten musicians, let rip with the entrance march. With that we all stand, deafened by the music, and not only us but probably all of the residents of Baku.

Enter the Bride and Groom

The bride and groom walk under an archway of flowers to the top table. The food looks delicious. Cold chicken, bacon, beef, fish, salad, and much more. I'm hungry so without knowing it I almost committed an unforgivable sin. I was about to grab the nearest chicken leg when a hovering waiter caught me in the act. He gave me an admonishing look and with a polished flourish served me with the starter of cold fish. I felt like a kid caught red-handed with his hand halfway in the cookie jar.

From that point onwards I wallowed in the waiter's personal service. I didn't have to lift a finger. No sooner had I finished the fish then he was there with the next dish. Would I like something to drink? Well now, there's a question. Don't even bother to ask. Just fill the nearest glass, young man. Would I like champagne? I nod enthusiastically. The music obliterated any attempt to be heard. He filled my glass and in commendable expat style I demonstrated my ability to down the drink before he had time to take his first step away from me. He was quick to discern that here we have a thirsty drinker and without as much as a blink of an eye he re-filled my glass.

Drinking Vodka

The wedding guests are drinking champagne and are in a happy mood. The food never stops coming and I've eaten so much I can hardly move. My colleagues clearly intend to make the most of the occasion and are on their first vodka toast. I have been through the Baku vodka experience before and ruefully remember my hangover the next morning. So without wanting to give offence I decline their invitation to join them, preferring to limit my alcohol intake and stay sober. So its cheer's, and down goes their first vodka.

One of the guys from the office is Angelo, from the Philippines. He's a nice guy but he clearly hasn't experienced the Azeri vodka-drinking custom. One doesn't sip it, one has to swallow it in one go and before you can catch your breath there's another toast - also to be thrown straight down. The mood gets mellower and mellower and I can see that the guys are getting into their stride. Angelo is not to be outdone and my colleagues keep the waiter very busy with the diminishing vodka bottle. Rather them than me.

Believe me, this band could win any competition when it comes to loud music. Forget about talking, even thinking, when they are playing! But it's clear to see that Azeri's love their music, and they love to dance to it. And this is where you have to give them credit because it's hot in here and when the band plays a number it goes on and on and on! Maybe it's part of Azeri culture.

And you should see the way they dance! The first thing you notice is that a whole gang of folks will take to the floor. No-one has a partner. You hold your arms outstretched at about shoulder level and you move your arms, hands and fingers in time with the dance rhythm. I just can't do it. But over there I catch a glimpse of Angelo with the guys from the office formed in a circle dancing together. This may sound strange but in Baku it's common practice for men to dance this way.

My Office Friend rues the Vodka Toasts

Angelo is the star, his first time at such an event and has already perfectly copied the dance of the Azeris. He's now raising his glass in another toast. Better him than me. Now it's time to go home and I'm looking for him. He's already left. I'm not surprised because I would be under the table with the amount of vodka that he has consumed.

Next day in the office he looks very jaded, has a rotten hangover. I'd like to bet you that the next time he will ease up on the number of vodka toasts. On the other hand, he excelled himself on the dance floor for which I am happy to appoint him as a True Expat, worthy of his place in the Hall of Fame. Should Dunya and Ahmad be reading this story then may I thank you once again for your wonderful wedding reception.

CHAPTER 24

THE PALACE OF SPORTS GYM, BAKU

Introduction

For many years I have frequented gyms both at home and overseas. Don't get me wrong. I'm not Mr. Universe. Far from it. You won't see me pumping iron. No, I would describe my workouts as fairly genteel. There are occasions when such an approach comes in handy, take for example my membership of the gym in the Palace of Sports, Baku, Azerbaijan.

I meet Teymur

The first time I visited the Palace of Sports located at the end of the Boulevard in Baku I found that there was absolutely no one around. About to give up I stumbled on a group of guys drinking tea on a terrace. That's when I met Teymur. In my beginners Russian I asked him if I could join the gym. He gave me a puzzled look, not understanding what I had said. So I resorted to my normal practice and did a few exercise motions to get my point across. His whiskered face broke into a broad smile and he promptly led me down some winding stairs to the basement which housed the gym.

Teymur – multi-tasker

To describe its facilities requires a comparison. All I can say is that if you wanted something better then you had best go to Baku's Hyatt Hotel gym which undoubtedly is the jewel in the crown when it comes to the gyms in the city. They have young enthusiastic staff, spotless changing rooms, lockers, towels, showers, and much more. All newcomers are given a mandatory introduction session to show you how to use the exercise machines.

Teymur's gym had no changing rooms, no showers, no towels, and I definitely did not have an introductory session. The staff consisted solely of Teymur. He was the gym receptionist cum gym instructor cum everything. Having pointed me towards the exercise machines he promptly disappeared back up the stairs intent on rejoining his tea-drinking pals on the terrace. In about five minutes flat I was a gym member. So, without further ado, I commenced working out on an exercise machine. It wasn't until a couple of weeks later that Teymur raised the subject of gym fees, having given me time to settle in.

An Evening's work-out

My friend Teymur, the Azeri gym instructor greets me tonight, smartly dressed in his one and only suit. His hair is carefully combed and his shoes shine like new. He must be expecting a visitor because normally he dresses casually in his track-suit and trainers. Regardless of his dress code I have never actually seen him doing any work. He's just there and that seems to be the only requirement of his job. Unless, that is, you count collecting my monthly gym fee as work. Teymur is always friendly towards me and tonight he is in a particularly talkative mood as he jabbers away in Russian. I try to make conversation but he knows that my language skill is being sorely tested. Teymur departs and I greet my Azeri gym friends, select my first exercise, and commence my work-out.

No Women present

As I look around the gym I'm not surprised to see that there are no women here this evening. Not a single one. Doesn't that tell you something? Only men are silly enough to go to a freezing cold gym on a winters evening like this. From this I conclude that woman have more sense than men. I did see a couple of expat wives here a while back. It was late summer and the temperature in the gym was just about as good as it gets. On that occasion the Azeri guys, unaccustomed to having the company of females, pampered to their every need, vying with each other to help them master the stubborn exercise machines. But they haven't been back since. My theory is that the attention was just too much for them because back home they manage very well thank you without the men's help.

Gym Equipment

Thinking of the Palace of Sports gym reminds me that its equipment is as ancient as can be. Elsewhere it would probably be liable to a law-suit because the exercise machine that I'm about to use is an accident waiting to happen. As I set the weights I mentally note that the lifting cable is dangerously frayed. So I proceed in a genteel manner, with extreme caution, prepared for an almighty crash should the last brave strands of the cable finally refuse to take the load of the weights.

When I mentioned it to Teymur he had that air of a man who knows that it is pointless to complain. Nothing in the whole world is going to change that. He knew that if the government, who owned the sports centre, wouldn't provide a new cable then there is no point in getting upset about it. Wait until it finally breaks, then you might stand a chance of getting a new one. But don't waste your time trying to get it replaced while it's still working, no matter what condition it is in.

Electricity Supply

Another example of life's realities in Baku is that of the electricity supply. One evening I read an article saying that the power company had threatened to cut off the supply to those residents who had not yet paid their bills. In mid-winter this would be a harsh action.

I asked an Azeri colleague what he thought about this threat. He explained that part of the problem is due to the actions of certain power company employees. He had personally experienced this because he had only recently visited the electricity office whereupon he was told that he had to pay a fine. He asked why. The answer was that he hadn't paid his bill on time. He pointed out that he had only just received the bill. The guy then told him that in that case the fine could be reduced. My colleague was suspicious so initially he refused to pay. It wasn't that the contrived fine surprised him because unfortunately it was a fact of life.

The reality was that he had no choice but to pay the fine or risk his electricity being cut off.

A Bizarre Twist

There's a bizarre twist to this story. I was playing basketball with my Azeri gym friends in the Palace of Sports one winters evening when suddenly all of the lights went out. We found ourselves in pitch-black darkness. We called for Teymur who eventually surfaced from his basement hideaway, torch in hand. Off he went to determine the cause and 10 minutes later he returned to tell us that the power company had cut the electricity supply because the Sports Centre hadn't paid its electricity bill. Now bear in mind that the power company is owned by the government and so too is the Palace of Sports. Ah well, never mind. What you see (if you have electricity!) is what you get.

CHAPTER 25

THE VOLLEYBALL MATCH

Introduction

Baku city, Azerbaijan, is a place of ancient wonders. Not far from my apartment I discovered a Caravanserai which is now a restaurant. This ancient stone building was a stop-over for merchants and traders from China and India who, from time immemorial, transported their products on camels along the caravan routes of the Silk Road, heading for Constantinople. They came with silks, spices, ceramics and much more. It's interesting to think that Baku was considered at one time to be the world's greatest trading centre on the Silk Road. But it wasn't the silks of old that interested me on a summer afternoon as I made my way to the Palace of Sports on the boulevard ...

Women's Volleyball

There are certain locations when being an expat in the oil and gas industry is not as bad as some make it out to be. But please keep this to yourself. You'll understand that cautious expats never tell the management back in head office that our overseas life is tolerable. On the contrary, an outward appearance of hardship must always be employed. However, if I'm honest, life in Baku the capital of Azerbaijan was thoroughly enjoyable.

Take for example the international women's volleyball tournament at the Palace of Sports. A friend at the office encouraged me to see some games so on a pleasant Saturday afternoon I strolled along the boulevard, purchased my entry ticket, and soon found myself seated high up above the volleyball court. Around me were a happy bunch of Azeri supporters. Mind you, you could hardly hear yourself think because the sound system only had one setting – very loud!

The Sequined Cheer Ladies

Out there on the centre of the volleyball court are the cheer-ladies. Dressed in sequinned tops and skirts the alternate colours of turquoise, green, red and blue sparkle in the lights that blaze down from the ceiling. Waving their hand-held rosettes, they dance in unison with the music. Absolutely charming. The fascinating thing is that not one of them can be more than nine years old, and surely that little girl in the centre can't be more than four years old! She's not quite in step with the older girls but she's trying her hardest. She moves her hips as she dances, her pony-tailed hair swinging gracefully. She's the darling of the crowd there's no doubt about that.

Freddy Mercury – we will Rock You

There's a guy on the other side of the court with a beat-up old drum. Let's just say I'm sure that he's never had drum lessons because he's making a terrible discordant din. The guy next to him has a huge Azerbaijan flag under which those near him disappear as he waves it enthusiastically. This evening we will see the semi finals between Austria vs. Yugoslavia, and Azerbaijan vs. Poland. The sound system is now deafening us with Freddy Mercury of Queen "We will, we will, we will rock you." The crowd clap in unison. Without realising it I'm joining in, caught up in the excitement surrounding me.

Now the first semi-final is underway. Yugoslavia are playing well, they're in the lead. Austria are fighting every inch of the way. Yugoslavia serve for the final point. The players are jumping, falling, shouting for the ball. A Yugoslav player smashes the ball across the net, and despite a bone-crushing dive for recovery the Austrian girl simply can't return it. It's all over, Yugoslavia are the winners.

The Azeri Team are on Court

The air is now tense with excitement. A huge roar from the spectators fills the stadium – it's the arrival of the Azeri team. Their shirts are emblazoned with the insignia of Azer-rail, their sponsor. The sound system now blasts out an Azeri song. Next to me a young guy has one of those whistles that are favoured at kids' parties and he's really giving it his best. The noticeable thing is that the supporters are mostly all men! Hardly a woman in sight, yet it's a woman's tournament. I guess that the women of Baku prefer to stay at home, or do their Saturday shopping.

I have come to like the Palace of Sports, not only for the gym down in the basement but because I have also played five-a-side football here with some Azeri guys from our office. But there is a difference - we never have any spectators! Well, I tell a lie. At our first game a stadium employee enquired of one of my much younger fellow players "what age is that old guy playing in defence?" My friend called out to ask me and I replied that I was sixty-one. This caused my pals to laugh heartily. I guessed that they were having a bit of fun at my expense but nonetheless were happy to have me along.

My attention is caught by a guy near the front row dressed in a Mickey Mouse costume. He is bobbing around punching his fist into the air in tune with Freddy Mercury. The audience clap and stamp their feet in unison with the music. Great atmosphere. We now have the Azerbaijan chant "Az-zer-bai-jan."

A guy adds to the noise with a raucous blast on a trumpet. Over on the other side of the court there's a guy wearing a cylindrical tube, only his head and his feet are showing. On the tube is an advertisement encouraging the Baku citizens to purchase some product or other. Encouraged by the crowd's support Mickey Mouse begins energetically punching both fists into the air. There's now three Azeri flags waving opposite me. The cheer-leaders are back and I make a guess that the little girl stands just three feet in her bare feet!

Azerbaijan vs. Poland

The game is about to start. The guy in the carton jigs up and down to the music. The cheer leaders dance. "Az-zer-i, Az-zer-i" chant the crowd. The Polish girls are introduced onto the court. Loud boos from the crowd. Next it's the Azeri girls and each gets a loud ovation. The game has started. It's very evenly balanced and the lead swings from one side to the other. Azerbaijan win the first game 26 – 24.

What a roar of support from the crowd. Tina Turner is now giving it her best. There's a break in the play and the cheerleaders are back on court, swirling coloured ribbons to an Azeri tune, their ponytails swinging from side to side. Azerbaijan start the second game. It's a time-out. Azerbaijan lead 6 - 4. Freddy's briefly back on again. It's now 8 - 5. Another time-out. This time it's a pop version of "Rock-around-the clock."

Remembering Bill Haley

Does a song remind you of times past? I remember the movie "Rock Around the Clock" with Bill Haley and the Comets. To those of us teenagers living in the quiet backwater of the Isle of Wight it was our introduction to rock-and-roll. We danced in the aisles of the cinema. In those days this was a shocking thing to do. Jock, the dour Scottish cinema attendant tried to make us sit down but as soon as the music struck up we were back on out feet again.

The Azeri Girls Win

The volleyball game is evenly balanced, now Azerbaijan are only one point ahead.
The tension and excitement is contagious. Without realising it I'm applauding the Azeri's points and groaning when Poland score. All of the girls are extremely fit. It's definitely not a game for the faint-hearted. You have to be prepared to fall quite hard onto the floor when you try to recover an opponent's shot. Another time-out. Freddy's on again. The blue, red and green flag of Azerbaijan is everywhere. A huge roar goes up. We are all on our feet. Azerbaijan have won!

That little Girl captured our Hearts

The game is over. I'm pleased that I came because it's the first time that I have seen a live international volleyball tournament. Azerbaijan now go on to the European tournament next year, and I'm really pleased for them. We all file out in a happy mood. And that little girl, what can I say? If she only knew how she captured our hearts. May it forever be so.

CHAPTER 26

TOILET FACILITIES

Introduction

Midsummer in Baku city centre can be uncomfortably hot so what better than to escape for a day to the cooler climate of the mountains? So on any given summer weekend there is an exodus northward of buses and cars - their destination is the town of Ismailli. From there they head off to their favourite mountain picnic spots. It's a stunning place to visit, forests, rivers, and wildlife abound. However, when it comes to public facilities travelling there and back can be a challenge. None more so than for my friend Rajiv...

A Day Out

When I arrived at the gates of the Old City in Baku that hot Sunday morning it was exactly 8 am. We were going on a day to the mountains – we being a mini-bus full of my Azeri friends. I had been introduced to them by Rajiv, a friend from our church who had worked in Azerbaijan for a number of years. Squeezed together like sardines we set off for Ismailli, a three-hour drive north of Baku. This was my first drive outside of Baku and once in the countryside the condition of the roads deteriorated alarmingly, with a profusion of potholes.

Dodging Potholes

Fortunately, our driver was unfazed by the road conditions. This has left me in no doubt that the pre-requisite for any Azeri driver is to master what I shall call the *"swerving to miss potholes"* technique. This, I can assure you, is an absolute necessity in Azerbaijan! Let's say that when you are driving you see a pothole ahead of you. Of course you don't want to damage the underside of your car which you undoubtedly would because those holes go down a very long way. So what should you do? Simple. Without reducing speed, you expertly swerve to avoid the hole. The normal result in doing so is that you end up on the wrong side of the road.

So there we were, one moment serenely driving along, the next we were given the fright of our lives because our driver on approaching a large pothole had instinctively swerved across to the wrong side of the road. The fact that there were vehicles bearing down on him from the opposite direction didn't seem to worry him at all. One might have expected him to signal his intention to avoid the hole. But why should he? After all, your average Azeri driver doesn't bother to signal anyway!

And the truth is that the guy coming from the opposite direction was also dodging pot-holes in the same manner, so he wasn't in the least surprised when he encountered someone else doing the same thing.

We reach our Destination

Upon arrival in Ismailli we needed to stop for directions. After gesticulations in various directions by a number of bystanders we at last arrived at our destination, a farm which was owned by a relation of one of our party.

We settled down in a field under the shade of some trees. Nearby a river wound its way down from the mountains, passing Ismailli on its way to the Caspian Sea. My Azeri pals were busy at the barbecue so I joined them. The feast was about to begin. Did I say feast? Apologies, because I'm afraid they didn't cook the meat long enough.

I took a quiet look around me and when no-one was watching I sent my half-raw offering sailing through the air into the nearby bushes.

We buy Lamb from the Roadside

At last it was time to go. Some of the party wanted to purchase some fresh lamb which we had seen for sale at various points along the road. When I say fresh it doesn't come any fresher because your local farmer sells the fresh meat on a daily basis. It's a common sight to see a slaughtered sheep suspended from the branch of a roadside tree, the farmer removing the fleece. I too had decided to buy some lamb - for my neighbours Ruislan and Ileyna.

The driver stopped and we all piled out of the mini-bus into the farmer's open air shop. Soon I had purchased my joint of lamb, but not before having had advice from the female members of our party. You have to admire those women. They inspected the meat in minute detail, smelt it, and cross-examined the farmer in great detail followed by a rigorous flurry of bargaining.

Buying a Duck for Lunch

One of the woman wanted to buy a duck, so further down the road we stopped at some road-side stalls. The woman made enquiries - but the stall holders couldn't help. Standing nearby was a young girl no more than ten years' old who offered to go and get a duck. Would it take long? No, she only had to go over there - her out-stretched hand indicating some houses set on the other side of the road. We waited for what seemed an age. We had time to refresh ourselves with soft drinks, buy the odd item for consumption on the way home, and generally exhaust any excuse for staying longer. But still no sign of the girl.

We were just about to resume our journey when she appeared hurriedly crossing the road with a live duck firmly held under her arm. Not exactly what the woman had in mind! Fortunately, a nearby stall-holder offered to help and, making his way to the other side of the road, quickly took care of the task. Upon his return I couldn't help noticing that in addition to the duck he took great care in placing the decapitated head in her shopping bag! Did she, I wondered, intend to cook that too?

We make a Toilet Stop

We again took our seats in the bus and soon we were in a convoy of other vehicles carrying day-trippers back to Baku. We make a toilet stop. Did I say toilet? It's not until one has actually experienced an Azeri roadside ground level toilet that one can appreciate the exquisite perfume, the water-less hosepipe for cleaning purposes, the water-less cistern.

Need I say more? Rajiv and I were just bursting and being the first to reach this simple convenience I entered only to find that one had to be very careful where one placed one's feet. Get the picture. Well, I wasn't going to let this trifling matter beat me. Upon emerging into the fresh air I gestured to Rajiv to enter. He took one look inside and his face instantly grimaced in distaste. He turned around declaring that he would rather wait until the next toilet stop. I chastised him for his lack of adventure but he was adamant that nothing, absolutely nothing, would induce him to use that appalling public convenience. One had to admit that he did have a point.

And so our road journey ended with our return to Baku.

Some Advice

Should you ever decide to take a hire-car holiday in Azerbaijan you would be wise to practice your pot-hole swerving technique beforehand. I'm sure that it will be put to good use. And one more piece of advice – be prepared for the roadside toilet facilities!

Finally, for his discerning choice in public conveniences I think it only fair to make Rajiv a True Expat. An impeccable member in the Hall of Fame.

CHAPTER 27

CHECHEN REFUGEES

Introduction

Until I worked in Azerbaijan I had never met any refugees. I had no idea what it must be like to live in a foreign land having fled one's home and country because one's life was in danger. But a plea from our priest in Baku brought me face to face with a Chechen family who had fled from Grozny (the capital of Chechnya) to exile in Baku, Azerbaijan.

Sponsoring a Refugee Family

I had been anxiously waiting for the meeting for quite a while, ever since I first heard about the family that I had never met. It was at church in Baku, Azerbaijan that our priest, Father Daniel, asked if anyone would like to sponsor a Chechen refugee family. I volunteered and was subsequently shown a photo album containing dozens and dozens of photographs of refugee families. Looking back, I guess that was a defining moment. The family I chose that day didn't know me nor I them. But what mattered was that they needed financial help. I wasn't to know at the time just how vital that help was to be.

I meet my Isa, Malcan, Abu-Bakar, Asset and Murray

Having chosen my family, Father Daniel made arrangements for me to meet them and a couple of Sundays later, waiting for us after Mass, was Isa who had come to the church to show us where they lived. Our taxi dropped us at the roadside and Isa ushered us through a low-level entrance door built into a large metal gate.

Once inside there was a stone-flagged yard and on the right was their home. If you could call it a home. It consisted of one main room and a small adjoining room which housed the kitchen, the toilet, and the bathroom. We were ushered into the main room and offered two old rickety chairs to sit on. There weren't any more. Sitting on a single bed were their four children. In the centre of the room was a double bed. Finally, there was a small dilapidated scratched table on which stood an old black and white TV. And that's it. Nothing else.

This one room, windowless, was their home. Father Daniel talked to Isa in Russian and interpreted for me. I asked about the children. The eldest was Abu-Bakar, the only son, aged nine years. Next came their daughters: Asset, aged seven, Marray, aged five, and little Fariza, just one and a half – the baby of the family. I told them in my broken Russian about my family in England, that I had a son, three daughters, and seven grandchildren. The children looked at me wide-eyed, shy. I noted that they were clean and well looked after. But I didn't see any toys.

Isa introduced us to Malcan, his wife. Her head was covered, her dress ankle length befitting a Muslim woman. There in that room in Baku I could see with my own eyes what it was like to be a refugee. It seems to be a fact of life that refugees are not generally welcome, wherever they go. Yet the Azeri government, many of whose own citizens were refugees following a war with Armenia, still offered refuge to those thousands who arrived homeless and penniless from Chechnya.

I ask why they are Refugees

The government's resources were swamped so they had sought international help from NGO's - non-government organisations. Such charities as USAID, Save the Children, and many others from around the world who were doing a marvellous job in difficult circumstances. Sitting in that windowless room, waiting whilst Malcan prepared the tea, I asked Father Daniel to find out a little about Isa's particular circumstances, why he and his family had come to Baku. I couldn't imagine why anyone would want to leave their own country to live in such awful circumstances.

Isa explained that in Grozny (where they came from in Chechnya) the people suffered from frightening Russian oppression. Chechen males were arrested and held in detention for days or weeks. Rarely were there any charges made or reasons given for arrests.

Some of the men were never seen again. Worse still the Chechen freedom fighters were also feared. They would coerce the Chechen men to join their ranks and if they did not then they would be threatened. Isa, having escaped such danger several times, had no choice but to take his family to Azerbaijan.

At the beginning one of the charities helped them but they were overwhelmed and had to stop funding the family. Without food to eat Isa though Muslim turned to our Roman Catholic Church for help.

Isa couldn't get a Work Permit

One day at work I asked an Azeri colleague how the Azeri's felt about the refugees. The reply was that generally they were not welcome. Sounds familiar doesn't it? Isa had no income at all. He could not get work because he couldn't get a work permit. There were thousands of unemployed Azeri's and understandably Azeri policy was that they came first. Poverty is an awful thing. When you have no money life is miserable.

We think of the Children

Malcan has made us tea which she serves in chipped glass cups. It is made without sugar but I have learnt what to expect. On the table is a plate of sweets. In fact they are some of the sweets that I brought with me for the children. I take one, and as I drink the tea, the sweet dissolves in my mouth, sweetening the tea. Also on the table are the biscuits I brought, placed on an old discoloured plate. Neither Father Daniel nor I took one. Silently we must have both had the same thought - that the children should have them.

The Children were their Treasure

As we left Isa's and Malcan's home I was touched by what I had seen. And then Isa said something very moving. We were having our photo taken and the children were standing smiling at their parent's side. Isa turned to Father Daniel and holding Malcan's hand he looked at the children and told us that their children were their treasure. Sometimes life puts things into perspective for us, doesn't it?

Bags of Children's Clothes

I'm thankful that there were some happy times to follow. Over the three years that I lived and worked in Baku I became very fond of this family and tried to make their lives a little more bearable. An example being the story of the children's clothes. I couldn't help noticing that the four children had a very limited stock of clothes so I determined to do something about it. I contacted my twin daughters (Charene and Shenya) back on the Isle of Wight and asked them to give me all the clothes that their children had grown out of. And why not, whilst they were about it, ask all the other mothers at their children's school if they too could help.

Can you imagine my amazement upon going home on my next R&R when I found my home flooded with bags containing clothes of all descriptions? I could barely get in the door. And so started the deliveries to Baku. I didn't need to take any personal luggage instead I had two large holdalls that I jam-packed with the kid's clothes.

When I went through Customs at Baku international airport I was given some odd looks by the Customs guys. But once I had explained that the clothes were for refugee children I was allowed to proceed.

The Look of Joy

The next time I visited Isa, Malcan, and the children I arrived with the bulging hold-alls. I urged Malcan to examine the contents and as she passed the clothes to each child I could see the joy on their faces. Malcan and Isa were overcome with gratitude. And so a shuttle service from my home on the Isle of Wight to theirs continued until I had taken the remaining garments. Meantime I wrote to the parents back home thanking them and at the same time begging them not to contribute anymore!

The Happy Times

Those moments gave me immense pleasure. Just before my contract in Baku ended the family returned to their home in Grozny. I haven't seen them since. Who knows, someday I may meet them again. Should I do so I will find that the children will be grown up by now. We might recall those days of the cramped windowless room in Baku but I will also recall the happy times enjoyed in each other's company.

CHAPTER 28

THE GHOST OF MAISY

Introduction

If I had arrived in Iraq in ancient times I would have been able to visit the then greatest city in the world – Babylon. It was there that Nebuchadnezzar constructed the hanging gardens, one of the seven wonders of the ancient world. Today the Babylonian dynasty, just like that of Saddam Hussein, has been consigned to the history books.

In 1983 Saddam began rebuilding Babylon on top of its old ruins to demonstrate the magnificence of Arab achievement. He installed a portrait of himself and Nebuchadnezzar at the entrance to the ruins, saying "This was built by Saddam Hussein, son of Nebuchadnezzar, to glorify Iraq".

Later, when the first Gulf War ended, Saddam wanted to build a modern palace called Saddam Hill over some of the old ruins, however his plan was halted by the 2003 invasion and occupation by US forces. So, exit Saddam from the Republican Palace in Baghdad. Around the Palace grew the Green Zone, a small area of the city accommodating US embassy and service personnel, and us expats, living cheek by jowl, holed up in its high security enclosure. Outside of the high concrete blast walls is the rest of the city, known as the Red Zone, where one doesn't go unless absolutely necessary – too dangerous. After the occupation commenced there arrived in Baghdad one of the most popular expats I have ever met.

Mind you, he did have the most amazing story to tell …

Ricky: Truly a Ladies' Man

Ricky is one those expats that everyone loves, none more so than members of the opposite sex. I have often tried to figure out what he has that the average guy doesn't. One couldn't say that he has film star looks or an envious physique, in fact the last time I saw him he was putting on a bit of weight. Even so he continues to be very successful in his numerous amorous relationships. Ricky would say (tongue in cheek in my opinion) that he is committed solely to his current lady friend who I gather is full of admiration for his, ummm, virility.

The Life and Soul of the Party

Ricky was the only expat that I have worked with in two different countries – Saudi Arabia and Iraq, over 20 years apart. To do so is unusual because when a project is completed we move on, spreading out across the globe.

I first worked with Ricky in 1977 on a construction site at Shedgum in Saudi Arabia. He had a passion for driving and his penchant was to get into his pick-up truck and drive like a bat out of hell from the office to the site, exceeding the speed limit along the way. Whilst being admonished for his speeding he was forgiven because one just couldn't stay mad with him for long. And if there was ever a social occasion, Ricky was the life and soul of the party - everyone enjoyed being in his company.

We meet again

Imagine my pleasant surprise to meet up with Ricky over 20 years later in Baghdad. It was 2003 and we were both employees of Foster Wheeler deployed in the fortified Green Zone where our team was project-managing the repairs to the Iraqi oil installations. Ricky hadn't changed one bit. If there was a call for an evening social get-together, he was the one who organized things.

At that time the US Army General Rule number 1 (no alcohol on base) wasn't in force so he would head off to a remote liquor store and magically return with a crate or two of beer. When the evening ended we mortals would slink away having consumed more beer than we should have whilst Ricky would still be going strong. Nor did this affect his mood the next day. Whilst we would creep into the office as quiet as church mice, suffering from a horrible hangover, Ricky would be his usual amiable self. We could always rely on him for dazzling stories of his amorous exploits but a spell-binding story he told us one lunchtime in Baghdad involved a ghost called Maisy.

Ricky holds us Spellbound

It was lunchtime in the Green Zone in Baghdad and we had made our way in our steel helmets and bullet-proof vests through the security checkpoints to the dining facility. Once there we had divested ourselves of this cumbersome protection, collected our food and taken our seats at a dining table. Someone asked Ricky where he was going on his next R&R (rest and recuperation).

It was a loaded question because he had over the years accumulated, how should one put it, a girl in every port. Ricky's response had us spellbound. This time he was flying back to the UK and from Heathrow airport he would hire a car and drive to west Wales. His destination was an old house which he had refurbished and in which he had installed a lady friend, ostensibly to look after the place for him whilst he was away overseas.

Whilst we were processing the real role of his lady friend Ricky calmly told us that they had now gotten used to sharing the house with Maisy. To be honest I naturally thought, knowing Ricky, that this meant that he had another lady friend secreted away somewhere. But no, it wasn't like that at all. Because Maisy, he said…was a ghost! This revelation was met with an awed silence. Did he say ghost? This was a new one. We hadn't had an expat ghost story before.

Noises in the Night

And so the story unfolded. The refurbishment was completed and Ricky and his partner had moved in. After retiring that first night they suddenly heard a sound coming from the bathroom. He reluctantly took leave of his partner and made for the bathroom only to find that the sound had stopped. Mystified, he returned to their bed. After a short while there was a sound downstairs like a door slamming. By now they were really alarmed. He gingerly crept down the stairs only to find that the kitchen door had closed. They were so on edge that they gave up on further amorous activity…and that's when the noises stopped. Eventually they fell asleep.

It was with trepidation that they retired to bed the next night. The house was silent and both lay awake, holding their breath, striving to hear even the slightest sound. They didn't have to wait long. This time it was the sound of the refrigerator door closing. Ricky was at a complete loss. The next night they were kept awake again which caused Ricky to remind us that the interruptions were depriving him of his rightful R&R rewards.

He jumped out of bed and bounded down the stairs only to get the fright of his life.

He saw a Ghost

Because there, standing in the dining room, was the ghostly-like figure of a young woman. She was wearing a plain gray servant's dress, her dark hair was drawn back in a bun and her apron reached down to her ankles. In a split second she was gone. But Ricky was absolutely certain that he had seen her. It was only then that they realized that each time they were ensconced in bed the ghost would attract their attention. They were being watched at night.

After yet another love-less night Ricky decided that enough was enough. Time was running out and he was soon to return to Baghdad. Immediate action was needed.

Call the Vicar

So the next day he took the problem to the local church Vicar. This action tickled me pink because I didn't see him as the religious sort but to be fair his situation was desperate. He begged the Vicar to come to the house and to tell the ghost to kindly desist from disturbing them at night.

The Vicar agreed and later duly arrived at Ricky's home to keep watch. Sure enough, around mid-night there was a sound in the dining room. On entering the room, the Vicar found no one there - but he politely requested the servant girl to cease her nocturnal annoyances.

But the next day Ricky was back at the vicarage in an agitated state. She, the ghost, was still up to her old tricks. He implored the Vicar to exorcise the ghost in order to make her leave. The Vicar was extremely alarmed at this request and strongly advised Ricky against this line of action. He was certain that to do so would give her great offense. His advice was better to leave things alone.

Maisy the Ghost

Ricky was at his wits' end. His last resort was to examine the archives in the local library. His research yielded an account of a long deceased occupant of their house. There had been a servant girl employed there who had, tragically died. Her name ... was Maisy. The clothes he had seen her wearing and her general appearance all matched. Her gravestone showed that she had been buried in the local cemetery. Ricky and his partner concluded that their uninvited ghost must be Maisy. They decided that she would be welcome in their home and could stay and live in the house in peace. From that point onwards Maisy's disturbances ceased.

We listened in silence throughout Ricky's story, utterly spellbound by the idea of a real ghost in his home. I'm only guessing but I think that Maisy was happy to stay, after all ... everyone loves Ricky.

Ricky my good friend - you're a True Expat, way up there in the Hall of Fame.

Footnote

My sister Jean, a dress-maker, was really impressed with Maisy's story. So much so that she obtained a life-sized shop model, dressed it as Maisy the ghost and one evening unbeknown to me put it in my bedroom. I returned on R&R so can you imagine how startled I was to see Maisy there when I retired that night. My first thought was to take her and put her out in the hallway but I relented. I decided there and then that she could stay with me for a while ... we would be company for each other.

By the way if you are a doubting Thomas please note there is an on-line site that has over *16 000* published ghost experiences. So, maybe, just maybe, Ricky wasn't spinning a yarn after all.

CHAPTER 29

LIFE IN THE GREEN ZONE

Introduction

The Green Zone (GZ) in Baghdad is a heavily fortified walled-off area of the city where I lived and worked for the nigh on three years that I spent in Iraq. It's there we find the Presidential Palace, one of many which belonged to Saddam Hussein. In one of my chapters called Death in the Palace I recall the events when a rocket exploded close to where I had been working only half an hour before. Such events allow those expats given to exaggeration to stress the difficulties of working overseas but this is really for the management (and wives!) back home. After all, the worse we make it out to be the more management are likely to improve our terms and conditions. In this chapter I describe my time in the Green Zone.

Threading a needle

I don't care what they say, there are some things I may never be able to master. For example, I'm in my hooch (our four-man accommodation trailers) in the Green Zone in Baghdad attempting to achieve an incredibly delicate task … to thread a needle. For the last five minutes I have tried and tried again. I wish that I could get my hands on the guy who designed this needle because the eye is ridiculously small. I'm prepared to bet that he knows the agonies of

175

impatience that I and others go through. Not that he is entirely to blame.

What about those who sew buttons onto shirts? Yes, they too must share some of the blame for not sewing them firmly in the first place. And because of the trouble they have caused me I have determined that they should suffer for their errors. If the opportunity should arise I'm going to get the needle with the smallest eye known to man and I'm going to have them flogged mercilessly until they thread it. Ah, at last, the thread is through the eye and I'm now happily sewing on the button, my negative thoughts all but forgotten.

To keep me company I'm listening to a CD which I bought in Malaysia, or perhaps Thailand, or somewhere else. I can't tell you exactly what country it came from because I can't understand a single word of the lyrics. But that doesn't matter because I like the music. Buying CD's from the countries that I visit is a habit I've acquired. But pity the poor shop assistants as I search for some music that appeals to me. I sit patiently, listening to just about every CD in the shop. You should just see the look of deep despair in their eyes as I shake my head and gesture for yet another CD to be played.

I can tell you one thing, they wouldn't be human if they weren't glad to see the back of me. But maybe they aren't because often a crowd of curious onlookers will gather to stare at this guy sitting with a huge pile of CD's all around him. This has at times encouraged them to make a purchase themselves. And none of your originals, if you don't mind. For a fraction of the price back home they will copy an original CD or DVD onto a blank disc.

Mind you, these copies don't always come without problems. For example, once, when my youngest daughter Zarita was visiting me in Malaysia, we had bought a movie and were looking forward to watching it. Well, it was laughable. Some guy had made the movie by videoing it in a movie theatre. You could hear the rustling of sweet packets, giggles, and general audience noise.

My Bicycle Saga

And what if you are an expat overseas and you need a local tradesman? Don't hold your breath. Take for example the saga of my bicycle which I purchased to get around the Green Zone in Baghdad. Shortly after arrival in the GZ I had gone to the PX (military shop) and found that they had no cycles in stock. I enquired how long before the next delivery.

No-one knew because the delivery trucks coming down from Turkey were being fired on by the bad guys. My only alternative was to try the Iraqi souk (later bombed) in a street close to our office. Can they get me a bicycle? Yes of course. They will bring one from the city. Just the same model as the PX but less expensive. How much? $115 ... plus $10 to assemble it. Excuse me? Doesn't one normally expect one's new cycle to be assembled? I'm told to *come back tomorrow.*

The next day I go back and there's my new bike. I set off on a trial run accompanied by loud encouragement from a crowd of Iraqi stall-holders. The bike had twenty gears but it engaged in only the lower ones, leaving me pedalling furiously wherever I went. So I asked them to fix it, and whilst they are about it can they kindly adjust the brakes and raise the saddle? Sure, no problem.

Come back tomorrow.

Next day, another trial run. Nothing had changed except that the rear brake is slightly better. It doesn't work efficiently but the look on their faces and expressive shrugs of their shoulders made me realize that it would be best to give in gracefully. If I persist I will have to endure more *come back tomorrow* requests.

Fixing the Saddle

But all was not lost. I had a plan. I would take the bicycle to the Green Zone garage and ask them to fix it. So the next day I went to the garage where I met Ali, a young Iraqi fitter, and asked if he could raise the saddle. I wasn't to know how excruciatingly painful, figuratively speaking, that this experience was going to be.

Not that Ali wasn't helpful. It's just that his skills were, shall we say, very limited. He put a spanner on the saddle nut but it was the wrong size, fitted loosely. The nut didn't turn but the spanner did, ruining the edges of the nut. Not to be defeated he replaced the spanner with a pair of pliers and proceeded to complete the removal of the corners of the nut. But he had raised the saddle and his look when I thanked him showed a genuine pride in his work. By the time I got back to my hooch the saddle had moved back downwards and was lower than its original position. Ali had not tightened the nut sufficiently.

Fixing the Pedals

The next day I had to go for more repairs – a peddle was about to fall off. My friend Ali was very pleased to see me. I attempted to explain that he should be very careful when he tightened the pedal lest he did irreparable damage. Well, I'll give him credit because at least he got the gist of what needed to be done. Imagine then my dismay when he turned to the workbench and selected his trusty pliers. Again he did more harm than good.

Ah for the Sparrows

But life in the Green Zone did have its pleasurable moments. One evening at dusk as I walked by the trees at the rear of the Palace I heard the happy chattering of dozens of sparrows. These little guys sounded so pleased to be alive. Next time you hear them you'll see what I mean. It lifts one's spirits. Wonderful, just wonderful.

CHAPTER 30

LEROY'S STORY

Introduction

The 2003 invasion of Iraq (ruled by Saddam Hussein) was completed on 1 May 2003 with the capture and military occupation of Baghdad. But soon the euphoria of Saddam's fall was replaced with danger for those of us living and working in the Green Zone. Many rocket attacks into the Green Zone were made by the bad guys from across the Tigris River. Believe me I found it very scary because one only had to be in the wrong place at the wrong time. Don't get me wrong, we had lighter even heart-warming moments often due to the interesting and colorful expat characters stationed in Baghdad, like Leroy from New Orleans...

Leroy – a Cool Dude

When I met Leroy in our offices in the Green Zone in Baghdad I thought that he was the coolest looking Afro-American that I had ever met. He had it all. Just turned twenty-nine years old he was seriously good looking, had a fabulous physique, and a positive personality. To add to that, he had an eye-catching dress sense. His adornments included a long gold necklace, a diamond earring in his ear, and a ring on each finger. His hair was neatly trimmed as was his moustache.

His hooch-buddy (the guy with whom he shared a room in a trailer) confided in me that Leroy spent ages every morning combing his hair, checking his appearance, and applying aftershave and deodorant. Yes, Leroy was one heck of a cool dude. But he wasn't a softy and you certainly wouldn't want to get in his bad books as he weighed in at around 220 pounds, stood six feet four, and was all muscle. And when you learnt about his tough upbringing you just knew that he could take care of himself.

Leroy was born and brought up in the lower ninth ward of New Orleans. Life there was tough, but such surroundings molded him, giving him a determination to succeed in life. At the same time, it provided an anchor to his past, reminding him of where he had come from. His momma admired him because, being the oldest of four brothers, he was forced by circumstances to become the man of the house. One day his papa had left to find a job "somewhere up near Baton Rouge" and hadn't bothered to return. That was when he was thirteen.

Kindness Remembered

One warm October evening as Leroy and I were sitting outside our rooms in the Green Zone he told me about those tough teenage years and about the racism that still lingered on in his neighbourhood. On one particular occasion he was returning from High school when he was threatened with baseball bats by three white boys. He had to flee for his life. They finally cornered him in a cul-de-sac and in desperation he ran to the nearest house and knocked on the door.

It was opened by a little old white lady. She could see that he was frightened and when she saw the three bully boys she calmly asked him to come into her house. Leroy had never before been in a white person's house but his momma had told him that most white folk were decent people. She would not hear a bad word said about them. When the bullies were gone the old lady sent him on his way, telling him to be cautious in case they were still in the neighbourhood. Leroy told me that he had never forgotten her kindness.

That evening he decided that he was never again going to be bullied. He enlisted the help of his younger brother who attended the same school. The next day as they walked back home the same three boys followed them. The two brothers stood their ground. The threats grew more ominous and just as they were about to be attacked Leroy and his brother took out the bicycle chains that they had hidden in their back-packs. They whipped the chains across their attackers.

From that day on Leroy was not threatened again. He never told his momma about the incident. She disliked racism as much as she abhorred any form of violence.

At school Leroy excelled in all sports. This occupied much of his spare time but having just turned sixteen he discovered girls and that, as he told me in a reflective moment, was the beginning of the joys, and the problems, of his life. If he had bothered to keep a diary of his romantic encounters you would be exhausted just by reading it. But little did he know what would become of an amorous adventure in Baghdad, Iraq.

Oil Rig Roughneck

Once graduated from High school he took a number of different jobs in New Orleans but didn't settle in any of them. After two years of drifting from one job to another he told his momma that he was heading off to Houston in Texas where he intended to try for a job in the offshore oil industry. His momma gave him her blessing providing that he kept up his attendance at the Baptist church. Leroy promised that he would. On arriving in Houston he was offered a job as a laborer, known as a roughneck, on the oil drilling rigs out in the Gulf of Mexico. His job involved hard manual labor and for the next eight years he worked his way to the top, the toughest of the tough.

When he got his first pay packet and R&R (his onshore leave) he knew that he had found a way of life that he loved. By his own admission he lived a wild life and had forgotten more girlfriends than he could remember. But he kept his word and whenever he was onshore he would attend a local church. He never forgot his love for his momma and each month she received a cheque in the post.

Applies for Iraq

When the second Iraq war ended in 2003 the word went around that jobs were available in Iraq. The next time he flew ashore for his R&R he headed straight for New Orleans. He had to talk to his momma. What would she think if he accepted a job in Iraq? She could see that he really wanted to go so without showing her inner fears she gave him her blessing. Leroy then travelled to Fort Belvoir in Washington DC to attend security checks and briefings, a mandatory prerequisite for Iraq deployment.

Hired in Iraq

After I had been in Iraq for nearly two years we needed to recruit an additional engineer. Within a few days several CV's arrived on my desk including Leroy's. We interviewed him and it didn't take us long to ascertain that he didn't have the right experience for our needs. He had been in Iraq for just under a year in which time he had done well.

I'm not one who believes in keeping an applicant hanging on a string so I explained to Leroy that he was not the man we were looking for. He really appreciated my honest reply and I was happy to learn that another department soon hired him. He wanted to stay in Iraq in order to save money to buy a house. I wasn't far wrong when I learned that it was to be in New Orleans and that his momma figured prominently in his plan.

Risked All for Love

And now the story has a bizarre turn of events. After Leroy had been with his new department for a few months I heard a whisper going around that he had been sent back to the US ... in disgrace. I never have concerned myself with what other folk do in their own time and therefore I was completely unaware of Leroy's leisure activities.

It transpired that he had met an Iraqi woman at work with whom he wanted to spend an amorous evening. His problem was that she lived in the Red Zone, outside of the heavily guarded Green Zone where we lived. Now, if anyone had asked me to jump into a vehicle and drive into the Red Zone then I would have rapidly declined. Such an action was extremely dangerous. Furthermore, if I were asked to do so alone rather than with an armed security team I would assume that someone had gone plumb crazy. But I'm not Leroy … and apparently that's exactly what he did!

Crazy Risk

The story goes that he took a crazy risk trying to smuggle his Iraqi lady love into his hooch from the Red Zone. I should explain that security surrounding the Green Zone consisted of a number of armed check points. Somehow he convinced the guards at Checkpoint 11 that she was a visitor and obtained a visitor's pass for her to enter the Green Zone. Once inside he drove to the security checkpoint at the entry to our main compound. He then used the visitor's pass to convince the guards that she could enter. To get into where we lived there was yet another security point.

And that is where he made a fatal mistake.

Just at that moment it so happened that one of my colleagues was about to pass through the security gate on his way to his room. Leroy asked him to lend him his security pass, not mentioning that he wanted it to pass his lady friend off as a resident. It was immediately obvious what Leroy's intentions were and so my friend declined, knowing that he would have been in serious trouble if he had complied. Unfortunately for Leroy the Ghurka guard could understand English and, refusing entry for Leroy's lady friend, radioed the guard commander. In no time at all the lady was taken to the Checkpoint and dispatched into the night. The next day Leroy was fired and on his way home.

Heart of a Romeo

In a way it's a pity that his intentions came to nothing. But the security risks were bad enough without adding to them. Had the lady in question been a suicide bomber many expatriates would have died. However, you can't keep a good man down and low and behold Leroy later surfaced again in Iraq, this time in the south in Basrah.

Ever the Romeo, it was rumored he soon resumed his romantic wanderings.

Personally I don't hold that against him. To his credit he had achieved a great deal since his tough days of being a roughneck on the oil rigs. I have no doubt that he persevered and has since bought that home for his momma. She probably doesn't know anything about his attempted extra-curricular activity in Baghdad. She doesn't need to, does she? I respect Leroy for his heart of gold, being loyal and loving to his mother.

Perhaps, some day, he will find the right girl and then settle down. When he does I would like to be the first one to congratulate him.

Meantime Leroy, you're a True Expat. Welcome to the Hall of Fame.

CHAPTER 31

KIDNAP IN BAGHDAD

Introduction

Iraq, post the 2003 invasion, became a very dangerous place, none more so than in Baghdad. For example, at that time an English guy against advice continued to live in the unprotected Red Zone. He thought that he would be safe, but he wasn't. He was abducted and beheaded by the bad guys. What happened to him was to become common place - the threat of such a death was very real especially for the ordinary Iraqi civilians. One of whom was Hassan...

Hassan

It was a hot summer's day at Abu Gharib. The white Toyota land-cruiser with the distinctive blue UN door markings had been standing in the sun from nine in the morning. Hassan, Khalil and Omar had just finished a site meeting with the building contractor, finalising the plans for the refurbishment of the Abu Gharib primary school. The UN had recently released the funds and Hassan, as project leader, was pleased that the work could now move ahead. It was sorely needed. For some time, the school had been closed and as a result the local children were not being educated. Poverty was everywhere.

Hassan saw children playing barefoot in the street. He thought of his own childhood, saddened that things had changed so much in Iraq.

But now he had a chance to help improve the future for these children who only knew of war and shortages and hardship.

Their driver, Ahmed, had the car air conditioner running as they made their return to central Baghdad. Hassan was anxious to get home before nightfall. Being out on the road after dark could be dangerous and his wife Leila would be worried if he arrived home late. He glanced at his watch. It was almost time for the evening prayers and he knew that she would be preparing for her devotions. Hassan never ceased to be comforted by her deep faith. Yes, she was a good wife and mother, and he counted himself a lucky man.

The Kidnap

His thoughts were suddenly cut short when he was flung violently forward. Ahmed had braked hard and swerved to avoid a black saloon car which had intentionally cut straight in front of their vehicle. Another car simultaneously screeched to a halt close behind them. Their path was blocked. Four armed masked men sprang from the rear car and ordered them to get out of their vehicle. They were stunned with the speed at which things had happened. Hassan glanced at the occupants of the front car, a typical family, the husband at the wheel and beside him sat a woman with a young child on her lap.

Shot dead

The masked men ordered them to lie face down on the ground. Ahmed hesitated and then suddenly he snatched at the mask of one of the men. Ahmed gasped, he had recognized the attacker and spat angry words at him. The man flew into a fury, deadly anger suffused his features. In that moment of recognition Ahmed had signed his own death warrant. Hassan then watched what happened as if he were held in a trance. He saw the un-masked man angrily push Ahmed to the ground, take a handgun from a holster inside his jacket, and shoot Ahmed three times at point blank range in the chest. Ahmed slumped, lifeless.

Kidnapped

The silence that followed the gunshots was soon broken. The leader of the masked men barked an urgent order for Hassan, Khalil and Omar to stand up. It was clear that the shooting necessitated an urgent haste to get away. Not one of them moved. They were terrified, frozen with fear, the shock of the killing etched on their faces. They could hardly comprehend what had happened. One moment Ahmed was alive, the next he was dead. Murdered - shot at point-blank range.

The masked men were in a hurry, they kicked them cruelly, forced them to stand. Each was thoroughly searched. Their captors were looking for cell phones. Hassan noted their cold efficiency and realized that this was not a chance operation. These men were prepared, ruthlessly pursuing their plan. Hassan handed over his UN cell phone but his heart was beating with fear because they hadn't noticed his personal cell phone in his trouser pocket. He was then forced to get into the trunk of the family car. Meanwhile Khalil was forced into the trunk of the other car. Whilst this was happening a masked man shot Omar in the leg, his cries of agony filling the air. He wasn't wanted. But he couldn't be allowed to escape and raise the alarm.

Instantly the cars set off. In the cramped confines of the car trunk Hassan took his cell phone and rang the number of the contractor's office, hoping that the occupants of the car wouldn't hear him speaking. The phone in their office rang and rang and Hassan despaired that they had all left to go home. Just as he was about to ring off the phone was answered. Hassan quickly whispered a brief desperate message.

Leila gets the Kidnap Call

Leila was in the kitchen preparing the evening meal. It was 5.45pm and Hassan wasn't home yet. She was accustomed to him sometimes being delayed, although he usually tried to phone her if he was going to be late.

Everyone in Baghdad knew of the car-bombings, the checkpoints, the traffic diversions. She tried to hide from Hassan and the children how worried she was for their safety. She watched on TV the carnage wrecked by the suicide bombers. Innocent people, young and old, being blown to pieces. She had deliberately closed her mind to the thought that Hassan might one day also be a victim. She glanced again at her watch, it was nearly 6pm. Should she wait for him, or serve the meal in his absence? Just as she decided to start without him her phone rang. She expected the caller to be Hassan.

It was a hammer-blow. She heard the words and froze with dread. Hassan had been kidnapped.

Brutal Treatment

Hassan felt the car come to a standstill. The trunk was opened and he was ordered to get out. He was searched again and his other cell-phone was found. The leader swore at him and viciously struck him in the face with his fist. The pain of the blow exploded in his head. His nose started to gush with blood. He and Khalil were then gagged and blindfolded and forced to get into the trunk of the family car. By now they realized that their lives were in serious danger, they knew that kidnapping often ended in execution.

Soon they were on their way again and gradually the sound of traffic increased. Hassan guessed that they were on the outskirts of Baghdad. After a while the vehicle slowed down and stopped and he concluded that they had joined a queue of cars at a check-point. They heard a policeman questioning the man and woman in the car. It suddenly dawned on Hassan why the kidnappers had used a typical family to be in the car. It was a façade of innocence intended to put the police at ease and making it unlikely that they would search the vehicle.

Torture and Interrogation

After another twenty-minute drive the car drew to a halt and the engine stopped. The trunk was opened and they were dragged into a house, hardly able to walk because their legs were so cramped. Inside the house the man who had struck Hassan then heatedly accused him of deliberately concealing the cell phone. Hassan was still gagged, he couldn't protest. His blindfold was removed and he found himself looking at a loaded revolver. He believed that he was about to be shot. Instead the man raised his hand quickly and cruelly clubbed Hassan across the head with the gun.

When he recovered consciousness his head was thumping with pain. A kidnapper removed his gag and he was told to sit on a chair. He then interrogated him. Why was he working for the Americans? There was cold hatred in the question. Hassan replied that he wasn't working for them, that he worked for the UN. The man swore at him and struck him in the face and head. Later another kidnapper repeated the same process. The questioning and beatings continued. Hassan was bleeding from the nose and mouth. His face was swollen and he could hardly see. His head was now pounding from the continuous blows that he had received.

He wondered how much more of this brutal punishment he would have to take. Then the leader told him that they knew where he lived, that they knew that he had a wife and three children. He left the words hanging in the air. Hassan was filled with dread, fearing for their lives.

Horrific Execution

Seven long days passed during which he was kept in complete isolation. The beatings continued. On the morning of the eighth day he was taken to a room separated from an adjoining room by a glass partition. He was joined by Khalil and another prisoner. In the adjoining room there was a man who was kneeling on the floor, blindfolded, head bowed, his hands tied behind his back. They were told that the man was on trial. That a judge would be coming shortly. Hassan wondered why they had been brought to witness the trial. He didn't have long to wait.

The judge arrived and after a short cross-examination ordered the kidnappers, all of whom were masked, to execute the man. A kidnapper wielded a sword and cut the man's head off. It was a horrific sight. Hassan vomited uncontrollably. He realised that these men would stop at nothing. They had their own laws, their own judge, and their own executioner. The horror of the decapitation appalled him. He dreaded the thought of suffering the same fate.

Anxiety and Fear

Leila was in the grip of anxiety and fear. She was desperate to know if Hassan was still alive. For one week no-one had heard from the kidnappers and she feared the worse. She had heard of husbands who had been kidnapped, tortured and killed by their captors, even though in some cases the families had paid the ransom. Her phone rang, she rushed to it and a man's voice asked her if she was Hassan's wife. Leila guessed correctly that these were the kidnappers. She confirmed that she was Hassan's wife, trying to remain calm. But her heart was breaking so she tearfully pleaded with the caller not to kill Hassan. The caller callously rang off without another word.

Relatives contacted

Tarik, Leila's nephew, knew that his Aunt was distraught with worry. His mother Fatima and Leila were sisters and were very close. By now the whole family were caught up in the stress of the kidnap. Tarik's phone was ringing. When he answered it the caller asked him to identify himself. Tarik asked if the caller's group were holding his uncle Hassan. Yes they were. They had found Tarik's telephone number on Hassan's cell phone. Tarik pleaded with the man to release Hassan, that he was an innocent family man with children. The caller told Tarik that they knew all about Hassan. They would think about releasing him.

Ransom demanded

Later that day a lady colleague of Hassan was at her UN desk in central Baghdad when she received a call – was she a relative? No she wasn't related, but was his friend. She sensed that the caller was one of the kidnappers and went straight to the point and asked how much money they wanted to release Hassan. The chilling reply was that they might not release him, but kill him. Two days later Tarik's mother, Fatima, received a call.

The ransom was one hundred thousand dollars.

Fatima was shocked. She replied that they didn't have that amount of money but would get as much as possible. The caller told her that she only had two days and if she failed they would kill Hassan. Without further comment the caller rang off. She wanted to ask for more time. On checking the caller's number, she discovered that it was from Hassan's cell phone. She tried to call the number but there was no reply.

Ransom Negotiations

Two days later the caller contacted her as he said he would. Had they got the money? No they hadn't, it was such a huge sum. The caller told her to instruct Leila to sell her apartment, her car. But Fatima was not one to be pushed around. She had a tough inner core. Her mind was made up; she would not back down in the face of threats made to her. She replied that the kidnapper's demands were unrealistic, that it was impossible to meet their demands in a few days, that it would take much longer. She emphasised that the sum was beyond their means. The caller backed down and then started to negotiate the ransom. First ninety, then eighty thousand.

Fatima stayed calm and asserted that the family could only manage ten thousand dollars at the most. The caller hung up. That same evening the man called again. He would accept sixty thousand dollars. Fatima replied that the most they could raise would be twenty thousand dollars. With this the man hung up without comment. At this point the whole family started to collect the ransom money. Leila sold the family car for five thousand dollars.

Hassan's parents, now living in Holland, sent ten thousand dollars. The family in Iraq raised the balance. Two days later it was Leila who received the call – did she have the money ready? Leila confirmed that they had collected twenty thousand dollars. She was then told that it wasn't enough, that the final price was thirty thousand dollars.

Once again the family rallied around. Hassan's parents sent another five thousand dollars, his brother, also living in Holland, sent three thousand dollars and the family collected the balance.

The final call from the kidnappers came in the middle of the night. Leila reported that she now had the thirty thousand dollars.

Ransom drop-off Point

The instructions for delivering the ransom were precise. She was to come alone. No one was to be with her, or follow her. Leila objected, told them that a woman should not travel alone, asking if it would be acceptable for her to bring her brother. The caller agreed to this and gave her instructions to deliver the ransom to an open area at a specific place on the outskirts of the city. She was to be there at exactly 6am in the morning, she was to drive slowly to the drop-off point, drop the bag on the ground, and without stopping drive off, back to her home. If she tried to trick them they would kill Hassan and her as well. Before Leila could ask if Hassan was to be freed the caller rang off.

Dropping off the Ransom

Leila was charged with nervous tension as they left her home to go to the drop-off point. She did exactly as instructed. As they approached the drop-point she searched for any sign of Hassan. The place was deserted, he wasn't there. What if they didn't release him? What if they kept the money and killed him? She was going through agonies in her mind, not knowing what to think. Her brother drove slowly until they saw the exact place to drop the bag containing the ransom money. There was no-one in sight as Leila opened her door and dropped the bag on the ground. Her brother accelerated, heading back to her home. Leila was desperate to know what was going on. She rang Hassan's number on her cell phone. A voice answered and told her that Hassan would be released in one hour. She must conform to instructions and return home immediately.

Hassan released

Meantime the kidnappers released Hassan, giving him the taxi fare to get home. He found that he was in a district of Baghdad called Hay Al-Adeal and whilst waiting for a taxi he gave thanks for his life being spared. At home Leila was consumed with worry. Would they keep their word? Would Hassan be released?

The whole family had gathered to welcome Hassan. The taxi drew to a halt in the street and as Hassan disembarked his strength finally deserted him. He felt terribly weak, hardly able to walk. Slowly and with great effort he climbed the stairs of the apartment building, his heart thumping, his emotions welling up to the surface. He found himself crying, tears of relief streaming down his cheeks.

Reunited

He came at last to his home and had hardly knocked before the door burst open and Leila threw herself into his outstretched arms. Hassan was overwhelmed. The sleepless nights, the beatings, the mental torture, had taken a heavy toll on him. He saw the family cheering and clapping, smiles of relief and tears of happiness on their faces. Leila felt him weigh down on her arms. He had passed out. The emotional stress of the reunion coupled with two weeks of pure hell had taken their toll.

Warning

Later that day he told the family of his ordeal, of what he had suffered and what he had seen others suffer. Amongst his relatives was a niece, Raina, who listened intently to his story. For days she hadn't slept, worried that the kidnappers would torture Hassan and learn that she worked for an American company in the international Green Zone. But he hadn't said anything. It could have been her death warrant.

Hassan told the family that he had been warned by the kidnappers that he had better get out of Iraq. He feared his life would now always be in danger. They might kidnap him again, and next time he probably wouldn't be freed. Over the course of the following four weeks he didn't stay at his own home, but with relatives, moving from one to the other for security reasons.

Leaving Iraq

After one month Hassan, Leila and the children left Iraq for Syria where he sought specialist medical attention for his recurring head pains. The treatment was successful and they stayed for a much-needed period of rest and recuperation. The kidnapping changed their lives forever, they couldn't return to Iraq, it would be too dangerous. Hassan's parents were in a position to help and advised them to leave Syria and to fly to Holland. When they boarded the KLM flight Hassan's ordeal was behind him. A new life lay ahead for them.

Thanksgiving

Later that same day at our office, Raina, an Iraqi colleague, brought round a plate of Arabic sweets, offering them to us. We asked her what the occasion was and she replied that she wanted all of us to share in the thanksgiving for the safe release of her uncle Hassan. Over the next few days Raina told me this account of Hassan's kidnap.
This account is based on a true story. Names have been changed. The year was 2005.

Footnote

Decapitation: it may be seen as barbaric. Different cultures have differing perceptions. Reports kept in Baghdad's main morgue show that June 2005 was the peak month for corpses found beheaded.

Hassan's Back-story

Married at 21, Hassan subsequently graduated from the top Iraqi military academy. When Iraq's leader Saddam Hussein went to war with Iran, Hassan was commissioned as a Colonel and fought against the Iranians for two and a half years. Then he was captured, tortured and almost beaten to death. He spent 14 years in captivity as a POW. Ironically during that period, he was promoted several times, reaching the rank of General by the time he was freed!

At the time of this story he was working for the UN.

CHAPTER 32

DEATH IN THE PALACE

Introduction

Following the 2003 invasion of Iraq the Republican Palace, sitting beside the Tigris River in Baghdad, was occupied by US embassy staff, armed Services personnel and expat civilians. Surrounding the Palace was a large area known as the Green Zone. Heavily fortified, this was where I lived, worked, ate and slept for the duration of my work in Baghdad. Within its blast-proof concrete perimeter walls, its heavily guarded entry points, and its numerous watch towers one was relatively safe. Surrounding it was the city of Baghdad – the Red Zone, some say the most dangerous place in Iraq.

My employer in Baghdad was Foster Wheeler – an international engineering and construction Company. They had been awarded a Contract by the US Army's Project and Contracting Office (PCO) to provide a management team monitoring the reconstruction of Iraq's refinery and oilfield infrastructure. A few months after my colleagues and I had settled into the PCO a suicide bomber wearing a bomb-vest blew up the popular Green Zone café. It was located a very short distance from our office. There were fatal casualties. We were extremely shocked - it could have been us in the PCO because we had no armed guards to protect our building. Our repeated requests to the Security managers to provide protection fell on deaf ears.

*But matters were brought to a head on the eve of parliamentary elections —
renewed rocket attacks on the Green Zone were predicted. For our protection at
work we were temporarily moved to the safe haven of the Palace building. We were
very relieved, figuring it a much safer place to be. But little did I know what was
to happen that evening …*

Attacks on the Green Zone

It's January 29th 2005, the eve of an Iraqi parliamentary election. The
Green Zone security team has an Intelligence report warning of a
significant increase in insurgency activity right across Baghdad. As a
result, our security grading has been raised to the highest level. For
those of us working in the Project Contracting Office (PCO), indeed
throughout the Green Zone, this warning predicated further danger.
Many of us felt that our office building would provide us with scant
protection if struck by an incoming rocket from across the Tigris
River. And to add to our fears a suicide bomber had somehow
evaded Security and killed himself and others in the nearby Green
Zone café.

Enough was enough. We collected our files and around mid-
afternoon made our way to the Palace. Upon arrival we found that
we weren't expected - there was no office space available.

I find a vacant Workstation

After persistent enquiries we found a sympathetic ear and were
directed to an empty conference room but we couldn't continue our
work because there were no computers available. My colleagues
draped themselves disconsolately around the conference room table.
Time dragged. Then, fed up they called it a day and left to go back to
their rooms. But I had to complete some presentation slides for a
management meeting slated for early the next morning.

Should any of you reading this have worked in the PCO you will
doubtless recall the constant pressure to produce reports every
morning, noon and night! We dubbed this task as "feeding the
dragon," aptly named because there was a voracious appetite for
information which was digested and then transmitted to Washington.

I was under pressure. I had to get my slides ready. Fortunately, a sympathetic US Army Colonel offered me a computer desk. I settled down and completed my presentation slides just after 7pm intending to collect my files early the next morning I tidied my desk and left for my room. Little did I know of the tragic event that was soon to take place.

The Rocket Attack

I can only guess what happened. Baghdad city after 7pm was still busy. Soon it would be quiet because the curfew would start at 8pm, earlier than usual. By then the residents had to be off the streets. This heightened security measure was based on the same Intelligence report that we had received earlier in the day. But only the bad guys, not the Intelligence people, knew of their intention to launch an attack on the Green Zone. Under cover of darkness their nondescript Toyota pick-up was parked on some waste ground close to the bank of the Tigris River.

Across the dark-flowing waters life and work went on 24/7 in the Green Zone. The four occupants sat silently waiting, alert, they needed to pick their time to avoid detection by the US Army patrols. In the back of the pick-up a loose tarpaulin was draped untidily hiding a rocket-launcher. The men checked their watches. 7.30 pm. It's time. They uncovered the rocket-launcher and fired the rocket into the Green Zone.

Fatal Casualties

Not everyone had left the office area in the Palace where I was recently working. Amongst them was Lieutenant Commander Keith E. Taylor, USNR, a U.S. reserve navy officer, and Barbara Heald, a U.S. government civilian employee. Work must go on around the clock. Across the Tigris the night air was punctuated by the sound of the rocket launch. Death screamed through the night air. At one thousand miles per hour the rocket pierced the side wall of the Palace, landing near Barbara and Keith. They were both fatally injured.

After the attack it was quiet in the office, deathly quiet.

The air was filled with dust. Debris scattered everywhere. But amazingly the office staff in adjacent rooms survived. Shocked and frightened, they surveyed the devastated scene. The emergency sirens immediately wailed their lock-down message across the Green Zone. Everyone rushed to their nearest shelter. In any attack there was always the fear of further incoming rockets. But this time none came.

Collecting my Presentation Slides

The next morning at 6.30am I made my way to the Palace to collect my paperwork. I had no idea that the rocket had landed in the Palace or of the deaths it had caused. I found a US Marine sergeant stationed at the office door with orders to stop anyone from entering. Upon questioning him I learnt that the rocket had exploded where I had been working the evening before.

In writing this account I am sadly reminded of Keith and Barbara. I didn't know them but had probably seen them at their desks the evening before, dedicated to their duties. It could have included others, or me. Should their families ever read this account I humbly ask that they forgive me for any inaccuracies and wish them sincere condolences for their loss.

I hung around and badgered the Marine sergeant to go and look for my papers. Incredibly he found that my workstation whilst damaged was not destroyed and returned with my paperwork. Apparently the rocket hadn't actually exploded.

That morning we all returned to the PCO office where security guards were now stationed. Right across the Green Zone work resumed as normal. It made one think, after the previous evening's tragedy that between life and death there is just a fine dividing line. I would like to honor Keith and Barbara posthumously as True Expats, with a very special place in the Hall of Fame.

CHAPTER 33

DANGER & HUMOUR IN BAGHDAD, IRAQ

Introduction

Following the 2003 invasion and occupation of Iraq there was a need for Private Security Forces, PSF's. The PSF guys, mostly experienced ex-servicemen, were well paid but the risks were high. Some paid with their lives. In Baghdad they did an outstanding job, providing security for VIPs, venturing from the safety of the Green Zone out into Baghdad city itself, the Red Zone – where the bad guys lay in wait. The funny thing is that when I met one of their guys he wasn't the fearsome type that I expected; in fact he had a great sense of humour. So here's his story – which had us all laughing …

US Military Language

All civilian expats who went to Baghdad following the second Gulf war soon learnt an additional language because we were billeted and worked with the US military. So, when one entered Iraq one was then **"in Theatre,"** one worked in the **GZ** (green zone), one lived in a **"hooch"** (a four-person trailer) and one ate **chow** at the **DFAC** (the dining facility). General information was called an **"All Hands Alert"** and the security levels were denoted by **Green, Amber or Red**.

We flew from Kuwait International Airport (KIA) into the BIAP (Baghdad International Airport), and became acquainted with the PSF (private security forces). Phew!

The Brave Expat PSFs (Private Security Forces)

Speaking of the PSF guys reminds me that they were both mentally and physically tough. They had to be because theirs was a dangerous job. Those of us who lived and worked in the Green Zone had our scary moments when the bad guys fired mortars and rockets at us. But at least we were protected 24/7 by the ten-foot-high concrete blast walls, the armed guards at the checkpoints, plus manned watch-towers.

Outside was Baghdad city, the Red Zone, where danger stalked every street. Roadside bombs, suicide attacks, kidnappings, not a safe place to be. It was into the Red Zone that the PSF guys went every day because their role was to provide security whilst escorting their VIP passengers to various destinations, for example the MOO (Ministry of Oil) or Baghdad Airport.

The road to the airport was known as one of the most dangerous roads in Iraq. Not without reason. In a terrible two-week period alone the bad guys had killed sixteen PSF guys on that road.

The Pastor & the Baptism

One evening, at a church meeting, we were joined by Johannes, an Afrikaner, one of the South African PSF guys. Still wearing his revolver, Kevlar bullet proof vest and helmet, he arrived a little late – he had only just returned from a really dangerous mission into the Red Zone. Yet despite the trauma of his day he was able to tell us the funniest story of an event back home in South Africa.

Johannes recounted that in his church in KwaZulu Natal it was the custom to be baptized by complete immersion in a deep baptismal font. However, the Pastor had over the years become disillusioned with being soaked to the skin every time one of the more well proportioned members of his flock decided that it was time to be baptized. But in an article in the latest church magazine providence played its hand because what should he see but an advertisement describing waterproof baptismal leggings, guaranteed to keep one perfectly dry.

The problem was that they were only available for purchase from the USA and were not cheap to boot. The Pastor wanted them but would his parish council approve of the purchase? Throwing caution aside he called an extra-ordinary meeting and eagerly put the matter to them. After much debate they took the big decision to make the purchase. The whole church congregation was informed that future baptisms would be different – new fangled baptismal leggings would be used.

None could have known what was to come …

Weeks passed and the Pastor, indeed the whole church community, waited expectantly. Concerns grew, would the order ever arrive? At last a package was delivered to the presbytery. The Pastor and parish councillors gathered and eagerly unpacked the package. The relief was palpable because the delivery contained the water-proof leggings. But their delight turned to concern (and to some a guarded amusement) when the Pastor, of medium height and slimly built, tried on the leggings. They were several sizes too big for him. This now posed a dilemma.

Should they send the leggings back and ask for a smaller pair? What if they were lost in the post or what if they did get back to the US and the Company didn't respond? The decision weighed heavy on their minds. They eventually persuaded a doubting Pastor that they should keep what they had.

You can imagine that the news of the oversize baptismal leggings soon got around the whole church community. Thus (Johannes recounted) when the baptism of Mrs. Abali Wiataba was announced for the following Sunday, a large crowd pressed into the small church to witness this unique occasion. The service started with the usual prayers and hymns and then the Pastor stood to address the faithful from the pulpit. An expectant hush came over the congregation. You could have heard a pin drop.

"Brothers and Sisters, today we welcome Abali into the Church". All eyes were on the Pastor as he and Abali made their way to the font, which had been filled with several feet of water. The senior church elder solemnly assisted the Pastor into the gi-normous leggings. Many a smile was suppressed amongst the congregation because the leggings nearly reached up to the Pastors chin. Furthermore, they fitted so loosely that you could have easily fitted two people inside and still have room to spare.

Abali descended the font steps into the water followed by the Pastor shuffling along with great difficulty in his leggings. Johannes then described the physical differences between the two. Abali was a woman of more than ample proportions, typical of African women in the parish. She dwarfed the Pastor. And he was only about half her weight. Now the time had come for the baptism. Standing in the waist-high water the Pastor proclaimed "Abali, I baptize you in the name of the Father, and of the Son, and of the Holy Spirit".

At this point the person being baptized is supposed to lean back in the water and briefly fully submerge themselves, supported by the Pastor. Abali leaned back but rather than entering the water with a graceful movement she suddenly lost her balance and fell backwards with an almighty splash, promptly disappearing under the water. The Pastor was taken completely by surprise. He was holding her but he was not strong enough to support her full weight - so he too disappeared beneath the water. The congregation then gasped upon seeing the Pastors feet emerge from the water, given buoyancy by the air trapped in the leggings.

Meantime Abali had surfaced, coughing and spluttering. For a moment she was disorientated but then her attention was drawn to the two feet, waggling frantically in the air. With great presence of mind, she grabbed the Pastor and pulled him to the surface. Weighed down by the water that had entered the inside of his leggings it was as much as he could do to stand.

Abali, being strong and as broad as a barn door, picked up the spluttering Pastor, threw him over her shoulder in a Fireman's lift and calmly carried him up the font steps to safety. The congregation burst into spontaneous applause, greatly appreciative of this baptismal entertainment. When the next baptism was announced there was no mention of the leggings. The pastor's mind was made up. They never saw service again.

When I saw Johannes sometime later at the gym, I remarked that I would never forget the story of the baptismal leggings. He smiled. Apparently the poor Pastor hadn't been given the chance to forget it either.

Well done Johannes, you certainly are a True Expat – welcome to the Hall of Fame.

CHAPTER 34

THE ANNIVERSARY CAKE

ANDY AND THE PIPERS – STORY 1

Introduction

Sooner or later I, like fellow expats in the oil and gas industry, returned home to the UK after working overseas. Many can be found working in the home office engineering departments. One of my favorites is Andy. I met him - along with his fellow draftsmen - called Pipers - working in the piping design department of John Brown Engineering, located in Portsmouth city centre.

Andy was a great story-teller of outrageous yarns that had you splitting your sides.
Andy and the Pipers would take the mickey out of their boss David – and his deputy Alan - at every opportunity.

In this story, The Anniversary Cake, and the next two chapters you will learn just how wicked - and funny - they could be.

The Pipers feel the Heat

It was a hot UK summer's day and the sunlight was pouring in through the tall windows of the piping design department. The five-storied Portsmouth office building had been constructed before the introduction of double-glazed windows and the architect had clearly miscalculated their affect because the staff were roasted in the summer and half frozen in the winter! Not that this bothered Andy because, as he often informed his pals, he had experienced much worse conditions overseas.

Sensing an opportunity for a wind-up they replied that it might not be too hot for him but what was he going to do about *their* discomfort?

Andy was quick to reply, he would take the matter up with their boss David and that twerp Alan, his deputy. If they had any regard for the Pipers, then they would have at least supplied them with a couple of portable fans to keep them cool. What could one expect, he added, from management of such low caliber? This oft-repeated rhetorical question was as usual greeted with a chorus of agreement from his pals.

Robbie, gifted with handsome good looks and a strong liking for the opposite sex, suggested that they should complain and demand that David extend their lunch break to compensate for their discomfort. Andy however suspected that Robbie had an ulterior motive, namely to pursue the attractive new barmaid at their favorite city-centre pub.

David's upcoming Wedding Anniversary

That same morning David was in a good mood. He discretely asked Alan to come to his office. Closing the office door, he explained that he would be going out for a while. He wanted to visit a cake-shop. Alan agreed but was curious to know: why the cake shop? David glanced through the glass panels of his office in the direction of the Pipers, lowered his voice and confided that today was his silver wedding anniversary and that he wanted to surprise his wife with a nice anniversary cake. At the same time, he didn't want that reprobate Andy and his buddies to know anything about it.
"Of course not," concurred Alan, "Mum's the word!"

This assurance brought little relief to David because he knew that Alan was no match for Andy and his pals because they never missed any opportunity to create mischief.

Alan spills the Beans

After David had left the office Alan made his way to where Andy and his pals were working at their drawing boards. They agreed that yes, it was a nice morning, but what about providing some fans to keep them cool? After all, they added innocently and with a large degree of license, weren't they working their butts off to meet the impossible deadlines that David had set them?

Alan smiled at this response. Having come up through the ranks of the Pipers he was aware that whatever he said he would have the mickey taken out of him. So he responded by changing the subject, saying that he had been left in sole command of the piping design office. This was met with groans of mock incredulity by the Pipers. Why, they asked, would David be so irresponsible as to leave the department in the hands of such an incompetent deputy?

Not in the least fazed by this comment Alan calmly assured them that it wouldn't be for too long because David had only gone out to buy a cake. This news was greeted with hoots of derision from Andy and his pals and after they had composed themselves they enquired cunningly why David needed a cake. Surely, said Andy with masochistic fervor, shopping should be the job of one's wife? Alan declared that if a man wanted to buy a cake for his wife on their wedding anniversary, then what was wrong with that! Too late he had let the cat out of the bag.

The Cake

Meanwhile David was gripped by indecision. It wasn't until he was in the cake shop that the thought occurred to him that his wife might be buying a cake too. By this time the shop assistant had that look which says that if this customer doesn't make up his mind soon it would be better for her to die. Finally, he selected a large decorated cake which the girl promptly placed in an impressive cake-box, tied with pink ribbons. As David walked back to the office his spirits lifted. He was pleased with himself and sure that the cake would be well received by his wife. Upon his return Alan made his way to David's office where David proudly pointed to the cake box sitting on the windowsill.

Robby spies the Cake

At that very moment Robby wandered into the office. He casually enquired if the weekly progress review meeting would be taking place in David's office that afternoon. "Yes," said David, "and make sure you're not late!" This was a reference to the previous week when Robby had over-stayed his lunch time in the pub because he was talking to the new barmaid.

Suddenly Robby, feigning a look of complete surprise, asked David: "So what's in that box on the windowsill, David?"

David explained with pride that he had bought an anniversary cake for his wife. Robby, who was by now almost through his third marriage and truth be known probably had a couple of lady friends on the side, sincerely congratulated David, adding that they were both alike in that he too never forgot his wedding anniversary. Alan, trying hard to suppress a smile, couldn't help thinking which of his marriage anniversaries Robby might have in mind!

The Meeting

No sooner had the meeting started than Robby, in accordance with a predetermined plan, remarked on the heat in the office and shouldn't David provide fans to keep the Pipers cool? Before David could reply Andy jumped up and made his way to the windows saying: "Let's get some air circulating!"

Andy comes a Cropper

With that he approached the office windows which were the old-fashioned metal-framed type, rising right up to the ceiling. It wasn't hard to work out that Andy couldn't reach the catch of the upper opening section. So without pause he clambered awkwardly up onto the window sill and as he reached for the window catch he appeared to lose his balance. David's face showed his alarm.

He was just about to issue a warning when Andy trod right on the centre of the cake-box!

David's Despair

David let out a strangled cry and several well chosen expletives. Orchestrated despair broke out amongst the Pipers when David explained that the crumpled box contained an anniversary cake. Hearing this Andy's face became a picture of abject apology. He assured David that had he known of the contents he would have chosen to fall, possibly breaking a leg, rather than have trodden on the box. His heart-rending words and willingness to sacrifice his own safety almost brought tears of sympathy to the eyes of his pals.

The Pipers can't stop laughing

Alan consoled David and suggested that they adjourn the meeting to see if they could salvage any of the cake. David agreed and the Pipers solemnly trooped out of his office. Back at the drawing boards Andy innocently commented that wasn't it a dreadful shame that David's beloved anniversary cake had been so cruelly squashed. His pals couldn't suppress their mirth any longer and to a man they were convulsed with uncontrollable laughter.

The Pipers' Joke revealed

Meanwhile David got up from the conference table and, with a face as long as a fiddle, disconsolately untied the bow from the crumpled cake box. He was in no doubt that the cake was ruined. Suddenly he gasped, completely taken by surprise. Because the box was empty except for some squashed newspapers! His face showed a dawning realization and with determined stride was the first out of the office door closely followed by Alan.

But there, holding the original cake box stood Andy surrounded by his smiling pals. Offering it to David he said with a grin... *"I believe this is yours."*

Footnote

The days of drawing boards are now a thing of the past. Andy and his pals have long since moved on to computer-aided design. But the merciless mickey-taking never changes. *No-one* is spared. Andy had concocted a plan. Whilst David was out at lunch Robby was chosen to go to the cake shop and charm the shop assistant. She thus willingly provided an identical empty cake box and David's original found itself temporarily hidden away. All's well that ends well. It was reported that David and his wife thoroughly enjoyed their anniversary and their guests roared with laughter when David described his moment of abject despair when Andy accidentally lost his balance and expertly trod on his beloved cake.

CHAPTER 35

THE INTERPRETER

ANDY AND THE PIPERS – STORY 2

Introduction

There are occasions in John Brown's Engineering office when possessing a second language comes in useful. Recently the company had been awarded a very important contract by an Austrian client and within a few days their piping engineers were due to arrive to review progress in the piping design department. The problem was that none of the Pipers spoke a word of German. No one, that is, except Andy, or at least that is what he led his pals to believe ...

Andy - the Interpreter

For the past few days Andy's pals in the piping department had been talking non-stop about the impending visit of the Client's piping engineers from Austria. In their view their department manager David must have overlooked the fact that there would be a problem of communication.

Andy, busy on one of his drawings (masterpieces as he described them) joined the conversation. There would be no problem at all, he said confidently, because he could speak fluent German. From the look on their faces you could tell that the Pipers had serious doubts about this linguistic claim. They had come to accept Andy's fanciful stories because believe them or not you couldn't help enjoying them. Chas couldn't contain his doubts so he asked Andy where he had learnt to speak German. The Pipers, to a man, were suspicious. How would he answer the question?

Andy paused from his masterpiece, put on one of his old-timer looks and patiently explained that years ago he had worked as an expat in Germany. That was where he had learnt the language. Furthermore, every year he returned to Germany for two weeks of his annual holidays to brush up on his German. Before his pals could say another word he added that he was so fluent that his German friends wouldn't believe him when he told them that he was English. Looks of benevolent admiration flooded over him but not one of the Pipers believed a word he had said.

Whilst this conversation was taking place Alan, David's deputy, had joined them and upon hearing Andy's claim to speak German hurried off to David's office. This, he suggested, was a perfect opportunity for David to turn the tables on Andy by calling his bluff - he should challenge him to make use of his skills as an interpreter.

David loved Alan's suggestion and word went out that if anyone spoke German they should come forward. Upon hearing this Andy's pals joined him at lunch time in the pub. Conveying David's message they cunningly encouraged him to make the most of this wonderful opportunity to use his German. He should go straight to David's office after lunch and offer his services. It was with great interest that upon return from lunch Andy's pals saw him make his way into David's office.

David was in a confident mood as he warmly thanked Andy for his time and after some small-talk got down to business.

"We are in an awful fix," he said. "The guys from Austria hardly speak a word of English and as you are fluent in German could you help with translation?"
By experience Andy suspected that David was up to something. How did David know that he spoke German, who had told him? It must

have been that rotten creep Alan. Andy had to respond quickly. He confirmed that he was very fluent in German but, first of all, where in his job description was there a reference to translation duties?

David was caught unawares and before he could reply Andy laid his trump card and told David that should he require German translation then it would require a significant salary increase because he wasn't going to do the translation for free! David was snookered. He was out-manoeuvred once again.

Back in the design office the Pipers were waiting in eager anticipation to hear the outcome and immediately asked him what had happened. Andy gave them one of his disapproving looks, one reserved for those of little faith.
"Well," he said, "that miserable creep Alan must have told David that I speak excellent German."
"And did you actually agree to translate for him?" they asked.
"Of course not," replied Andy, "if he wants me to translate then he will have to pay me for it, won't he…"

They all smiled in admiration. He had done it yet again. They had been prepared to bet that Andy hardly spoke a single word of German, but it didn't matter any more. He had pulled off another one of his victories over David - and that was good enough for them.

Footnote

The Pipers eventually learned never to point out to Andy the improbability of his stories. Initially they mounted carefully orchestrated attempts, but they failed. So please, don't go there. Save your doubts. Become a convert like the rest of us. Speaking for myself I now believe every word that he says. For that reason, I have made him an honorary True Expat, one of the most absurd story-tellers in the Hall of Fame.

CHAPTER 36

THE WAZOMETER

ANDY AND THE PIPERS – STORY 3

Introduction

The time came when Andy and the Pipers from the John Brown Engineering Piping Department at Portsmouth were needed at the nearby Fawley Refinery in the UK. They managed to turn this into a series of outrageous and memorable events that included:
Inventing the Wazometer
The Pipers in hilarious Fancy Dress
A Passionate Kiss

Andy outwits David

When the piping draftsmen were asked by David, their department head, to join a newly formed project team at the Fawley refinery for a one-year period they had all to a man resisted his request. This mock act of defiance was based on the principle that whatever the terms and conditions were, they weren't anywhere near good enough. As usual it was Andy who was their spokesman. His irreverence for David was a joy to his pals and they knew from past experience that their best plan was to leave it to him to get the most advantageous conditions for them.

David knew that he had a dedicated adversary in Andy. Thus when he called a meeting with him to discuss the Fawley project terms and conditions Andy was ready to out manoeuvre him. Except on one vital issue – the Pipers usual lunchtime visit for a pint or two at the local pub. At Fawley refinery the time needed to leave and return to the premises would take longer than the one hour allowed. This dire news was met by a stunned silence. Any decent Piper worth his salt cannot possibly survive without a lunchtime pint. David was secretly pleased with himself, could he have at last outsmarted Andy?

A compromise was needed. Suddenly the answer came to Andy. They would be prepared to stay on site and take a shorter lunch-break from Monday to Thursday if on Friday they could have extended time at the pub. David had no choice but to agree. Friday lunchtimes at Fawley were to become the best that any of the Pipers could ever remember.

And I often joined them.

That first Monday morning at the Fawley refinery site office was something of a subdued affair. The Pipers drifted in and due to their normal excesses over the weekend could only manage a grunt of acknowledgment to each other. After they had made their first cup of black coffee Andy closed the office door and reminded them that they had an important decision to make - which pub to choose as their Friday watering hole for the next year.

Chas, morose as ever and wearing his normal undertakers' face looked at Robby for his view. Robby expounded the benefits of attractive barmaids. His pals benevolently allowed him to consider himself an authority on the female species, a magnanimous gesture given that he had already notched up two ex-wives and was tottering on the brink of a third.

After much debate Andy called the Pipers to order and proposed that their new pub should be the Flying Boat Inn at Calshot, known as the

FBI. The Pipers immediately agreed. Ironically if their partners had asked them to re-new the lounge curtains they would have taken months to decide. But ask a Piper any question concerning choosing a pub and one will get an immediate response.

Little did the landlord of the FBI know what was coming because the Pipers were soon to descend on his quiet Calshot pub.

Inventing the Wazometer

Now that the pub decision had been made the Pipers' mood again became subdued. Andy was worried. The sparkle was missing and the usual good-humored mickey-taking of all and sundry was absent. It was Chas who hit on the idea of the Wazometer. Soon a design was enthusiastically produced and the Pipers chewed it over until they were satisfied that every detail was correct.

And so the maintenance man was given his instructions with a promise of free beer on Friday at the pub. He thus took an immediate liking to the Pipers and the next morning he proudly mounted the Wazometer at the front of the piping design office. In size and appearance, it closely resembled a dart board, but having four equal divisions. The first, in clockwise direction, proclaimed in bold letters "Bad day," the second "Good day," the third "Very Good day," and the fourth "Excellent day."

The stage was set for some of the most hilarious moments ever seen in a piping engineering office. No sooner had the Pipers finished congratulating the maintenance man than Horace, the likeable personnel manager, who was constantly being mauled by the Pipers, breezed into the room. A groan of false agony went up and Chas switched the Wazometer pointer to 'Bad day'. A round of applause followed. Andy was pleased; things were getting back to normal.

Friday lunchtime couldn't come soon enough and as the Pipers trooped up to the bar of the FBI the landlord beamed with happiness. Chas fixed him with a melancholy gaze and ordered the first round of drinks. The Pipers sat in a large circle and without missing a beat they were back to debating their favorite subjects.

Leonard, recently married, mentioned the fact that his wife always insisted on him going shopping with her every Saturday morning, something he had tried but failed to avoid. Andy, contented and with a pint of beer in hand, gave him a fatherly look and pronounced that there was a simple answer to the situation. The Pipers were all up for this one because they quickly realized that here was the perfect subject for a great wind up. What course of action, they craftily enquired, would Andy recommend to Leonard? Andy finished his pint and sent Leonard off to get the next round.

When he returned Andy was sitting back in his chair with the air of an ancient sage. The answer, he explained, was to let the wife know that the husband was the boss. One of the Pipers, with mischievous intent, enquired if Andy was the boss in his marriage. There was a hidden meaning in the question because Andy had often asserted his superiority but his pals had their deep suspicions - because he was still married.

Surely any Piper who had survived over thirty years of wedlock couldn't possibly be the boss.

Andy was quick to head off this devious attack and steadfastly confirmed that there was no way that he would ever agree to going shopping with his wife. That, he proclaimed, was a woman's job. Looks of mis-belief washed over him but he ignored their doubts and, patting Leonard on the shoulder, advised him to do the same.

The Pipers in hilarious Fancy Dress

That first Friday at the FBI was a great success. An extra round of drinks worked wonders and by the time the Pipers returned to the office they were all in a mellow mood. The Wazometer was set at Very Good and their misgivings about working at Fawley were forgotten. Pipers are ever creative and Andy then had a brilliant idea. Why didn't they have a fancy dress competition on the last Friday of the month? This proposal was endorsed with enthusiasm and so it was that come the last Friday the Pipers were fully prepared for the event.

Unfortunately, what they hadn't bargained for was an unwelcome visit to site by their boss David. Try as they might they couldn't discourage him from doing so. Andy realized that David would be in for the surprise of his life because to a man they would all be in fancy dress. Chas suggested a resolution to this dilemma, why didn't they invite David to be their guest at the FBI at lunchtime? A ring of approval sealed this proposal. David accepted.

And so the scene was set.

Those of us familiar with the eccentricities of the Pipers were nonetheless not prepared when on that Friday morning we saw Dracula walking into the office, black robes flowing, splashes of blood copiously applied to his mouth and clothes. We just creased up with laughter. Next came a monster with a bolt driven right through his head, his masked face contorted in a menacing grimace. Next came Elvis Presley in a white sequined suit, curled lip and blue suede shoes.

Fantastic. And so it went on, one after the other. Little Bo-peep, Al Capone, Mr. Universe, the Three Musketeers. Never before or after have I seen such an event in an engineering office. But more was yet to come as David drew up in his car. The Pipers had closed their office door and as David entered they were all silently beavering away, pretending to be working hard at their drawing boards.

According to Andy the look on David's face was something to behold. His mouth dropped open in amazement and he was completely lost for words. Just at that moment Cliff, an instrument engineer, had the misfortune to walk into the piping office. To a man they gave him a huge round of applause. He was dumbstruck and had no idea why the Pipers were applauding him.

Andy smiled, vigorously shook his hand and gesturing towards his shirt and tie announced to one and all that he was the winner of the Friday fancy dress competition. The poor guy had chosen to wear a bright pink shirt mis-matched with a grey tie having black irregular slashes etched across it. Had you searched for a hundred years you could never have found two items that clashed so much.

He left the office muttering to himself that the Pipers were just about the oddest bunch of people that he had ever come across, accompanied by gales of uncontrollable laughter from Andy and his pals. The Wazometer was hovering between Very Good and Excellent but none could have foreseen the culmination of David's visit.

Come lunchtime I joined the Pipers as we set off in good spirits in the minibus, with David sat in the front passenger seat. This position was always fought after but Andy had suggested that it be given to David as their guest of honor. It took a while for the landlord of the FBI to overcome his initial shock at the boisterous arrival of Dracula, Elvis Presley, and the rest of the Pipers, not having ever experienced such a distinguished clientele before. Robby bought the first round and soon David was enjoying the jokes and the merciless mickey taking that he was subjected to. They left the pub in high spirits and boarded the minibus. Chas, more inebriated than the others, climbed in the back next to me.

The Passionate Kiss

Raising his voice, he announced above the general ribaldry that he was about to do something he'd long wished to do. This declaration resulted in raucous encouragement from his pals. With that he grabbed me and planted a passionate kiss right on my lips! My face contorted in absolute disgust and, wiping my mouth, I gave Chas a great shove. The Pipers were convulsed with laughter and as soon as they got back to the office they immediately set the Wazometer to Excellent.

As for me, I swore that if Chas even so much as touched me again I would personally be responsible for killing him. Chas couldn't have been more pleased with himself. Even to this day those who were there swear that he actually smiled! Never before had the Pipers had such an eventful Friday lunchtime.

Andy Exposed

We finished the project and went our different ways. A couple of years later I happened to be in Portsmouth and as I wandered around Littlewoods superstore who should I bump into but Andy. He gave me a sheepish grin and straightaway I could see why. In each hand he was holding shopping bags. His wife's shopping bags!

After swapping small talk I innocently asked him if he was doing some shopping for himself. He squirmed and gave me an embarrassed look. Glancing towards his better half he mumbled that he was on a shopping trip with his wife. But he was quick to recover and assured me that she would soon have to fend for herself because he was just off to the pub to have a pint. Just in case you are reading this Andy your secret is safe with me – there's no way that I would tell your pals that I saw you shopping with your better half …

Footnote:

Sadly, those Friday lunchtime sessions at the FBI can't be repeated. A local newspaper reported on July 16th 2001 that fire-fighters were called to tackle a blaze that destroyed a well-loved pub - the Flying Boat Inn. But please don't worry. Neither earth, wind, nor fire will deter our Piper. Rest assured that he will have found another pub in which to enjoy his lunchtime pint.

PART 2

GLOBAL TRAVELS

CHAPTER 37

EXPAT IN OZ

Introduction

The Azal Azerbaijan Boeing 757 lifts off from Baku in darkness. It's 10pm and I'm off to Dubai on the first leg of my journey to Sydney, Australia to see the 2003 Rugby World Cup. As the waters of the Caspian Sea recede from view I reflect on how I have grown to like the Azal airline. True, it isn't as well known as the main airlines but what it does have is a very friendly cabin crew. There's a polite niceness about them, sincere and always ready to help.

A Long Wait

The Azal airline stewardess informs us that we are about to land in Dubai. I brace myself for the thrill of having to spend yet another long airport wait. For those of you who have been to Dubai you will know that it has a show-piece airport. But believe me, the novelty soon wears off when you have to wait ages for your connecting flight. I now have about six hours to wait - which is good compared to the eighteen hours wait for my Baku flight when I come back.

Melbourne, Australia

Having made it to Sydney I have a few days to spare so I have taken a flight down to Melbourne where I'm sitting on a green bench-seat at the junction of Bourke and Elizabeth Streets. It's just past five in the afternoon and the clanging of the tram-car bells mingle with the sounds of the early evening traffic. I relax and enjoy the warm sunshine. Melbourne is certainly a pleasant city and the Aussies here are the usual friendly crowd. Unable to fathom your street map you may ask an Aussie for directions. Their friendly response will be "G-day mate, where are you heading for?"

The Christmas decorations hang above the streets and there's an artificial Christmas tree some thirty feet tall standing just down the road from the Town Hall. It's late November so it's not only back home that Christmas gets earlier every year! But there the similarity ends because here in Melbourne you don't see snow or rosy-cheeked children wrapped up in winter clothes. On the contrary, it's a glorious summer day, the sky is blue and the sun is shining.

The Great Ocean Road Bus Tour

After a brief but boring visit to the Victoria State Parliament Building I'm on a Bus tour that takes us from Melbourne along the Great Ocean Road. Jack, our driver, is great company and an affable raconteur. We learn that devastating bush fires are quite common. Apparently the one back in 1983 had razed an entire village – except for three houses that were left standing untouched.

Koalas, Kangaroos & Aussie Pies

We saw koalas, perched fast asleep in the branches of eucalyptus trees, only waking to eat. We saw kangaroos, the females with joeys in their pouch. And it would be remiss of me if I didn't mention that when we stopped for lunch I once again chose for my favourite - an Aussie meat pie. Oh how I love those Aussie pies!

The Urban Myth of London Bridge

I'll never forget Jack's most entertaining (and probably enhanced) story of the Great Ocean Road – a story that has been recorded as a typical Urban Myth. It involved the unfortunate stranding of a couple on a rock formation known as London Bridge, a popular tourist site at Port Campbell in Victoria. Apparently they had gone there believing it to be a perfect place to meet when, in January 1977, it suddenly collapsed, leaving them stranded out at sea, with no means of getting back onshore.

The Rescue Drama

An eye witness on the spot alerted both the Victoria State emergency services and the Channel 10 TV News station in Melbourne who saw this as a spicy news item and sent their own helicopter and Reporter to the scene. Several hours later after they were finally rescued and returned onshore, the couple refused to be interviewed and fled as fast as they could in their car - much to the disappointment of the growing crowd of curious on-lookers.

But their drama hadn't ended. Apparently the News Station Reporter eventually tracked down their identities. His investigation and headline TV news report had Australia laughing.

The guy involved had rung his boss that very morning saying that he was taking a Sickie (a day off) because he was feeling unwell. But meantime he had left his house in the morning as if he was going to work.

And the woman he was with…wasn't his wife. And thus the urban myth was born.

November 22, 2003 – the Rugby World Cup

Back in Sydney, it's a day that I will never forget, November 22, 2003, the final of the Rugby World Cup. As I disembark from the bus at the impressive Telstra Stadium my adrenalin is flowing. It's so exciting. Everywhere you look are thousands of England supporters, known down here as the Barmy Army. We are here to support our English team. I have waited all of my rugby life for this day – to see if England can prove themselves the best rugby side in the world.

Mixing in Harmony

The kick-off is at 8 pm. Australia versus England. Can we defeat an Aussie team that is brimming with confidence? According to the Aussie media we have no chance but that's just the expected POM (Prisoner of Mother England) bashing.

The Aussie fans are now singing "Waltzing Matilda" and the Barmy Army are determined to outdo them as they sing their anthem, "Swing Low, Sweet Chariot."
The atmosphere is electric. Both sets of fans are mixed together without a trace of trouble.

I ask you, what other sport can you name where the opposing fans mix in complete harmony?

An exciting Finish

The game at full time is seventeen-all. We are shattered because we've lost the lead we had and now we have to play extra time. Tension is etched on the face of every fan, Aussie and POM alike. Can we do it? Can we win? It's anybody's game now. There's two minutes left. The English forwards storm down the field and the ball comes back to our kicker Jonny Wilkinson. The tension is unbearable; we are a tortuous breath away from victory. And then Jonny kicks the drop goal that every English supporter there will never forget.

The Barmy Army explodes in joy. England have won. Complete strangers hug each other, slap each other on the back. The tension has been unbearable. The final whistle goes and right around the stadium there's a sea of red and white English flags.

Nothing, but nothing, will surpass this moment in my rugby life.

Back to Baku

The next day on my return to Baku, still on a high, I didn't notice the long wait in Dubai. Upon returning to the office I couldn't help rubbing it in, reminding my rugby pals that whilst they were stuck in Baku I had been in Sydney and was present when England won the final. This of course elicited some fairly profane responses.

CHAPTER 38

WEDDING IN THE PHILIPPINES

Introduction

What if you met and were married in a foreign country where you didn't understand a word of the ceremony? They say love conquers all... but still... as the bride, you'd long for a second wedding surrounded by your family and friends wouldn't you? Which is why in this story I'm going to describe the colourful "second wedding" of two of my closest expat friends, Scott (an American from Texas) and Riza (a Filipino from the exotic island of Negros Occidental), a forty-minute flight from Manila. Scott and Riza met at our church in the small village of Kerteh which is situated in Terengganu State on the East coast of Malaysia.

I travel from Malaysia to the Philippines

Let's say that you were a pig residing in the Philippines and you have travelled to someone's village home for an important occasion. Beware, because your chances of making it through the day are pretty slim. Because in the Philippines a pig roasted on a spit is a treasured meal, especially at a wedding.

It was 2001 and I had travelled from my workplace in Malaysia, where I first met Scott and Riza, to the Philippines island of Negros

Occidental, some forty-five minutes by air from Manila. I was there to be best man at their second wedding.

Their first marriage in Malaysia

Whilst they are both Christians their first marriage ceremony, held in Kuantan Malaysia, was a civil, not a church, event. Scott therefore needed a sponsor so he had asked a Malaysian friend, Mohamed, to help with the formalities. When we arrived at the Kuantan government office at 9am on that Monday morning we were met by a very polite Malaysian lady who was to conduct the proceedings. But ...we had no idea that she would conduct it in Bahasa – the Malaysian language.

Consequently, neither Scott, Riza, nor I understood a single word of what was being said. Riza was, as you can imagine, somewhat perplexed by the whole thing. I didn't help because afterwards, whilst we were enjoying their wedding breakfast at a nice restaurant, I happened to joke that for all we knew we could have mistakenly been in the vehicle licensing department. I made amends by telling them that should they be brave enough for a second attempt then I just had to be there.

So that's how I got to be their best man at their Philippines wedding.

Their second marriage in the Philippines

This time there was no mistake. There, in Riza's village church, Scott and Riza were married for the second time and we were so grateful that the priest conducted it in English. Not only was I best man, I was also godfather to Riza's daughter Tala. She had not been baptised so Riza took this opportunity to arrange a baptism after the wedding. Tala is just twelve years old and is a lovely girl. I'm pleased that I am her god-father.

The Wedding Reception

The formalities completed we walked the short distance from the church to Riza's parents home. The priest has joined us and is having a beer, socialising with the wedding guests.
Danilo, one of Riza's six brothers is calling me to the rear of the house and there, recumbent upon a roughly hewn bamboo pole, is the deceased pig, about to be placed on a spit above the charcoal fire for roasting. There's none of your motorised spit-turners if you don't mind. Here we have a machete cut into the end of the bamboo pole and Danilo squats at the side and turns the spit by hand.

By now the wedding reception is getting noisy, aided by the San Miguel beer and Tanduay rum. Riza's mother has set up the karaoke. If there's one thing I have learnt about the Philippines, it's that they love their Karaoke. Right now Scott has the mic. Mind you, he can't sing very well but then neither can I for that matter. Not to worry, the guests don't care anyway because everyone's having a good time.

The roast pig, ready for the feast, is carried into the house. When I say house I mean the bamboo houses that are common in the villages. The roof is of corrugated iron sheets, the walls are of slatted bamboo designed to allow the air to circulate, and the beds, table and bench seats are also made from bamboo. Outside, down the garden, is the toilet. The door is a canvas screen which one closes for privacy.

Scott is now giving it one hundred percent on the karaoke. Tom Jones would have had heart failure as Scott murdered the last words of the song "Forgive me Delilah, I just couldn't take any more."

Quite right Scott, none of us can take anymore, now get off. Give *me* the microphone. If that's the worst that you can do, then just listen to me!

Now Lechon, a pork dish, is being served. Oh how the Filipinos love Lechon! Next trays of
steaming hot rice, fish, vegetables, noodles and chicken are put onto the tables. How did they manage to cook such delicious food? The kitchen is a small bamboo building about one metre from the house.

The heat for cooking comes from sticks collected from the undergrowth at the rear of the house. Riza asks if I would I like to eat Balot. It's a boiled fertilized egg, much loved. No thanks!

I'm having a great time, and so too are Scott and Riza and all the family and friends. These folk are not well off but what they lack in material things they make up for in their generous hospitality and friendliness. The party's over but there's a visit Scott wants me to make. Just along the road is their soon to be converted future home. I say future because right now it's an abandoned rice mill standing on about half an acre of land. It's a substantial concrete building of two floors.

The upper floor will have five bedrooms, kitchen, lounge, bathrooms. The lower floor will consist of garaging and a workshop. It promises to be a palace and when it's finished I'm coming back to stay with them.

We visit Boracay Island

But I didn't have to go back to Malaysia yet so Scott had arranged for us to go to the island of Boracay, famous for its white sandy beaches. Mind you, we might not have made it there because of that taxi debacle. When I say taxi it's actually a small motorcycle with a passenger sidecar attached.

So there we were, Scott, Riza, Tala, Danilo and myself all cramped aboard the taxi bound for the Catamaran terminal when there was a loud explosion, just like a pistol shot. Simultaneously the taxi wobbled violently. The driver, probably accustomed to the situation, just managed to avoid our descent into a deep roadside storm gully. It was a blow-out in the rear tyre. We disembarked, relieved that we were all still in one piece. Sure enough the tyre was as bald as it could possibly be. Not a trace of tread on it.

So, having changed taxis we made it to the Catamaran terminal and crossed over to Puna Island. Once there we hired a mini-bus to take us on the five-hour journey to the north of the island. Waiting at a jetty was the bum-boat for Boracay. We donned our life-vests and boarded and rolling in the ocean waves we crossed the blue waters to Boracay Island. There at the jetty is yet another motor cycle taxi.

Once again we lever ourselves into position. Off we go, the pot-holed road jarring my bones. As we approach a hill the taxi driver desperately revs up the engine to increase speed. But the incline wins the day and we slow down to a snail's pace. This calls for action so Danilo jumps off the taxi and assists the ascent by pushing the taxi until it reaches the top of the hill. Where else, I wonder, does a taxi passenger have to provide such a service to the taxi driver?

I visit Corregidor Island

Our Boracay visit over I part company with Scott and Riza and fly back to Manila. There's one more place I had to visit - Corregidor Island. It was here in May 1942 that the U.S. – Philippine forces finally fell to Japan. The US supreme commander of Allied forces was General MacArthur. He was forced to flee Corregidor but he made that famous promise "I shall return." And he did when he returned to liberate the Philippines in 1944. If you ever visit Corregidor you will find a statue of MacArthur, erected in his honour.

My R&R is almost over. To get back to my hotel in central Manila I take a Jeepney which is a popular, and cheap, public transport vehicle. At a guess I would say that it carries around twenty passengers. One should pay homage to the Jeepney driver because he is also the conductor. How they manage to drive in the hectic Manila city traffic, and take fares, and give change, I'll never know. The method of paying the driver is interesting. If you can't reach the driver, you pass your fare to the guy next to you. He does the same until it reaches the driver. If there is change required, then this procedure takes place in reverse.

The next day I boarded my flight back to Kuala Lumpur in Malaysia. I have a lot to be thankful for. I've been a best man at a wedding, a god-father to Tala, I've eaten Lechon, avoided Balot, survived motorcycle taxis, and basked on the sands at Boracay. It doesn't get much better than that!

CHAPTER 39

KAVA IN FIJI

Introduction

When I worked in Baghdad I came across some of the friendliest guys you could wish to meet – Fijian soldiers seconded to the UN. These were big strong men employed to keep us civilians in the Green Zone safe from the attacks by the bad guys. Yet there was a peaceful side to them because they were all very committed Christians. Those of us who attended church heard that they had a choir and that they had the most wonderful singing voices. So a couple of days later I made my way to the Palace and joined a 6am service for an inter-denominational group of Christians.

After the formalities of the service had been completed the Fijians solders were invited to sing for us. It was just wonderful. As we departed the service I spoke to the soldiers and told them that I had visited Fiji and whilst there had heard the singing in a church and had received the friendliest of welcomes. Here's the story...

R&R Holiday in Fiji

I'm off on another R&R holiday. I've flown an arduous journey from Baghdad, Iraq to Seoul in South Korea and then on to my destination - Nadi airport in Fiji. Let me tell you that it's the friendliest airport that I have ever been to. Why? Because in the arrivals hall we were greeted with welcome songs by a group of colourful Fijian musicians.

After my protracted journey the infectious music was just what I needed. I had in my hand the address of the Downtown Backpackers hostel which I showed to a cheerful taxi driver and twenty minutes later I was being checked in by Charlotte, their lovely receptionist.

I was very tired and all I wanted to do was to get some rest. I was about to head for my room when she implored me to hold on a minute because first I must drink Kava. To be honest I'd never heard of Kava, but not wishing to give offence I agreed. Charlotte's colleague, Dave, brought the Kava drink, then saying Bula (which means welcome), he clapped once and handed me the Kava cup. I was told to empty it in one swallow, which I did. We then had to clap three times. I had now been welcomed as a friend.

In time I was to learn that Kava is a national drink and the Kava ceremony is part of the culture of the Fijian people. Kava is made from a root which is dried, then pounded into a powder, then mixed with water. At first taste it reminds you of an awful medicine given to us as kids. But if you are brave enough to drink a second cup (usually from a half-coconut shell) your taste-buds adjust to suit.

Protractors claim that Kava numbs the mouth and tongue and that's the reason why it seems to get better. Thinking about it, there may be some truth in that!

After spending a few pleasurable days in and around Nadi I took the bus to Suva, the capital of Fiji. As it was lunchtime I made my way to a restaurant. The radio was playing in the background and the DJ had a lovely Fijian-English accent. The view was amazing, across a pleasant park beyond which was the blue of the Pacific Ocean. The temperature was around 28C which reminded me very much of Malaysia. The climate, the forests, sunshine, humidity, houses built on stilts, animals roving freely in the villages, and schools where you can see children doing their PE outside on the playing fields. Imagine, PE in that heat. If you want to lose weight, then those playing fields are just what you need!

After another few days my R&R in Fiji was over. The next leg would take me to Samoa. Should you go to Fiji take a moment to listen to the warm welcome songs at the airport, and then make for the Downtown Backpackers hostel, ask for Charlotte and Dave and you'll soon be drinking Kava like a Fijian. Oh, and when greeting your Fijian friends don't forget to say "Bula."

CHAPTER 40

BAGHDAD TO MALAYSIA

Introduction

My expatriate days in Baghdad left an indelible mark on my memory. I mobilized there in 2003 after the second Gulf war and spent about three years there. We lived, worked, ate and slept in the Green Zone, a heavily fortified area of the city. We experienced rocket and mortar attacks, scary journeys to and from the airport, and two suicide attacks very close to our office. But we survived. Not so for the many Iraqis who have died or suffered terribly. What a wonderful people, what a terrible tragedy.

Because of the stress, our employment contract with Foster Wheeler Engineering gave us a work cycle of 28 days on and 20 days off for R & R (Rest and Recuperation).

This story, in which I travel from Baghdad to Malaysia for my leave, is dedicated to my Iraqi colleagues with and for whom we gave our best to restore the oil production facilities of Iraq.

My first R&R

Travelling in and out of the Green Zone was a dangerous and nerve wracking mission in itself. It often took me 3 tiring travel days to reach my holiday destination, as in this story.

I check my watch. It's 9.30 pm, time to go. I'm off to Malaysia on my first R&R leave. I shoulder my backpack, turn off the light in my room, and lock the door. I'm to be picked up at the security gate of our accommodation block. I climb into the Chevrolet Suburban and introduce myself to the US Army staff sergeant who will drive me to the Rhino base. He's a hardened soldier with 22 years' service.

As we drive the short distance I ask him if he will re-up, re-enlist. "Hell no, man," he replied, "Uncle Sam can take a hike … I want out of this army."

On arrival at the Rhino base I take a seat in the waiting room and glance at the notice on the check-in desk. It informs passengers to report at 2300 hours. Furthermore, just in case you have been remiss and are not wearing your battle-rattle (bullet proof vest and steel helmet) you are bluntly told "No battle-rattle – No Rhino!"

Rhinos

I stretch out and try to relax, knowing that it's going to be a long night. At 11pm two guys man the desk and I check in. After doing so it's another wait until around two in the morning. Standing silently outside are the black-painted Rhinos - looking like some pre-historic monsters of the night.

These armor plated buses are the designated means of safe travel along the roads in Iraq, safe in that they are escorted by armored Humvees and helicopters. The Rhinos will be our transport from the Green Zone to the Baghdad international airport (BIAP). Once outside the Green Zone death may only be one roadside bomb explosion away. To minimize the risk of attack by the bad guys the Rhinos had recently been restricted to travelling in the early hours of the morning, when road traffic was lightest.

Things have improved since I arrived

Thankfully things have improved since my arrival and first journey into the Green Zone. I had disembarked from the US Airforce C130

Hercules transport aircraft and was about to clamber into one of the Rhinos when the driver stopped me.

"Sorry sir, ain't no more room aboard, all the rhinos are full, yuh gotta ride in the Suburban."

"Uh, err, Suburban, aren't we supposed to travel in the Rhino?"

Full of anxiety I cast a furtive glance from the Rhino to the Suburban. If I asked you to compare the two you'd probably agree that the Suburban looks mighty vulnerable by comparison. Already shoehorned into the Suburban were five bulky Army guys so with great difficulty I squeezed in next to them. My helmet touching the roof and my knees up under my chin. Next to me was a US Marine Corps lieutenant in full battle gear, holding a M60 assault rifle. At his side he had a revolver.

I consoled myself with the thought that if we got into trouble he could defend both of us. It's time to go, we are about to take the infamous route between Baghdad airport and the Green Zone. The driver of the Suburban was a good humored guy from Michigan. It was his second week on the job.

"Hi folks, mah name is George Jablinsky and I'm your tour driver for this ride into the Green Zone. Now y'all settle back and injoy yo-selfs cos this is gonna be an interestin ride."

Fear Grips Me

I gulped and the cold grip of fear embraced me. Mind you I should have been prepared for what was to come because yesterday we'd had a security briefing in Kuwait before flying into Iraq. I'm afraid that it did nothing for my confidence. I understand that realism is important but I'm of the opinion that the guy giving the briefing had aspirations of becoming a partner of the Grim Reaper.

"Folks, y'all about to enter a war zone and ya gotta know that over thar in Eye-raq it's a dangerous place, yes sir, one hell of a dangerous place to be!"

I glance at the faces to right and left and see the same looks, serious, apprehensive, waiting for what's going to come next.

"When y'all git in the war zone yuh gonna ride the Rhino into the Green Zone. Now there aint nuthin to it man, just sit tight and them guys will git ya there in no time."

We all had the same thought - what the heck is a Rhino?

"That Rhino's a mean son-of-a-bitch and thar aint nothing them bad guys can do to stop it gettin y'all thar in one piece."

I wondered how safe a Rhino was because I had heard on the news that deadly attacks were regularly made against the US forces. As if reading my thoughts, the guy next to me had the temerity to enquire if riding in the Rhino was safe. The grim reaper brightened up, here was something that he could really inspire us with.

"Safe ... no problem sir. We've had a couple of attacks on the Rhino's but don't let that worry ya, that dang beast was hardly damaged, the armor plating is awesome man." This assertion was accompanied by a look of pride intended to put us at ease.

But he didn't mention anything about riding in a Suburban. To be honest at the time of my first journey from the airport to the Green Zone I didn't appreciate that the Suburban was also armor plated or that we would be in the very competent hands of the US Army.

Convoy Protection

Radio communications were checked, the convoy officer gave the signal and we were good-to-go. At the front and back of the convoy were armored Humvees (a US army truck carrying sophisticated communications and weapons systems) manned by young American soldiers. Overhead we were shadowed by a helicopter gun-ship. This was serious protection indeed. Nonetheless as our convoy swept at full speed from the airport onto the highway I saw every civilian vehicle as the enemy, about to blow us all to smithereens.

From the Green Zone to Baghdad Airport

But that was then – and this is now. I know that I survived that first scary journey into the Green Zone without incident, so waiting to depart, I feel more at ease.

Firstly, we are definitely travelling in a Rhino – not a Suburban.

Secondly we're not driving in broad daylight but at 2am under cover of dark, with very little traffic on the roads.

The Rhino took us to the Stables, a US Army encampment close by the airport. I disembark and I'm met by Francisco, a cheerful Philippino driver who drove me to a transit tent. It's now after 3.30am. I select a vacant bed, thankful that at least it has a proper mattress which is a big improvement on the hard army camp-beds of the past. I sleep fitfully and rise early for breakfast. Then Francisco's dayshift buddy dropped me off at Baghdad airport where I was manifested for my C130 flight to Kuwait.

Flight from Baghdad to Kuwait

I'm not looking forward to the flight. Yes, there is a chance of a missile attack but the real reason is that I get nervous flying in the C130. It goes back to when I made that first flight to Baghdad from Kuwait. When we descended towards Baghdad airport the pilot banked sharply to the right and simultaneously dropped from the sky.

You would think that I would have gotten hardened to the C130's delights, but not me!

Our aircraft has arrived and in single line we are guided to the rear loading ramp. The moment the incoming passengers are disembarked we are boarded. The flight deck keeps the engines running. As soon as we are strapped in the ramp is closed and we are ready for takeoff. As usual we are packed inside like sardines, wearing our full battle-rattle and perspiring profusely in the heat.

The flight from Baghdad to Kuwait went without incident. We landed at Ali Al Salem, better known as Tent City, the base for thousands of US service personnel. I and others on route to Kuwait airport were assigned to a transit tent, with beds, but no pillows or bedding!

I tried to rest, using my backpack as a pillow, but by midnight I gave up and trudged off to the dining facility where I passed time drinking tea. At 2am I returned to the transit tent, collected my backpack and battle-rattle and headed off for the departure tent. At 6.30am we boarded a bus and an hour later we arrived at KIA, Kuwait International Airport.

Sleep in the Safir Hotel

I'm very tired because I have had two nights with virtually no sleep. Polish George, one of my expat colleagues stationed in Basra and a promising travel adviser, had told me that on arrival at Kuwait airport I should contact the Safir hotel. So I found a phone and rang their number. Yes, they had a room, but which hotel did I want to stay at because there were four Safir hotels in the city! George's travel advice went down a notch. I said that I didn't mind which one as long as I had a comfortable bed to sleep in!

Soon a Safir driver arrived and drove me to the hotel. By 10am in the morning I'd had breakfast, in my room - because it was Ramadan in which Muslims spend the daylight hours on a complete fast. Then I slept like a log right round to the following morning.

From Kuwait to Kuantan, Malaysia

My journey now entailed an evening flight from Kuwait to Dubai, from there to Bangkok, and then to Kuala Lumpur in Malaysia. I resigned myself to another night without sleep because when flying I just can't get comfortable. So true to form I get up and down all night long, stretching my legs and chatting to the cabin crew. After arrival in Kuala Lumpur I have a domestic flight to Kuantan, on the east coast of Malaysia, arriving at 10.30pm. I'm very relieved that at last my journey is over - nigh on three days after I left my room back in the Green Zone!

Car Hire

Leyli and Lee, my lovely Malaysian friends, with whom I am going to stay, are waiting at Kuantan airport to pick me up. After a warm Malaysian welcome we set off on the one-hour drive to their home in Chukai. The next morning, I feel refreshed and the plan is to collect a hire-car that Leyli, bless her, has sourced for me. Had I known what was to come I would have gone directly to a car hire company and hired a decent car. But this was hire-a-car Leyli style. As we set off to collect the car I asked if we could stop at a bank but Leyli was ever-helpful.
"Wha you wan money for, is no problem, you pay car hire later."

Umm. Very strange. More so when I learnt that I didn't need my driver's license either. We made our way to Chukai town centre and there on Mederka street was Leyli's friend Ephraim, waiting for us - beside his personal car. We exchange pleasantries and without so much as a deposit or a document to sign I was given the car keys and off we went!

You can imagine that I was itching to ask Leyli exactly what sort of hire company this was. It transpired that Ephraim was a friend who had a large family to support. So Leyli, always ready to help those in need, had decided to do him a good turn and arranged for the hire of his car to me for the duration of my stay. A perfect plan. I would have transport and he would earn some money. In theory it sounded good but there was a problem - Ephraim was not a great believer in car maintenance!

The first thing that I noticed about Ephraim's car was that my vision was impaired by a nine-inch black sun-visor painted at the top of the windscreen. Being tall I found that the only option was to peer under the visor in order to see the road ahead. Ummm. The car had an empty gas tank so our first port of call was a gas station.

I must have had a premonition because I asked the attendant to check the tires. Sure enough one was nearly flat, which he inflated. So far so good. We were now good-to-go so we set off for Leyli's home. It was a hot day so we put the air conditioner on but it would only blow hot air. No matter what setting we selected it still didn't get any cooler. In the end we gave up. In this battle of minds, the air conditioner definitely won.

Ready with my Handkerchief

Soon we arrived back at Leyli's home just minutes before ten in the morning. She seemed in a great hurry to get indoors. We had bought a takeaway breakfast in China-town and with the speed of light it was laid out on a coffee table which was strategically placed between the settee and the TV. Within minutes both Leyli and Lee were engrossed watching their favorite daily TV Soap.

I was to find that there was another in the afternoon and it didn't take me long to realize that the formula for both was broken hearts causing lots of weeping. Someone had run off with someone's girlfriend or boyfriend. Heart-breaking stuff! One of the Soaps came from Indonesia, the other from the Philippines and both had subtitles in Malay. During my R&R I got to appreciate them because whilst Leyli and Lee were glued to the screen I could relax and read the newspaper, always ready with my handkerchief in case the sobbing became too much and I was induced to join in.

Kampong Berserah

Whilst working in Malaysia previously I had discovered a charming fishing village - Kampong Berserah. To get there I would first drive to Teluk Chempedak (known as TC), a very popular seaside resort just ten minutes from Kuantan city centre. Then I had found a wonderful walk which took me two miles or so along the beach to Kampong Berserah. So the next day I set off from Leyli's house and drove to TC intent on making the same walk again. I hoped to visit with my friends who were the owners of a small beach-side food stall. Plus, I just had to stop by and see if my bovine friend Berserah the water buffalo was still around. *(See Chapter entitled The Water Buffalo).*

When I reached TC I parked the car under the shade of some trees behind the beach-front shopping kiosks. Before starting my walk, I applied my sun-lotion, knowing from experience that I should protect against the UV. Next, with revenge in mind, I applied a liberal coating of insect repellent to my legs. The last time I walked this beach I had been bitten by some very vindictive sand-flies and by that evening my legs were covered with painful red sores. The discomfort didn't clear up for several days.

Should I ever have an enemy I will send him along this beach…and fail to mention the sand-flies!

At the start of my walk from TC there was now a wooden walkway circumventing the original path which involved climbing and descending a series of rocky steps. Having reached the end of the walkway I headed for a jungle path that would take me towards Berserah beach. Trees towered above me, slivers of sunlight shimmering through the canopy above. Suddenly there was a loud swishing of tree branches as a troop of noisy monkeys moved far above me.

By now the heat and humidity caused me to perspire heavily. Twenty minutes later I emerged onto the golden sands of a long curving beach, gently lapped by the waves of the South China Sea. I was alone on the beach, there wasn't a soul in sight. Peace and tranquillity embraced me. As I walked I looked out to sea, curious to see if the fishing boats were coming into Kampong Berserah. I reached a headland and negotiated a winding path between the rocks. In the distance I could now see my favorite beach-side food stall.

I meet Berserah once again

As I approached the food-stall I could see that it was closed. I checked my watch and it was almost mid-day. By now I hoped the chicken soup would be ready - including the ever-present splintered chicken bones. But suddenly it dawned on me that it was Ramadan - meaning food is not served from dawn to dusk. Ah well, never mind. The next time I visit I'll avoid the fasting month. But my walk was not finished because I had yet to see my water buffalo friend. So I continued along the beach and then made my way through the sand dunes to the fish sheds.

There's a dozen or so workers loading a fish lorry bound for Kuala Lumpur and I stop and have a chat with them. I enquire if Berserah is still being used to pull the fish cart and they smile and direct me to the rear of the sheds.

Wow, there he was, contentedly chewing his cud and looking as magnificent as ever. He had been washed and his black coat was shining in the sunlight. Nearby stood the wooden-wheeled fish cart.

I recalled the first time I saw him, standing knee-deep in the sea, patiently waiting whilst the cart was loaded from the fishing boats with heavy baskets of fish. And when he was given the order to make for the shore he would first plunge his powerful head below the water, cooling himself, snorting loudly as he emerged. Then he would shake off the sea-water, his magnificent curved horns cutting the air. The cart driver would crack a whip above his head and with huge muscles straining he would make for the fish-sheds. Wonderful. May it never change.

Ephraim's Awful Car

A couple of days later Leyli and Lee took me to meet their friend Shang and his wife Chong Sai. They live on the outskirts of Kuantan in a lovely traditional Malaysian wooden home, standing on stilts. Shang's pride and joy stood outside - his new Toyota people-carrier which he wanted to show off to us.

The plan was to go and see the Sultan of Pahang's palace. I offered to use Ephraim's car but Shang, thankfully, would have none of it. We set off in heavenly comfort, enveloped in a stream of cool air from his air-conditioner. On return Shang wanted to collect some goods from a warehouse in central Kuantan so I suggested that this time we use my car. I was grateful when Shang offered to drive because I was not that familiar with the route.

We had only gone a short distance when Shang, perspiring in the heat, tried to adjust the AC. I looked on with growing amusement. This was going to be good. His first attempt came to naught. Not to be beaten he pressed, turned and adjusted just about every single item on the dashboard, but still no cool air. I could see exactly what was going through his mind and couldn't suppress my laughter any more. He gave a wry smile and commented succinctly that we had a very, very inefficient AC in the car!

We had just passed the soccer stadium when there was a loud thump-thump noise. Surprise, surprise, the deflated tire had given up the ghost. We searched amongst the contents of the untidy trunk and found a rusty wheel jack and brace. Shang looked at them disconsolately. By now he clearly had a very low opinion of the car. After the wheel was changed Shang drove to the warehouse and from there headed for home. But he couldn't contain himself any longer. He asked Leyli from whom had she hired the awful car. Just as she was about to explain Shang gave a sudden startled exclamation. The steering wheel had become loose in his hands! He was able to control the car but the look of concern on his face was something to behold.

Well, excuse me, but that was just too much! Leyli, Lee and I just creased up with laughter.

Steer clear of Ephraim's Car

Should you ever go to Malaysia for a holiday and decide to hire a car, please be careful. If you see a guy hanging around in Chukai with a white Mitsubishi, give him a wide berth. That way you'll sleep better at night!

CHAPTER 41

CARNIVAL TIME IN BRAZIL

Introduction

One of my most memorable and exciting destinations during my expatriate R & R (Rest and Recuperation holiday breaks) was the Carnival in Rio de Janeiro, Brazil, the most famous carnival in the world, attracting more than 500 000 foreign visitors a year. This is a spectacular wild event, spread over 5-days before the beginning of Lent, at the hottest time of the year in Rio.

Upon arrival I was soon caught up in the buzz and excitement of ongoing street carnivals and parades all over the city. But the highlight takes place at the Sambadrome every night from dusk till dawn featuring the floats and music of more than 100 Samba Schools all competing for the top prize.

Costumes are extremely imaginative and colourful, with mirrors, feathers, metallic cloth, silk and sometimes gems or coins. And as for the floats, huge, impressive and lavish, like you've ever seen in your life. Take my word for it, it's spectacular. Let me share the story of my visit with you.

And if you read to the end you'll learn how I sat next to Brigit Bardot and actually put my hand on her knee!

Brazilian Soccer

I was staying at the Copa Praia Back-packers Lodge near the famous Copacabana beach, on the outskirts of Rio. Eusabio, manager of the Copa Praia obtained tickets to a soccer match taking place at the city's Maracana stadium - the biggest in this soccer-crazy country. I jumped at the opportunity to go because this was the ultimate day in the Brazilian soccer season – the Cup Final, contested by two of Rio's top clubs - Flamenco and Fluminensa.

Flamenco 3, Fluminensa 2

It's a sunny Saturday afternoon and as we approach the Maracana the streets are filled with thousands of noisy soccer fans. We have got through the crush at an entrance gate and are now in the stadium, pushing our way through the packed terraces to our pre-booked seats. But they have already been taken. Eusabio doesn't try to get the incumbents to move. I conclude that one simply doesn't try that sort of thing here in Rio. So we stand.

I have never been in such a packed mass of people before, and frankly I don't reckon it's very safe. The place is just heaving with people. Many are standing in the stairways which should be kept clear but there's no way that anyone could make the people move. The teams emerge from the players' tunnel to a huge roar from the crowd. We get caught up in the excitement. We are right in the centre of the Flamenco supporters so you can guess who we were supporting! Flamenco score a goal and all hell is let loose. Firecrackers explode around us. Thousands take off their shirts and are whirling them around their heads. Thank goodness Flamenco won by three goals to two.

Exiting the Stadium

Eusabio had stressed that we must stay close together once inside the stadium and that to avoid being split up we should leave five minutes before the end of the game. Good advice because when we were entering the stadium a group of Flamenco supporters ruthlessly swept us aside as they surged en-masse towards the stadium entrance.

Thank goodness baton wielding mounted police kept them in check. On the way back to the Copa Praia we exchange thoughts on the game and all of us agree that it was a hair-raising – but exciting – experience.

Carnival Street Party

The next day I take the Metro from Copacabana into Rio's city centre and the street that I'm now on has been closed to traffic because there's going to be a Carnival street party. During the four days of the Rio carnival these parties attract thousands of people onto the street and believe me if this procession is anything to go by then they are all chaotic!

Up ahead I can hear the sound of music approaching so I stop and join the spectators jammed along the side of the street. I can now see an open-decked bus approaching and on the top deck is a band playing samba music. The bus is moving at a snail's pace, preceded by a swathe of people, young and old, dancing and singing. And man, it's hot! As the bus passes me, the music pounds in my eardrums. There's also a mass of people following the bus, smiling, singing, clapping, dancing.

I'll tell you one thing: you'll soon lose those extra pounds if you come and join in the Rio Carnival!

I meet Juan and Suzy

Feeling a bit peckish, I stop at a pavement food-stall in a quiet side-street. I order a burger with egg and mayonnaise. I sit and relax on the ever-present white plastic chair, a bit grubby-looking, standing nearby on the pavement, provided for discerning customers who prefer to eat-in.

The food-stall owner is a dark skinned guy who speaks some English. We get chatting and he informs me that by 2pm the street will be packed with people because there's going to be another street parade. His name is Juan "call me John" and he introduces me to an adjacent drinks vendor called Suzy. She's also dark skinned with long hair arranged in that style used by Rastafarians. Juan's wife is over there with her cool box of soft drinks. She has their youngest child of nine, a girl, sitting on her lap. Again introductions are made.

These folk are very friendly and Juan acts as the interpreter as we chat about the usual things, where I'm from, do I have a wife, a family? Suzy's mother has now joined the group and she asks Juan to tell me that she is a widow and, looking longingly at me, declares that she is seeking a husband. We have a good laugh. I like these guys so I decide to hang around to see the next parade.

Juan's Night Job

The street is now filling with people who have come to watch the parade. And with them have come numerous street vendors. I can smell the pungent aroma of sweet corn as a vendor steam-cooks them in a large saucepan. Just to our right is a pop-corn vendor, and further on a lady is selling cans of pressurised white foam which these Rio folk love to spray over anybody standing nearby. This is Rio, anything goes, it's Carnival time! Here comes an ice-cream vendor pushing a makeshift wooden cart on which is mounted his cold-box. Juan's hi-fi, which only has one setting (very loud), is playing a samba CD.

A drum band will lead the parade and the drummers are assembling about 100 yards down the street. I can guarantee that their drums will be going at full blast! I'm chatting to Juan in between him serving customers. He tells me that he normally works at night, setting his food stall up outside the hotel just down the street. Apparently the hotel doubles as a brothel and Juan, struggling to manage on his food-stall takings, supplements his income by finding customers for the women.

He asks me if I want "a nice girl." I decline. I have often tried to see the world through the eyes of the people I meet on my travels. So yes, if I were Juan, I too would do the same. He has to be street-wise in order to survive in Rio. He tells me that the local authority theoretically requires each vendor to have a licence to put a stall on the pavement. But there isn't strict enforcement. So there's dozens of them. It's very competitive.

The Greatest Show on Earth

Of all my experiences in Brazil the best came the following night when I attended the Sambadrome to see the main Carnival all-night parade. Perhaps I need to give you some background. Years back the communities living in the ghettos on the outskirts of Rio formed Samba Schools. These schools were steeped in the legacy of Afro-Brazilian music.

The Samba Parades started in Rio city centre in 1932 and by 1984 a Sambadrome was built to provide a unique venue for the parades. A league was established which organised the Samba Schools into one entity. Brazilians regard the Carnival as the greatest show on earth. Just imagine the size of the Carnival that night - fourteen Samba Schools! And just one School can have up to eight thousand participants!

The Samba Schools I saw were:

Portela – presenting Legends and Mysteries of Amazonia
Imperio Serrano – presenting Brazilian Watercolour
Tradicao – presenting Tales of the Sand
Viradouro – presenting the Ciriio de Nazare Festival
Sao Clemente – presenting pranks played in Braziluan life
Caprichosos de Pilare - presenting the Queen of the Little Ones
Unidos da Tijuca - showcasing inventions and inventors
Salgueiro - showing fuel alcohol distilled from sugarcane
Grande Rio – featuring Aids Prevention
Mangueira – featuring the Royal Highway that once shipped gold back to Portugal
Porto da Pedra - showing the History of Messengers
Imperatriz Leopoldinense - celebrating the 500th anniversary of Cabo Frio, the shipping of Brazil wood back to the Old World
Beija-Flor - presenting the Amazon Rainforest
Mocidade Independente - showing a Traffic-safety Campaign

The Carnival at the Sambadrome

I'm on my way to the Sambadrome with my ticket - I'm in Stand 13. Aline, who works at the Copa Praia, has told me that the Parade starts at 9 pm and will go right through the night. I push my way into the Stand and at last I'm sitting on the concrete steps that serve as seating. It's jam-packed in here and I'm now grateful for the crowd experience at the Maracana. There's a Brazilian family next to me and they offer me a can of beer. I wouldn't mind betting that they are not that well-off, but still they want to share with me. I thank them and decline. And now the first Samba school comes into sight.

How can I describe the fantastic costumes, the colours, the incredible Floats which keep coming, one after the other? And the music. Fantastic.

I Stay all Night

The people around me are dancing, singing, clapping, and cheering. At four in the morning I'm feeling tired and we are all somewhat subdued. Many of the smaller children are sleeping, their heads resting on their mothers' laps. We are told that the last School will finish at 5am but by 5.30 the Parade is still going strong! No-one has left. With the dawn I get my second wind, feel better, the tiredness leaves me. As I look around at the crowd I see that they too are rejuvenated, on their feet again, dancing to the samba music.

 Ah well, when in Rome, so I'm standing, clapping, and smiling along with those near me with whom I have made friends and talked to through the night. It wasn't until eight in the morning that the Parade finally ended. I stayed right to the end and as I left the Sambadrome the sun was rising above the city.

Hundreds of Samba School members were walking from the Sambadrome on their way home, carrying their costumes. As I passed the small café-bars that abound in every street I saw people having coffee, some dancing and singing to samba music. Up ahead of me a giant float is being pushed by about ten guys. They are taking it to a parking area where the floats will stay until the next night's parade.

I take the Metro back to Copacabana, tired, but thrilled because I've achieved another milestone. I've seen the Rio Carnival.

Relaxing in Buzios

To recuperate from all the carnival festivities in Rio, I head for the beautiful resort of Buzios, just over 100 miles by bus, north of Rio. It had been highly recommended to me by a colleague back at the office and I find it as idyllic as he had described.

I'm sitting in a sea-side bar enjoying a refreshing Skol beer. The water's edge is only twenty feet or so away and children are splashing around, having fun. And then there's the dog. He's sitting in a small boat moored about one hundred yards from the shore. With him are his two friends – a couple of young boys who have come for a swim - probably straight after finishing school.

These kids have a wonderful life here. The sun, the warmth, the calm sea lapping the sandy shore. You can feel that they are happy. More have arrived now, a mixed bunch of boys and girls aged from around seven to thirteen. They swim out to the boat and join the dog and his pals.

My Favourite Buzios Bar

This bar is not only a bar – it's a restaurant too. But you can't compare it to one of those fancy restaurants in Rio. No, this one-room bare concrete building is only about five metres by five metres square. Behind a narrow bar-top is the tiny kitchen where the food is cooked on a gas cooker. There are two plastic tables and several plastic chairs - the type that one uses in summer in the garden. The floor is plain concrete, and the front door is a metal shutter which the owner pulls down at night. But what the building lacks in sophistication is more than made up for in the friendliness of the man and his wife who run the place.

The wife is a shortish, round woman with a dark skin and curly black hair. She smiles a welcome as she brings my drink. Mind you, she didn't have to move very far because the beat-up refrigerator housing the beer and soft drinks is standing right next to where they have placed my plastic chair. I return her smile and exchange pleasantries, though neither of us understands the other. But smiles and body language are international aren't they? She puts a CD into the player situated up there on a flimsy shelf hanging off the wall. The music has that Latin samba beat.

The Dog's Name is Bobby

There are now four boys in the boat but the dog has taken to the water paddling lazily around with head held high. I ask for his name and the wife informs me that it's Bobby. Some men come into the bar, get a beer and then go back to the beach to work on their boats. The children are now straggling in for their lunch – rice and fried fish. Bobby has swum ashore and is now sitting next to a guy who is working on an old fishing boat. It's definitely seen better days because the paint is peeling off. The sea and the weather have all but conquered this old tub yet I can see a name on the bow "Dom Kiko." I'm told that the boat will be ready for them to go fishing in a couple of days.

Better them than me.

Footnote: Brigit Bardot

In 1957 I was a first year Saunders-Roe engineering apprentice, on the Isle of Wight. How can I forget when Brigit Bardot entered our lives? A national newspaper published a full sized picture of her in her birthday suit - which we promptly hung in a prominent position next to our work benches.

However, the superintendent took a dim view of the nudity and had the photo removed, much to our disappointment. Little did I know then that many years later I would be visiting Buzios in Brazil where I would meet Brigit in person. I had my photo taken seated next to her and what's more I had my hand casually resting on her knee. Yay. Eat your hearts out you 1957 apprentices! OK, it was only a statue of

Bardot on the Buzios seafront (once her favourite beach), but the thrill was there just the same.

CHAPTER 42

WHITE WATER RAFTING IN UGANDA

Introduction

In this account I conclude my R&R holiday in East Africa with a trip to Uganda. I have been to many countries but Uganda was the only one where I actually stood on the equator. It passes through the exact centre of the Earth and divides it in half. So I had a photo taken with one foot in the northern half and the other in the southern. Cool eh. But I don't want to get too carried away because I made another of my mistakes – my decision to once again try white-water rafting...

White water rafting on the Nile River

The bus from Kampala, Uganda has just pulled to a stop at the boat landing near Jinja. There's five of us, plus four raft guides from a white-water rafting company. We are about to start our 30 kilometre trip on the Nile. This is in fact called the Victoria Nile because a few miles away the Nile River starts from Lake Victoria. I have been looking forward to rafting again ever since my exhilarating experience some years previously on the river Tully in Australia, up near Cairns in Queensland. Little did I know what the day would bring.

The Nile is not the same as the Tully, a fact that became evident when the guide told us that there are four Grade five rapids to be negotiated. Some of you may not know what a Grade five rapid is like and I certainly didn't because the Tully only had a maximum of Grade four. Well, I can *now* tell you that a Grade five rapid is one of the most frightening experiences that I have ever had. Things started off ok. We practiced the moves we should take as we encountered different situations at the rapids. But there was a new move that I didn't learn on the Tully. It entailed what action to take if the raft overturned and one was trapped underneath it.

Training Protocol

Over we go, and I'm under the raft. There's an air pocket into which we have been told to surface and breath. I do this and hear the raft guide calling to me to swim out from under the raft. I take a deep breath and swim under the upturned side of the raft and surface several metres away from it. Scary.

In writing this my mind goes back to the 1996 Vendee Globe challenge when Tony Bullimore's world turned upside down, literally, when his yacht overturned in the Southern Ocean. The yacht, Exide Challenger, hit a submerged object as it flew down the face of a cresting swell. He survived for four days huddled in an air pocket beneath the hull of his upturned yacht - in freezing Southern Ocean waters. The epic story of his rescue is among the greatest sea dramas ever witnessed in peacetime. Believe me, that guy had some guts. To keep one's nerve in those conditions, to wait for rescue for days, was an incredible feat of human endurance.

The Nile River where we are rafting flows steadily on its long journey but ours has just begun. The first four rapids are bumpy and the adrenaline rush hits as we are tossed about in the rush of water. Grade 3, then Grade 4, and now our first Grade 5. I had never been through a Grade 5 rapid before thus our raft guide had advised us what to do if our raft overturned. Let me tell you that in my opinion nothing can prepare you for your first underwater experience in a Grade 5 rapid.

As we neared the rapid we were told to paddle hard, really hard. We did our best but as the waves grew bigger the raft became unmanageable. Suddenly we lost control and the force of the water threw the raft upwards and sideways. The next thing I knew was that I was under the water, disorientated, and definitely very scared. I surfaced after what seemed an age and remembering what we have been told I looked to see if the waves were coming towards me before I took a desperate gasp for air. But I swallowed water and, gasping and coughing, tried to get more air into my lungs.

I saw the small rescue raft come alongside me and I grabbed the lifeline. The raft guide shouting to me above the noise of the rapids, warning me not to capsize it. I was then towed to our raft which was now upright. The guide pulled me out of the water. I was coughing up water, and seriously frightened by the experience.

Almost Drowning

I re-gained my composure, if not my confidence, as the raft guide informs us that we are now approaching the next difficult rapid. Several of us groan, not *another* Grade 5. The expression on our faces must have given away our feelings. The guide tells us to paddle hard, and we should get through all-right. The roar of the water almost drowns the exhortations of the guide "paddle harder, *paddle harder.*" So I try to dig deep into the water with my paddle. It's not that easy, one moment we are tilted to one side, and I'm high above the waves, next moment we lurch the other way and the water seems to be rushing by at the level of the side of the raft.

The next thing I know is that I'm under water again, being swirled around. The strength of the water disorients me. I try to swim, to control my movement, to get to the surface. It's an instinctive thing, but we were told not to do this, to conserve our strength, hold our breath until we surface. But nonetheless I try to swim to the surface. I'm scared. Again I swallow water. I surface downstream of the rapid and the rescue craft comes to my aid.

"Are you all-right?" asks the guide. I gasp for air, gulp up water. I tell him that I am not. I have little strength to offer when boarding the raft. He pulls me in, and the other four rafters join me soon after.

We all look exhausted and rest whilst we regain our breath, and our strength. Once again the myth of the stronger sex is exemplified by an Irish girl. She is about mid-twenties, married to a young French guy at her side. She too had been under water, like the rest of us, but she tells me that she wasn't frightened. That definitely makes me the weaker sex - because I was! We are feeling better now and the subject of the next Grade 5 rapid came up. Of the five of us in the raft, only one, a French guy, is willing to do it. The rest of us do not want to go through the experience again.

So it's agreed. We won't run the rapid but it means that we will have to carry the raft along the bank of the river, and re-enter downstream. This was easier said than done but believe me we were all very glad that we hadn't attempted it because it was much worse than the previous two that we had just come through.

Floating Downstream

We are now in calm water; the river is flowing at a steady rate. The sun is hot, maybe around 35 degrees or more, and we are trying to avoid sunburn. The guide tells us to get into the water and just float downstream with the flow of the current. It's lovely. Our life-jacket keeps us afloat. We just lie back in the water and take in the scenery along the river bank. Lush vegetation. Small villages. Local people fetching water - it's the woman's job to do this. They carry water in heavy containers on their heads, their children trailing along behind them with small water containers on theirs.

Can you imagine it? Every day they fetch water from the river, carry it in the hot sun back up the bank, maybe a mile or so back to their villages. And so our Nile trip ended. We bid each other farewell. I can't remember the names of my fellow rafters but I can tell you one thing – I will never forget those Grade 5 rapids!

My East Africa holiday was eventful. I won't forget my visit to Kirubel in Ethiopia, or the mugging at Debrezeit when I was robbed of all I had; I won't forget the abundant wildlife and chanting warrior tribesmen of the Masai Mara, or the rapids on the Nile in Uganda. But all good things must come to an end and so I boarded my flight back to Baku in Azerbaijan. As our flight touched down my mind was already at work. Like any True Expat I was already planning my next R&R - which I'll tell you about later.

CHAPTER 43

THE TUBBIES

Introduction

The islands of the South Pacific Ocean include Samoa where the people are of the Fa'a Samoa culture. Mythology says that Samoans are descended from the Gods and that, in my humble view, is why they are such accomplished rugby players! By the way, did you know that Samoa is the resting place of Robert Louis Stevenson, the author of "Treasure Island?"

How I loved that book.

When Stevenson passed away the Samoans buried him on Mount Vaea, a peaceful prominence high up overlooking the sea. But speaking of peaceful I just have to tell you about the Samoan women's seven-a- side rugby tournament...

I attend a Rugby Tournament in Samoa

I was on another R&R holiday and having travelled to the main Samoan island of Upolu I made my way to my hotel in Apia. I'm a life-long follower of rugby so you can imagine how pleased I was when told that a seven- a -side rugby tournament had just commenced. The next morning found me at the national stadium sitting in the main stand, surrounded by a boisterous crowd of Samoan rugby supporters. Mind you, the seating arrangements left something to be desired simply because there were no seats as such, just a rising series of rock-hard concrete steps.

I had taken the precaution of stuffing a hotel pillow into my backpack which I intended to sit on when my backside started to ache. The view from the stand embraced the main rugby pitch and a number of outlying pitches, beyond which was the luxuriant greenery of fields and trees stretching to the horizon. It had rained during the night and the pitch had been turned-up by the games that had already been played by the men's teams. Added to that were some muddy areas where the players were prone to completely lose their footing, sliding uncontrollably along the ground on their back-sides.

The Women's seven- a-side Teams

A roar of applause has just gone up from the rugby spectators because onto the pitch has emerged two women's rugby teams. Now I'm not talking about those dainty women that appear on the covers of glossy magazines. Oh no. Because your Samoan female rugby player is large, muscular, possessed of great strength, and very round in shape. One could describe them as the Tubbies. I hasten to add that you won't catch me mentioning that word in their presence because I certainly wouldn't like to be on the wrong end of a left hook from one of them!

The referee has blown his whistle and the Tubbies are pounded down the field after the rugby ball. Heavy, deliberate strides, their faces gritted with determination. This referee must have been selected from amongst the most lenient because the Tubbies disregard the rules of the game – they are for sissies. Late tackles, the odd punch or two, shirt grabbing, anything goes as the struggle for possession takes place. Samoan women's rugby is not for the faint hearted!

Tubby falls on her Bottom

By half time there has been no score. The second half is nearing the end and the crowd is transfixed as a sixteen stone Tubby makes a run for the try-line. An opposing player who is only about fourteen stones has made a desperate attempt to tackle her but our Tubby has steam-rolled right over the top of her. Our Tubby is thundering on, the rugby ball gripped firmly under her arm. Suddenly her feet slip from under her and she falls heavily onto her bottom, sending up a spray of mud and water. Waves of laughter around the ground. But all is not lost. A team-mate has arrived in support and has grabbed the rugby ball from her. The new ball-carrying Tubby wants to score the winning try. But can she do it? Legs pumping, she gathers speed. Two opposition Tubbies try to head her off but she evades them - exhaustion has slowed them down.

The Try is scored

The crowd is roaring encouragement which lifts the spirits of our rugby heroine. Now the try-line is only a few metres away with no defenders left. She triumphantly raises her fist in the air and dives over the try line - it's the winning try. The referee, sensing that both sides are totally exhausted, blows the final whistle. To a woman they collapse onto the ground in sheer exhaustion. After recovering they come off the pitch and our heroine is given a raucous ovation.

That evening I was invited to the Marist rugby club in Apia. As usual with all rugby clubs the drinking of beer takes place the difference being that one doesn't simply buy a round of drinks for one's pals, rather one buys a crate of beer! This is delivered to the table by the bartender whereupon everyone joins in. Eat your heart out you guys at the Isle of Wight rugby club!

That Dog Tried to Bite Me

Having spent a few days on Upolu I next visited the nearby Samoan island of Savaii. To get there I had taken a passenger ferry but the sea crossing made me nervous. Why? Because I'm a wimp, definitely not cut out to be a sailor. The first part of the passage was calm because we were inside a reef which gave protection from the Pacific waves. But once leaving the reef the ocean waves grew in size causing the ancient ferry to roll far beyond my liking.

Conversely my fellow Samoan passengers took no notice. Music was coming from a couple of rusty-looking speakers on the passenger-deck bulkhead. You hear their wonderful Samoan music everywhere, not least from the old-fashioned wooden-seated buses which run from Apia bus station out to the villages strung along the coastline of the island.

My thoughts were arrested from the music by a large wave which caused the ferry to roll sideways. I froze and gripped my seat. I had planned to make the trip and return the same day. In the event circumstances caused me to stay overnight. I should have known that it wasn't going to be my day when that dog tried to bite me. I was walking from my hotel to the Apia central bus station at about five thirty in the morning when suddenly three dogs emerged from the gate of a house and barked furiously at me. One, about the size of an Alsatian, sort of nipped my backside. Gave me the fright of my life! Anyway this slowed me down because I was concerned about rabies.

I had been given a rabies jab and advised that if one was bitten then one should get another shot. So there I was, in the grey of the dawn, trying to see if that inconsiderate mutt had drawn blood. Anyone who that morning might have seen a guy with his shorts down to his knees, staring intently at his backside would justifiably have had great doubts about him! I was very relieved to find that the skin hadn't been pierced albeit my backside was very sore.

A Huge Meal for One Dollar

Because of the delay I missed the bus that I had intended to get resulting in taking a much later ferry to Savaii. On arrival my intention was to visit the Saleaula Lava Fields so I took a bus and before alighting had agreed with the driver that he would pick me up later that day when he came back on his way to the ferry terminal.

Well, it was my own fault that I missed the bus. I had got chatting to a group of village women and noticing their cooking saucepans enquired if they had any food. Well, in no time, for about a dollar or so, I had a huge meal in front of me. A whole fish freshly caught from the Pacific, a slab of pork, and tarot, a root vegetable much-liked in that part of the world. You can imagine that it took me ages to finish that lot off! Then I was taken by Tasi, one of the ladies, to see the Lava Field. But that took longer than planned and that's why I missed the bus back.

The Law in Samoan Villages

I was born in the village of Rookley on the Isle of Wight and from about six years of age grew up in the nearby village of Godshill thus I have a great affinity with village life. So I felt really at home as I visited Samoan villages. Whereas in Godshill we had Police Constable Thatcher to keep the law I was to learn that invariably there isn't a policeman in a Samoan village. But there is a Chief who, together with the elders, keeps order. If there is a problem that demands a policeman then they can contact Apia main police station, but by the time a policeman arrives its two hours later by which time the matter has usually been solved!

No Swimming in the Sea on Sundays

Samoans are mostly Christians. Sunday is definitely the day of rest, and of going to church.

One Sunday afternoon I had gone for a walk and as I passed through a small village called Palolo (where no swimming is allowed in the sea on Sundays!) my attention was caught by the sound of hymn-singing from a church. So I slipped quietly into a rear pew. The scene was like something from the past. The church was full. The women were wearing broad-brimmed straw hats and conservative ankle-length white dresses. The men, too, were dressed soberly in their Sunday best. And the singing was wonderful. First the women sang a verse, then the men, then both. And where did you last find a rule forbidding one to swim in the sea … because it was Sunday!

Crossing the International Date Line

And so my R&R to Samoa was over. I have resolved that I will never again take that ferry across to the island of Savaii when the seas are rough. As to that dog that took a bite at my backside, well, I haven't forgotten him and should I return I have resolved to steer well clear of his neck of the woods. Most of all, having departed Fiji on Friday morning I arrived in Samoa on Thursday morning, the day before. No, I'm not joking because our flight crossed the International Date Line.

It doesn't get any better than that!

Footnote

When Samoa made their rugby debut in the 1991 rugby world cup they were unknowns on the international stage. Imagine then the shock when they defeated Wales 16-13 in Cardiff. Wales, one of the leading rugby union nations, were eliminated from the competition. So I have great regard for Samoa.

Oh, before I forget. Should the female rugby-players at the Marist rugby club in Apia read this story I fervently hope that they will forgive me for describing them as the Tubbies.

Mind you I'm no hero so just as a pre-caution I'm keeping my whereabouts a close secret.

CHAPTER 44

THE THAI POLICEMEN

Introduction

On my travels I have some unusual surprises. Like the time when by pure chance I met a bunch of off-duty Thai policemen and their families. In fact, at first I had no idea that they were policemen. What impressed me was that they could let their hair down, have a good time and include me in their revelry.

The Sports Stadium

Once again I had ridden my motorcycle from Malaysia northwards into Thailand, this time to the city of Narathiwat. The next morning, I set off on a sight-seeing ride and by pure chance I passed by a noisy sports stadium, bursting at the seams with activity. My curiosity got the better of me so in no time at all I found myself strolling amongst a noisy, happy festival crowd. Music was everywhere, groups of singers, guys bashing drums, others playing guitars. The overall objective seemed to be to make as much noise as possible! And there, under the shade of a tree, were a troupe of scantily dressed dancing "girls" wearing grass skirts, heavy make-up, and having enormous boobs. They were dancing to the rhythm of music coming from two large speakers located under an awning.

Handsome

Sitting with them were a group of guys with their wives and children, convulsed with laughter at the antics of their dancing colleagues. As I was about to walk past them a smiling face sought my attention, waved, inviting me to join them. I hesitantly walked over to where he was seated. My new friend, a handsome guy with a neat moustache, gestured to me to sit down with them. I was given the seat of honor, a broken paving slab lying on the ground next to him.

Handsome spoke some English. "Drink beer?" His invitation was accompanied by a gesture towards a rather dilapidated plastic beer barrel placed strategically in the centre of the group. I looked into the barrel and hid my concern when I saw that it contained a white colored liquid. It didn't look like beer and certainly wasn't the color of beer as we know it.

Should I risk drinking it? Would I suffer afterwards? As usual the problem was communication. Handsome and his pals wanted me to have a drink with them. But I wanted to ask them about this white beer - was it safe to drink, was it really beer?

Sensing my reticence Handsome gave me an encouraging smile and filled a rather grubby-looking plastic cup. The fact that he had taken the cup from one of his friends, who had been in the process of drinking from it seemed quite natural to him. "Good beer, Thai beer, you drink."

I took the cup and glanced hesitantly around the group of expectant smiling faces. I was about to lose face. This was a serious matter. I could be officially reprimanded as a disappointment to the legions of brave expatriate drinkers who had gone before me. Lead-dancer clearly believed that actions spoke louder than words and, taking the cup from me, drank half of the contents and handed it back as if to say that it wouldn't do me any harm. I gathered my courage and drank the remainder of the beer. I politely thanked them, smiled, and nodded my approval. This was an unwise move because without a second's hesitation Handsome had taken the cup, re-filled it and thrust it into my hand.

Now, I'm pretty lucky in that I don't usually get an upset stomach, wherever I go. Could the Thai white beer be my comeuppance? I told myself that I had better take it easy and with that I passed the cup to a guy on my right who I had come to know as Number 6.

The Numbering System

The allocation of the numbering system by Handsome had caused much merriment all round. It was whilst doing so that I learnt that this noisy beer-drinking happy group were all off-duty Thai policemen! They came from a police station in a nearby town called Ruso. And the numbering identified them by seniority. Handsome called over a middle-aged guy who was responsible for discordant clashes on a pair of symbols. Handsome respectfully introduced him as Number 1.

He was clearly the senior rank present. This introduction was met with happy applause. This clearly encouraged Handsome and he proceeded to introduce Numbers 2, 3, 4, 5, and 6. Number six was the youngest and Handsome addressed him in a tone of mock disparagement which elicited hilarious laughter. A joke that they all shared. I found myself relaxing.

Then followed a pronouncement only possible in such circumstances. Handsome firmly shook my hand.
"I love you," he proclaimed.
"And Number 1 loves you" gesturing towards Number 1.
"And Number 2 loves you." The rest of the Numbers apparently loved me too. There were beaming smiles all round.

"Where you from?" asked Number 1. I replied that I was from England. "Ah, Manchester United" exclaimed Number 6, clearly a ManU fan. He vigorously shook my hand and I gave him the thumbs-up sign. Not to be outdone, Number 3 added "David Beckham." With that I was seized with enthusiasm for Manchester United. Not that I supported them. But these policemen did.

Someone then grabbed my hand and pulled me towards the dancing girls. It was lead-dancer and he wanted me to join them in their dancing act. Knowing how hot it was and having seen them perspiring heavily I politely declined.

Number 6 asked me if I would like to eat and handed me a plate of rice, vegetables and small bits of chicken. In between mouthfuls I was encouraged to drink more beer. I looked in the barrel to find that the surface of the beer was covered with small leaves that had fluttered down from the tree above. These were succinctly dealt with by being skimmed off and thrown un-ceremoniously onto the ground.

A Town called Ruso

Number 1 asked me if I could let him have prints of the photographs that I had taken of the group. I readily agreed and after a search for a pen I wrote their police station address onto a scrap of paper. And that's how the next day I found myself in the town of Ruso.

Before I tell you about Ruso I must tell you about my over-night stay in Narathiwat. An amusing situation occurred. I had parked my motorcycle on the road outside the front of my hotel. I was about to go to my room when the reception clerk gestured towards my motorcycle and indicated that I should bring it into the hotel foyer! I did as requested. To be honest I couldn't recall how many hotels I had been to where I had seen a guest's motorcycle parked right in front of the reception desk! Wonderful stuff.

I rode slowly down the main street of Ruso and stopped at the express PhotoShop. Upon handing the guy my roll of film I was told to come back at noon so, with time in hand, I set out to explore the town. It was very hot, so I found a restaurant and ordered tea. I like to take in everything going on around me.

There was a young lad wearing a black and white striped football shirt. The bold lettering proclaimed "Newcastle Brown Ale." A cat lay asleep on a pile of newspapers beside me. It woke and nonchalantly climbed onto the adjacent tabletop and drank water from a glass in which there were teaspoons intended for customers to stir their tea! I made a mental note not to stir my tea in future. Outside, a woman drove by on her small motorcycle, her children sitting side-saddle on the pillion seat.

Just after mid-day I collected the photo prints and found that the police station was just across the road. I gave Number 1 the photographs, which were passed around. There were hoots of laughter when they saw themselves in the grass skirts. Calls quickly went out on the radio to the policemen who were on patrol. Lead dancer arrived at the station. This time he was smartly dressed in uniform. But the sight of himself dressed as a busty dancing girl left him weak with laughter.

Farewell

Number 1 asked me to have lunch with him and two colleagues. Afterwards I made my farewells and set off on my journey back to Malaysia. I'll always remember those Thai policemen and their kindness to me. Should you guys from Ruso get to read this story I hope that I have told the truth, the whole truth, and nothing but the truth. And don't worry, I can keep a secret, I won't tell a soul that you were the guys dressed as dancing girls.

CHAPTER 45

RIDING THE ORINOCO IN VENEZUELA

Introduction

I'm on R&R again, this time my destination is Venezuela, a country on the northern coast of South America, whose capital is Caracas. It's Sunday, around 5 pm, and I've just taken a flight from Montego Bay in Jamaica to Caracas airport in Venezuela. Having exited the airport terminal, I had a stroke of good luck when a taxi driver, Juan, approached me. Did I want a taxi? No thanks, I'm taking the bus. Do I want to change money? He says he'll give me a better rate than the bank – 2,000 Bolivar's to the dollar rather than 1,500. I'm on my guard as usual but decide to change 50 dollars. Actually he's a nice guy, and having taken me to the bus departure point, tells me the name of a Caracas budget hotel in the Sabana district. I'm to get off the bus at the Parque Centrale and then take a taxi to the Mountford Hotel.

Mind the Gap on the Metro

The bus ride up to Caracas takes place in a heavy downpour. Upon arrival I take a taxi from the Parque Centrale to the Mountford Hotel. Now I face the acid test - my first exposure to Spanish. The receptionist doesn't speak a word of English. But I manage and after a good night's sleep I'm up early the next morning, go out for breakfast, and ask for directions to the Tourist office. I am told to take the Metro (underground) to Bellas Artes station from where I must make my way to the 35th floor of the nearby West twin tower.

I won't forget that Metro ride in a hurry. The platform was jammed packed with commuters so I had positioned myself to be the first into the carriage. The underground train doors opened and I hurriedly made to step into the carriage but in my haste I stepped into the space between the carriage and the edge of the platform. My left leg went right down into the gap. No matter how I struggled I couldn't budge it. As you can imagine I had the fright of my life not helped by the fear that the train doors were about to close. With the assistance of unknown passengers (who I thank profusely) I managed to yank my leg free and as the doors were closing I plunged headlong into the carriage.

Was my Face Red!

You can imagine that I was somewhat in shock so it didn't occur to me that something was wrong. The train had remained stationary. Then I realised why - because nearby was the strident sound of an alarm bell. Approaching were two stern-faced train guards. When they reached me they stopped. I still hadn't registered where the alarm sound was coming from but one of the guards pointed to my backpack. Oh my God – it's my fault.

What had happened was that after the mugging and robbery in Ethiopia I had purchased a personal alarm which I intended to use in the event that I was ever attacked again. Somehow when freeing my trapped leg, I must have inadvertently activated it. All eyes were turned in my direction. With profuse apologies and acute embarrassment, I rapidly dug the offending alarm out of my backpack and silenced it. The guards kindly gave me a reassuring smile and in no time we were on our way. So please – don't make the mistake that I made. Should a guard tell you to *mind the gap* – then do just that.

Phone Rebecca

Phew. That was a close one. Soon I found myself in the tourist office. I didn't have a set plan so I asked the young girl at the desk (they are *all* young nowadays) what places of interest there were to visit. Keeping her attention was easier said than done because apart from talking to me she had to answer the telephone plus there were other visitors all clamouring for her attention. Standing in line behind me was a young Venezuelan guy who had overheard me mention the Orinoco River. In no time at all he introduced himself (Peter) and assumed the role as my travel adviser.

According to Peter, a trip on the Orinoco is an absolute *must*. He advised me to take the overnight bus to Tucupita where I must hire a boat to take me all the way down the Orinoco to the village of Curiapo, close to the Atlantic Ocean. He fished in his pocket and finding his address book gave me the telephone number of a friend, Rebecca "who speaks good English." Thanking Peter, I called Rebecca, yes she could organise my Orinoco trip and would meet me when I arrive at the Tucupita bus station - I'm to go to the CANTV office and call her.

I Shiver my way down to Tucupita

It's mid-afternoon, I settle my hotel bill and set off - I must take the Metro to Patare station from where I must take a taxi to the bus station - the Terminal de Oriente. Taxis don't have meters here so you have to negotiate the price before you start the journey. I'm getting quite used to this now so I give a hand sign signifying "how much?" The taxi driver, an amiable guy, wrinkle lines on his forehead and around his eyes, holds up four fingers. I nod in agreement – it's 4,000 Bolivars. About two dollars. I climb in. There's lots of room inside because this is a huge gas-guzzling ancient Chevrolet car which went out of production many years ago.

Rebecca has told me that when I get to the Terminal de Oriente I must go to the desk of the bus company called Expresos Los Llanos. I buy my ticket to Tucupita and at around 7.30pm we depart. The bus is air-conditioned and my, it's so cold in here! But my fellow passengers are well aware of this. They have come armed with blankets and pillows so that they can sleep. All night long I shiver my way down to Tucupita where we arrive at about 6am.

I meet Rebecca

On arrival in Tucupita I call Rebecca and in no time at all she and her driver Narang pick me up from the bus station and take me to my hotel. I learn that Rebecca lives with her parents who have a small hotel in the village of Curiapo and that she will accompany me there in a day or so when one of their boats journeys up from Curiapo. I can't go by road because, well, there isn't one! Everyone travels by river. Meantime Rebecca offers to take me sight-seeing around Tucupita.

I ask about the Angel Falls – the highest in the world. Access is by single-engine plane only. It's a six-seater – I decide against it because of the horrendous flight I had some years ago in a similar plane from Le Havre to Southampton. Later I learn that a flight to the Falls crashed with no survivors. We spend two days sight-seeing and the next morning at 4am in total darkness I board the boat for Curiapo.

I was about to see a part of the world I never knew existed.

Riding the Orinoco

The powerful twin 75HP Yamaha outboard engines burst into life and we set off at breakneck speed. I'm gripping the edge of the boat with one hand and the seat with the other. Thump, thump, thump – the river's waves hit the hull of the boat, shaking my bones. Neil, Rebecca's brother, is driving the boat at top speed.

Suddenly, dramatically, we swerve. White-knuckled I see that the reason is a mass of reed floating down-river. My heart is in my mouth. What if we capsize? My mind races through the possible scenario. The river is about one mile wide – maybe more. Could I swim to the shore? I doubt it. I have a small life-jacket on so I may be able to float. My thoughts are arrested by a more immediate problem because I'm feeling cold - we have had a rain-squall and I'm almost soaked.

New Moon and Starry Skies

Relentlessly we press on. Mile after mile. We cross a stretch of calm water. I relax and looking skywards observe that there is a new moon. The sky is clear and the stars are wonderful. For three hours we travelled, on and on. We cross the wake of another boat and our prow rises high in the air and then with a shuddering whack it comes down, hitting the water with a jarring crash. Ouch! At last, after what seems an eternity, Curiapo comes into sight.

Arrival in Curiapo

I climb stiff-legged off the boat and climb the jetty steps to the hotel entrance. First impressions are lasting, aren't they? All around me are wooden homes built on stilts - this is the village of Curiapo. On the bank on the other side of the river I see a line of simple homes perched precariously on stilts above the water's edge. They are mostly built of bamboo with roofs of bamboo leaf. Stretching back from the river's edge is the dense jungle - as far as the eye can see.

Welcomed by Birma and Kawall

Rebecca's home cum my hotel is called the Orquidea and upon entry her parents Birma and Kawall warmly welcomed me. I have found peace and tranquillity – just what I needed after the bumpy journey down from Tucupita. Birma and Kawall are of Indian, not Venezuelan, descent. Back in time their grand-parents were brought to Guyana from India by the British - with promises of jobs.

Life was very hard in Guyana so after their marriage Birma and Kawall moved to the Orinoco Delta to find work. They found the sub-tropical climate perfect for growing fruit so they started a fruit-farm. In this remote location they didn't have to buy the land or apply for planning permission to build a home - they just hacked down the surrounding jungle and got on with it!

Birma and Kawall re-build their Lives

They started a family and made a new life for themselves. But one day danger struck whilst they were away from the farm. Local Warao Indian tribesmen came intent on robbery. They killed three relatives and stole their boat and money. Once more they had nothing. So they moved across the river to Curiapo and started all over again. Through hard work they have built up their business – the hotel, a shop, and the boat transport cum trading business. They have six boats which they regularly use to transport petrol (illegally) from Venezuela where it's cheaper to Guyana where it's expensive. They also transport goods down from Tucupita, and occasionally a greenhorn tourist.

Birma's Hindu Faith

I'm shown to my room – double bed, small table, a fan. The toilet and shower are a low dividing wall away. There's no surprise when I find the shower water is cold. In hot countries this is often the case in budget hotels, and to be honest, once you have gasped your way through the first few moments, it's really refreshing. I have taken a liking to Birma. She's a very genuine person whose life is guided by her Hindu faith which she has inculcated into her three children, Neil, Rebecca, and Bimbo.

This is a nice family and I'm treated as one of them. After lunch I go with Kawall on his boat – he's looking for a special hard-wood tree for the roof timbers for a new shop which he currently has under construction.

Trips on the River

The boat has slowed to a snail's pace and we are entering a small waterway that penetrates the jungle. Trees tower above us and the undergrowth grows right down to the water's edge – brushing across our lowered heads. We disembark and walk into the trees. It's very muddy because the high tide floods this area. I'm being bitten by mosquitoes and as Kawall searches for the right tree I retreat to wait at the boat.

That was my first river trip from their Curiapo base. Subsequently I went out with them many times on the Orinoco, observing the tributaries which flow into the Atlantic. Long before the Spanish settlers arrived the Warao Indians lived here. Small in stature, brown skinned, they live today much as they have done for centuries. Their houses are single-storey, they sleep in hammocks, wash in the river, and fishing is an important part of their lives. They travel on the river by canoes chiselled from tree-trunks, large enough to accommodate the whole family. Even the small children can paddle the canoe.

Relaxing on a Saturday Afternoon

It's Saturday afternoon and I'm sitting under an awning with Neil at his uncle's house on the river's edge, some 30 minutes upstream from Curiapo. Several other guys who work for the family have come along, and now I know why. A bottle of rum has materialised. It's passed around without comment. A liberal splice is poured into an old chipped enamel cup. I'm hoping that Neil can take his drink because the ride back against the rising tide can be bumpy. I'm offered a ripe mango plucked straight from a nearby tree. Delicious!

Neil's uncle has a small farm here on which he grows coconuts, mangoes and vegetables, plus he keeps chickens which he sells for the meat. I'm thinking that his wife, Aditi, must have a singular existence – she's the only female here. Indeed, there are no neighbouring houses within sight.

Neil interrupts my thoughts "English, would you want to stay here?" I ponder on this question. All around me is the jungle, untouched by mankind. Groups of parrots, brightly feathered, make a lot of noise as they fly overhead. Across the river to the West the sun is setting, casting shadows across the rippled water. There is peace and silence all around. I try to couch my reply carefully. These are nice people. I don't want to offend them. I reply that I really like the peace and quiet here, but my R&R is almost over and that I have to return to Azerbaijan to my work.

The Bottle of Rum is empty

It starts to rain a heavy downpour. Sitting on a nearby beam are two tame parrots each constrained by a piece of string. They are clearly extroverts because they are making so much noise. Neil tries to entice them to speak and we all smile as one of them imitates the crow of a cockbird. The rain has stopped. I didn't know it, but my holiday coincides with the rainy season. It's after 5pm and I've been monitoring the bottle of rum - it is now empty. The guys are talking in Patois – a mixture of English, Spanish and Creole.

There's a lot of good humour going around and they tell me that I'll soon learn their Patois. I express my doubts, explaining that I'm the world's worst when it comes to learning languages. We return to the hotel Orquidea. The boat rides, prow-up, over the waves, the wind tears at my face. Neil expertly makes the turn towards the hotel and cuts the engine at precisely the right moment as we come alongside the jetty landing stage.

Farewell to the Orinoco

My trip down the Orinoco is almost over. I'll always remember Curiapo. For dinner we have fried fish, fresh from the river. And lots of vegetables. Afterwards Kawall and I sit outside the hotel and he breaks open a bottle of very nice fruit wine, made in Guyana. The next morning, we set off back to civilisation, as you and I know it. But down there they breathe clean air, eat fish caught daily in the river, thrive on healthy vegetables and fruit, and live in peace with each other.

And just imagine: there are no traffic lights on the river. Lucky them.

CHAPTER 46

ON SAFARI IN KENYA

Introduction

Having been to Ethiopia a couple of times to visit Kirubel, my PLAN UK kid, I made a plan that on my next R&R I would include a visit to nearby Kenya. I wanted to go on a safari. At the time I didn't realise that Kenya is Africa's most popular safari destination and I certainly hadn't heard of the Masai Mara Game Reserve. Having taken an African taxi from Nairobi airport into the city centre I wandered down a busy street, found a Safari company, and booked my place with a group of fellow tourists bound for the Masai Mara the very next day. But first I had time to explore the city. Come early evening I was pleasantly tired so what better than to relax and have a nice cool beer.

Kenyatta Road, Nairobi

It's Saturday evening in Nairobi, Kenya. The sun is setting as I sit in an open-air bar just off Kenyatta Road, drinking a cool glass of the local beer. Over there is a band consisting of six guys who are playing some great music - two guitars, drums, keyboard, African drums, and the lead singer who also plays the trumpet.

There's a good crowd here and I can see that they know how to enjoy themselves. The aroma of a barbecue wafts across to me but I have decided not to eat here, instead I'm going to a café on Moi

Avenue. I can get chicken and chips for 80 Kenyan shillings and a cup of tea will cost another 20. That's about one dollar! The guys are now playing a Spanish song and I'm thinking, as I survey the black faces surrounding me, that music transcends race, culture and the colour of one's skin. Three lovely Kenyan girls have just got up onto the small dance floor in front of the band. With rhythmic body movement they dance in unison to the music.

I have an early night – tomorrow at dawn we set off for the Masai Mara.

The Masai Mara Game Reserve

We are hushed as we watch the lions feeding. Here on the Masai Mara life and death goes on as it has from the beginning of time. The buffalo's eyes are sightless and the lions, three male and one female, are tearing at the flesh with their powerful teeth. One male is interrupted by another who wants to feed where he is feeding. So he growls deeply, a primeval, powerful, ominous tone. The tour driver tells us that the lions will spend the next four days being sick on their gorging and that it may be another two weeks before their next kill.

We traverse the vast expanse of the Mara and see lion, elephant, giraffe, gazelle, impala, wildebeest, warthog, waterbuck, and cheetah. We visit the river Mara and see the hippos and crocodile. But perhaps the most unusual sight of the safari was our meeting with "Pork Chops." We had stopped at a safari Lodge and had sat down in the lounge area for drinks.

Pork Chops

And there, lying fast asleep on the floor next to our coffee table was a warthog. I'll bet that there are very few of us who keep a pig in our lounge. At least, not where I come from anyway! We pat this sleeping beauty but no amount of attention would rouse it from its slumbers. It transpired that it was found when it was very small by a guy who lives and works at the Lodge. There was no mother around so he took it and raised it as a pet. Nowadays it is treated like royalty by the staff. At night it is locked up to protect it from the lions.

You might say that Pork Chops is a very lucky pig indeed.

The Masai Tribesmen's Village

No visit to the Massai Mara would be complete without what we are about to experience. I'm standing just outside the small gap in the thorn perimeter fence that denotes the entrance to a Masai village. It's not a fence as we understand the meaning, rather a circle of thorn branches, some hundreds of metres in diameter encircling the village houses. We are waiting for the Massai tribesmen, in warrior costume, to perform their tribal dance for us. And here they come, in single file, their red cloaks draped across their shoulders, chanting as only an African can chant. It's fascinating.

The warriors stamp their bare feet on the dry earth and sing a welcome song to us. The lead warrior sings the verse and then the others, in perfect unison, chant the chorus, and as they chant they continue to stamp their feet and at the same time advance a few feet towards us. In their hands they are carrying their weapons - spears sharpened to a razors edge.

I'm captivated by the raw power of these men. Now a warrior steps forward and the singing changes tempo. Without pause he jumps into the air, legs together, feet parallel with the ground. Four, five, six times he jumps vertically, almost twelve inches from the ground. Amazing. Then another steps forward and takes over the role, and this continues until all of the warriors have completed this ritual. They reform and do another tribal dance, and after they have finished I take the opportunity to mix with them and, holding a spear, have a photo taken.

Mind you, I wasn't fit enough to do the jumping thing, that must be born in them. I was enthralled by the setting, the warrior costumes that they wore and the sound of their voices as they sang and chanted.

Next came the visit into their village. We entered through the gap in the thorn fence and were shown a typical village house. Of circular shape, the structure is made of wood, the walls are lined with cow dung, and the roof is made of long coarse grass. We are told that the smaller room, on the right as we stoop to enter, is for the calves, a special security for the most vulnerable of the herd. Not that we can see much because inside it's almost pitch dark.

In the main room there are no windows but as our eyes grow accustomed to the light that filters through the space between the walls and the roof we see that it is divided into two parts. To the left is the cowhide bed laid on the earthen floor. On the right is the larger part - the living area. Here the wives cook the main meal of the day which is taken after the evening milking (done by the women) to a communal gathering where all one hundred and fifty families in the village eat together. There is no water, electricity, or toilet in their houses. Surprisingly one cannot smell the dung walls.

Everyone drinks milk daily and, on special occasions, cow blood is mixed with the milk. We learn that in a Masai house you rotate two sticks against each other to ignite the wood for your fire – one is soft and one hard. Water for cooking, drinking, washing, comes from a nearby stream. And your wealth is measured by the number of cattle that you own. The Massai tribesman can marry only when he has cattle to give as a bride-price - the current rate being ten cows. We met a young guy who told us that he wasn't married - yet. He has some young cattle – not fully grown. So he has to be patient before he can get a bride.

Safety on the Masai Mara

It's a potentially dangerous place to live on the Masai Mara. Out there are hungry lions that are free to wander wherever they wish. There are no fences to keep them away from the tribesmen's village so the protection of their cattle is of paramount importance. By day they are guarded as they graze out on the Mara. At night they are brought back and to protect them from attack by lions they are secured in the centre of the village, within a circular thorn fence. Outside the cattle enclosure are the village homes lying in a circle surrounding the central area and protecting them is the outer circular thorn fence through which we entered on this tour of their village.

Every morning the village men drive the six hundred or so cattle out to graze on the vast expanse of the dry grass-land of the Mara. That evening our final sight was to witness the tribesmen driving the cattle back into the village. The sun was getting low and as they headed for the village we could hear the cow-horns clanging, the men whistling and shouting commands, the dogs barking. We are told that about one cow a week is killed by lions, and that two years ago a tribesman was killed by lions whilst trying to protect his cattle from attack.

As the cattle enter through the village I note that they all have scars on their hides – these are the owners marking, a simple identification system. And whilst I watch the shoeless children standing, observing us tourists, I become aware that there are lots of flies around the cow-herd because that little boy over there has flies settled on his face. And what of law and order? Well, there's no police force here. But they do have a village chief, elected by the villagers for a two-year period. They abide by his rulings. Yes, it's another world isn't it? If only ours was that simple.

CHAPTER 47

EXPAT IN JAPAN

Introduction

If you need advice on how to navigate around Tokyo's central underground station, then please don't come to me. It's a nightmare! Such was the situation when I disembarked from the underground train intent on finding the exit that I had been advised to take. After walking around in circles and getting nowhere I finally in desperation asked an old guy for advice. He stopped, smiled, and put me right. With that he rapidly disappeared up an escalator - I swear he wasn't a day under ninety...

Trip to the Live Volcano

As I relaxed in my Kagoshima hotel room I was pleased that the weather forecast for the next day was dry and sunny. Having arrived in Tokyo on R&R my decision to head to southern Japan was largely because the north was still in the grip of winter snows. The tourist office at Kagoshima rail station suggested that I should visit the live volcano on nearby Sakurajima Island.

To get there I must first take a ferryboat and then a bus to Arimura village from where I was assured I could get the best view of the volcano's eruptions. I couldn't wait because I had never seen a live volcano before so the next morning I found myself disembarking from the ferry and making my way to the nearby bus terminal. The timetable informed me that I had nearly an hour to wait. So rather than stand in an empty queue I had decided to pass the time by taking a stroll along the sunny water-front.

Nine very slow old Ladies

When I returned the situation had changed because I now found about nine tiny Japanese ladies in the queue. Surely not one of them could have been a day under ninety years of age and I'm not exaggerating when I say that all of them were no more than five feet tall. It was evident from their bulging shopping bags that they were on their way home and meantime, whilst waiting for the bus, they were chattering away ten to the dozen. On joining the rear of the queue I checked my watch and sure enough the bus drew into the bus station right on time.

The procedure for disembarkation and embarkation was something to behold. First the driver stopped the bus for the exiting passengers and upon opening the rear door they disembarked. He then closed the rear door, pulled forward all of four feet and then opened the front door for passengers to embark. The very frailest of the ninety year olds was at the head of the queue. Grasping her shopping bag, she reached up for the bus handrail with her tiny hand. With grim determination she managed to get one foot up onto the first step. She then paused for breath before gathering her strength to raise the other foot. Meantime the bus driver, selected I'm sure for his patience, observed the procedure with an experienced eye.

I counted the remaining old ladies and calculated that at this rate of progress I could be kept waiting for ages. I thought of offering to assist our great grandma but having at last ascended the first step she found the final two steps easier to achieve. With a solemn indifference she passed by the driver and slowly headed for her seat. Clearly that's exactly what he expected. Raising a white-gloved hand he indicated that before sitting down she must first swipe her bus pass.

Meantime the second old dear had climbed aboard and she too had to be hauled back to swipe her pass. Goodness only knows how many times they had enacted this procedure but I have come to the conclusion that if I were to return on their next shopping day then things would be exactly the same. At last all of the grandmas were on board, the door was closed and we were on our way.

Farewell Old Dear

I settled back in my seat thinking that in no time I would be at the volcano. Wrong! Little did I know what was to come. As we approached the first village one of the old dears rang the bell indicating that she wanted to alight at the next stop. It was then that I had to witness *the* most excruciatingly-slow disembarkation from a bus known to man! First the bus stopped, then the rear door was opened. But before our old dear disembarked she had to perform the farewell ceremony. Rising to her feet she slowly passed along the bus and bowed in turn to her chums at the same time having a chat with each one of them.

I was in agonies, wondering what they still had to talk about. Slowly, one by one, she made her farewells and finally she bowed to the driver. With infinite care our old dear descended the rear steps one at a time and at last stood at the roadside, waving a cheery farewell to her chums. The driver moved off and I realized with despair that I still had to witness the departure of the remaining old ladies.

Pedestrian Control

Following my visit to the volcano I decided to return to the ferry terminal on foot. Upon approaching some road works I was intrigued by how the Japanese controlled the traffic. At one end stood a guy holding two flags, one red and the other white, whilst at the other end his buddy was similarly equipped. I naturally assumed that these guys were there to control the traffic, never thinking that they also controlled pedestrians.

Thus imagine how impressed I was to find that I too received the full flag-waving treatment! Our man brandished his white flag high in the air indicating that I should proceed, directing me to a temporary footpath. It would have made my day if I had caught sight of the guy at the other end of the road-works raising his red flag in order to stop a pedestrian coming from the other direction! Anyway, our flag-man was friendly and his sun-tanned face beamed a warm smile as he politely bowed to me. And how could I miss noticing the ever-present white gloves?

A Hot Tub beckons

That return walk took ages! At last the terminal was in sight and believe me I needed a rest. As chance would have it just a hundred metres or so before the terminal I noticed a large sign displaying some natural hot water baths. In no time at all I had made enquiries at the reception desk. I have to admit that initially the thought of Japanese communal bathing, in one's birthday suit, was a tad off-putting. But I was exhausted so I quickly dispelled that thought and without further ado I was in the men's changing room, showered, and ready to enter the bath area.

Tiny Towel

Whilst paying my entry fee the receptionist had asked if I would like to purchase a towel. It seemed like a good idea so I agreed. However, when it was handed to me I could hardly contain my surprise because it was so small. Which part of my body, I asked myself, should I attempt to dry with it!

The bath was about twelve feet square and full of hot water. When I say hot you have no idea how hot! It took me ages before I could immerse myself but having done so I was in heaven. Hot water was being pumped into the bath by jets something akin to a Jacuzzi. Suitably rejuvenated I took the ferry back to Kagoshima from where I headed north, looking forward to the real reason for going to Japan, my visits to Nagasaki and Hiroshima. How can one forget that in 1945 atom bombs were dropped on these two Japanese cities? The thought of even contemplating using these terrible weapons again is beyond belief.

Nagasaki and Hiroshima

At the Nagasaki exhibition I saw the terrible destruction caused by the bomb. I sat and listened to the recorded stories of the survivors. Unforgettable, tragic, heart-rending. From ordinary people, like you and I. As I travelled onwards to other places one often saw plaques proclaiming that Japan should never go to war again, that all nuclear weapons should be destroyed.

The irony for the city of Nagasaki is that is wasn't a primary target. The intended city was Kokura but it wasn't bombed because it could not be seen due to cloud. So the aircraft proceeded to Nagasaki which was clearly visible. Hiroshima, the other primary target, was bathed in perfect sunshine and both were completely destroyed. The suggested time for each exhibition was two hours, but I can tell you that I was so engrossed by what I saw and learnt that I was at each visitor centre for many hours.

Fond memories of Japan

My R&R in Japan helped me to widen my perspective. I certainly found the people there to be very courteous and helpful. After Kagoshima I also visited Fukuoka, Osaka, and Kanazawa from where I returned to Tokyo, considerable distances. I learnt how to eat noodles with chopsticks and proudly contend that I can now easily empty any restaurant with the loud slurping noises which I make. Plus, I am contemplating opening a string of natural cold-water spas across the Isle of Wight. I hasten to add that I won't personally be using them because I dislike the cold.

However, if you are interested I'm looking for volunteers. And should you be a long-suffering commuter fed up with your tiresome daily journey to work just take the Shinkanshen. This excellent Japanese super-express rail system runs *exactly right on time*.

Looking back my fondest memories of Japan are those diminutive old ladies. They might have been ninety years old, and not as sprightly as they once were, but they were still going strong!

CHAPTER 48

EXPAT IN JAMAICA

Introduction

I'm off on my R&R again, this time to Jamaica, the birthplace of my favourite Reggae artist, Bob Marley. Born February 1945 in Saint Ann Parish, Jamaica, to his parents Norval Marley, a White Jamaican and Cedella, an Afro Jamaican. Growing up in Trench town, a suburb of Kingston, Bob and his childhood friends forged a distinctive song writing and vocal style that would later resonate with audiences worldwide.

Later when he moved to England to pursue a solo career it culminated in 1977 with the release of the album Exodus *which established his worldwide reputation as one of the best-selling artists of all time. At the age of 36 he passed away. He received a state funeral in Jamaica.*

My visit to the Bob Marley Museum

My Jamaican holiday kicked off at Montego Bay where I chilled out and swam in the warm waters of the Caribbean. From there I moved on to Kingston. I had a good reason to go there – I simply had to visit the Bob Marley Museum. I really didn't know what to expect so imagine my surprise when I found that it is situated in what was his home. It was such an interesting experience. Moreover, I hadn't realised how popular his music was, and indeed is to this very day, until I mixed with fans who like me had come to Jamaica from around the world just to visit Kingston and the museum. I have at home a CD of his greatest album, Exodus. Unfortunately, what I don't have is a sound system similar to that in the museum. Awesome!

Trench Town

Having been to the museum there was another place I wanted to visit and that was Trench Town, where Bob Marley grew up - and immortalized in his music. At the time I wasn't aware that whilst people from all over the world have heard of Trench Town few have ever been there. I wondered why. The answer came when I asked my taxi driver to take me there:

"No way man!" came his forceful reply.

"Why not?" I asked.

He replied "Hell man, those people down there, they don't even like each other - it's too dangerous man. No way, I aint takin you there."

He was right of course. What I learnt was that in Trench Town gun crime and shootouts between rival gangs occur every day and every night. It's this hostile warfare that has turned it into one of the most dangerous places in the world. This is where Bob Marley grew up. So I left it at that. I had made my pilgrimage to his home and I was happy for having done so. Why not explore the island instead?

Bus to Port Antonio

Having spent a couple of days in Kingston I decided to take the bus across to the other side of the Island and head for Port Antonio - a journey I'll never forget! Our driver, a young handsome guy who I'll name Dreadlocks for his long dreadlock hair, is driving at a furious pace reminding me that my brochure said that Jamaicans are crazy drivers. Well, OK, it didn't exactly say that but you get my point don't you? Once out of Kingston the road twisted and turned, following a valley before commencing the long climb up the Blue Ridge Mountains.

Crazy Driving

Pity the poor vehicle driver in front of us because Dreadlocks, who probably invented tail-gating, wants to overtake him. But he's having none of it and obviously isn't going to give way. Dreadlocks is not to be outdone. He crashes down a gear and swings out to overtake. My heart is in my mouth. Surely we will never make it? To our right there's a steep incline down into the valley and I'm scared that we could be down there at any moment because there's a guy coming towards us who is not going to give way either. I have my feet hard on the floor, willing Dreadlocks to brake... anything.

But he doesn't. Having managed to just pass the guy in front of us he makes a dramatic last-second swerve to the inside lane. Phew!

Next to me a young attractive Jamaican woman sits, quietly composed. I breathe a deep sigh of relief and remark that we came very, very close to a collision. She smiles and in that wonderful Jamaican Patois replies "welcome to Jamaica, man." I thank her, whilst silently hoping that we will get to Port Antonio in one piece.

A Shoot-Out in Kingston

Dreadlocks has turned the radio on and the news is now being read. There's a shoot-out in Kingston. Two guys are dead. The police are advising motorists to take a diversion around the area because the shooting is still going on. After the news the DJ told listeners what I thought was a funny yet awfully sad story. She quoted from a newspaper cutting which referred to a decision, by a long past Governor of Jamaica, to allow 2,000 slaves to be brought from Africa to work in the sugar plantations ... "providing they are capable of becoming good Christians!"

Next stop - Venezuela

I found Port Antonio very pleasant. If you ever visit Jamaica do go there. There's some fun tours to go on and compared to Kingston it has a very different feel to it. And so ended my R&R in Jamaica. Next stop – Venezuela. You'll read about it in another chapter.

CHAPTER 49

DANGER IN ETHIOPIA

Introduction

It had taken me two years to overcome the grief of losing my wife Jan in 1997 and during that time I remained in the UK for family reasons.

For the next eight years I threw myself into contract work as a full time expat in the oil and gas industry where you are given time off, commonly known as rest and recuperation (R&R). For income tax purposes I could only spend a relatively small number of my R&R days per year in the UK.

Backpacking

Thus I used my time off to travel the world as a back-packer. For those of you who have not back-packed I can tell you that it is great fun. You meet fellow travellers from around the globe, share your adventures, pass on useful tips, and gamble on the next back-packing lodge being what you hoped it would be! But there are dangers too. This chapter recounts a visit to Ethiopia - I was there to see Kirubel, a lovely Ethiopian boy who I had been sponsoring for a number of years through a charity called PLAN UK.

Little did I know what was in store for me...

Bus Trip from Addis Ababa to Debrezeit

Have you ever been mugged before? Well I hadn't - until this trip. I have travelled quite a bit and have always been confident that I take precautions regarding my personal safety. But they say that one is never too old to learn. Some years back my wife Jan and I decided to sponsor a couple of children through a charity called PLAN UK. My wife's child, Kulsum, lived in the Dinajpur region of Bangladesh and mine Kirubel, lived in Addis Ababa, Ethiopia.

Prior to this visit to Ethiopia I had already met Kirubel and his family on two previous occasions and in doing so had come to know Addis and the surrounding areas quite well. The day after my arrival I had free time so I decided to once again visit the beautiful lakes near a town called Debrezeit. I informed the hotel manager of my plan and then made my way to the Le-Gare bus station in the city centre.

Now I must tell you that this is not a bus station as most of us know it. On the contrary, this is a bus station - African style. Space is at a premium. Buses are packed side by side like sardines. There are no white lines denoting the bus parking bays because there isn't a paved surface onto which the lines can be painted. Just a hardened earth surface. And one has to admire the bus drivers because they have an incredibly difficult job in getting into or out of it! And forget about scheduled bus departure times in this part of the world. The system is customer-driven.

The driver and his conductor stand outside the bus and shout out their destination. When the bus is full they leave, no matter how long the process takes. Next the exciting bit starts - getting out of the bus station. First the driver spends about five minutes trying to find room to get the bus facing the exit followed by twenty minutes of verbal battle with other incoming and outgoing drivers with respect to who has the right of way. Eventually it all gets sorted out despite the angry shouting going on. Just another day in Ethiopia! Eventually we are on our way, driving the forty-five kilometres south to Debrezeit.

I reach Debrezeit and the Lakes

I disembarked upon arrival and as I headed for the dirt track leading to Lake Hora a couple of young local guys started to walk alongside me. They enquired if I wanted a guide. On my travels I have often been approached in this manner and I have always declined. So I told them that I didn't but thanked them all the same. After a while they stopped walking with me and returned towards the roadside where I had first encountered them.

Reaching the side of the lake I watched as about twenty or so cows were being washed, the cowmen splashing water over them, driving them against their will into the deeper water. I then walked along the lake side and after a while stopped to sit down under the shade of a tree to rest and observe the lake birds, cormorants, herons, moorhens, and many others. Altogether a very peaceful and tranquil scene. But then these two guys appeared again. As I got up to continue my walk, they followed me. I stopped and told them that I didn't like being followed, sensing that they were becoming a problem. They turned around and went back the way they had come.

A Violent Mugging

In hindsight it was at this pivotal point that I made a serious mistake because I continued walking, eventually coming to a narrow path close to the edge of the lake. Unbeknown to me the two guys had been following me. Without warning they raced from behind me and in an instant I was violently flung backwards to the ground. As I fell they both stood menacingly above me. One was holding a large stone in his hand, ready to smash it into my face.

One said "Give me money, I want money." I refused and instinctively tried to protect my pocket which held my money but one of them viciously bit my hand. The other guy ripped off the button of the pocket and seized an envelope in which I had US dollars. I was very scared. I was alone and there was no one to help me. I quickly realised that these guys would become violent if I resisted further.

I was in danger of having my face rearranged. So I ceased all resistance. The guy with the stone took the contents of another pocket. This was more serious because in addition to Ethiopian money it contained my passport and credit card. They had stolen every penny I had. As they made their rapid departure they threw the passport and credit card onto the ground. Thank goodness for that!

Why did I carry the valuables with me?

You are probably wondering why I had all of my money, my passport and credit card with me. Yes, it was big mistake and a lesson learnt that I will never forget. But there was a reason – I was not happy with the security of my room in the hotel, and they didn't have a place, in my opinion, which was secure enough to keep my valuables. I must add that on my previous visits I had never felt at risk.

Looking back, if I hadn't taken that lonely footpath, if I had stayed amongst other visitors, then I would have been safe.

Light or dark skinned?

Can I just tell you an amusing anecdote which occurred during the hours and hours that I spent in the Debrezeit police station? I was being questioned as to the appearance of the two guys who stole my money. What did they look like? The police officer elaborated on his question - were they light skinned or dark skinned. I looked around the room for inspiration. There were about six or seven policemen there but what was I to say - to me they all looked the same, black complexions and short curly black hair. But apparently they were not the same.

That policeman, I'm told, has a light colour skin, whereas the guy over there has a dark skin. Well, you could have excused me for seeing the funny side of this because until now I saw all these folks as dark skinned.

Ah well, you live and learn, don't you? I doubt if my muggers were ever apprehended.

Visiting Kirubel – a heart warming experience

Finally, I was free to move onto the reason why I had come to Addis – the highlight of my trip - to visit Kirubel. The PLAN director in Addis had been incredibly helpful after the mugging and a colleague back in Baku (thank you Michael) wired me enough funds to complete my R&R.

The PLAN visit coordinator has collected me from my hotel and we have driven to the outskirts of the city. We disembark from the car and awaiting me is Kirubel, his brother Ibrahim, their mother, grandmother, and an assortment of relatives, neighbours and friends. We talk, coffee is slowly made and I give the boys some presents, and then take photographs. They look at the presents, anxious to play with them.

These children may be very poor but when it comes down to it kids are the same the world over aren't they? Sponsoring Kirubel has been a most humbling, heart-warming and rewarding experience for me.

The next day I moved on to my next destination, safari in Kenya. I had forgiven the guys who stole my money, after all life is for the living isn't it?

CHAPTER 50

A HAPPY ENDING

Introduction

Sometimes something happens in our life that we hadn't planned. Call it destiny. Or fate. Or maybe it's Que Sera, Sera, whatever will be, will be. Whatever it was it manifested itself in a major turning point in my life when I found and eventually married Caryl, my beloved and darling wife.

10 Years Alone

Following the sad death in 1977 of Jan, my first wife, I had been a widower for 10 years. During this time, I worked continuously overseas as an expatriate in the oil and gas industry. I had also made many endearing friends when I travelled extensively during my R & R breaks as I've described in this book.

During this time, I discovered the international travel site, Couchsurfing.

Couchsurfing

Couchsurfing is an organisation dedicated to helping members meet locals on their travels by staying as a guest (no cost) in their homes and in return offering to host travellers. In both cases the term used

313

is to "surf" or stay on a couch - though comfy beds are often on offer.

Online Dating?

It was in Baghdad in early 2007 that Bill, a good friend, turned a discussion around to my somewhat lonely personal life.

"Hey Nick. Why don't you try to find a partner with whom you can share your life?"

"Oh, I don't know, it's very difficult to meet anyone, living this overseas expat life."

"Then why don't you try Internet dating?"

I wasn't convinced because to be honest I didn't think that it suited me. But Bill persisted and eventually we put pen to paper and wrote the most glowing profile known to man – and hopefully one special woman!

It was fun and I warmed to the idea of meeting my future soul-mate and love of my life. Who would she be, from where, and how was I to meet her were all unanswered questions. But Bill, always positive, imbued me with confidence and we sent my irresistible message out onto a dating website.

From the replies that I received it would have taken me ages to actually have a date because, whilst I was located in Baghdad, the respondents came from all over the world! This setback cast a cloud over the proceedings but Fate decreed that I was still destined to meet my soul-mate, Caryl.

Caryl in Cape Town

Meanwhile in Cape Town, South Africa, a blonde, beautiful, single woman in her 50s called Caryl was dreaming of travelling the world, writing inspirational books and meeting *her* true soul mate. Later I found out she often played a Moody Blues song... *"I know he's out there somewhere...somewhere..."*

She had also put her profile on Couchsurfing. As I was intending to couch-surf in South Africa in 2007 I contacted her.

And so began our unusual cyber-space courtship between Baghdad and Cape Town. I found out she was originally from Zimbabwe, divorced with two grown up children and a grandson, and a former photo-journalist. At the time we met she had a thriving PR practice promoting and organising workshops for international self-help authors and was herself busy training and coaching people in emotional-energy healing. All foreign concepts to me!

But something clicked between us and our love grew via emails and weekly phone calls (I didn't have Skype in those days). This was from March to August 2007.

The path of love was not without its challenges, however.

When I eventually visited South Africa later that year, Caryl was in the UK which was a disappointment for both of us. But I met up with her family and we continued our long-distance courtship, growing ever closer. Caryl was becoming the love of my life – but we had yet to meet!

We Meet – and Marry

To and fro went our emails and in this way we built our relationship. Eventually Caryl and I met in the UK in August 2007 when I was home on R&R. It was strange at first, we knew so much about each other and felt deeply connected - yet we had never met face to face.
We had a week together in Wales - and then we parted - I went back overseas whilst Caryl, now working in the UK, waited for my return on my next R&R. This time we had two happy weeks together, now planning our future lives. Once more I went back overseas -this time to Yanbu in Saudi Arabia.

Meantime we had decided to spend the rest of our lives together - and the day came when I officially proposed to her - by email!

Caryl and I were married in a small gathering of family and friends (mostly hers but my daughter Zarita flew out to be there) at a dream Cape Town destination in Noordhoek called Monkey Valley on December 16, 2007. And our honeymoon continues...

Babyboomer Honeymooners

Now, 9 years later (as I write this in 2016), we feel blessed that it all worked out so well and jokingly call ourselves the "babyboomer honeymooners."

Happily retired, living an ideal life, we split the year between Newport on the Isle of Wight and Fish Hoek in Cape Town, following the summer sun. Yes, you got it - we don't experience winters anymore - just an eternal summer - or what South Africans call being a "swallow".

Cool eh?

Thanks Bill

Wherever you are Bill I want to acknowledge that, perhaps unknowingly, you were instrumental in changing in my life to what it is today - happily married. Thank you. Bill you have a special place in the Hall of Fame. A True Expat.

Time to hang up my Hard Hat

After our marriage my expat wanderings were about to end. In 2008 I went to Saudi Arabia, for the last time, to work at Yanbu on the Red Sea coast. And there my expat journey ended.

Life and love at home with Caryl beckoned.

Farewell

This brings to an end my tales of an expatriate life in the oil and gas industry. I hope you have enjoyed reading it as much as I have enjoyed writing it.

And to all you True Expats in the Hall of Fame - thanks for enriching my expat life - it was a great pleasure to meet you.

THE END

About Nick Westmore

Nick Westmore was born on the Isle of Wight, UK, where he grew up in the picturesque village of Godshill. He served an engineering apprenticeship following which he later moved into the Oil and Gas industry as a project planning engineer.

His career in the Oil and Gas industry spanned forty years working all over the world as an expatriate.

He also travelled extensively.

Now retired, he spends his time between the Isle of Wight in the UK and Cape Town in South Africa, enjoying his favorite pastimes of gardening, hiking, croquet and tennis.

8083009R00188

Printed in Germany
by Amazon Distribution
GmbH, Leipzig